The
WORLD
at my
FEET

The WORLD at my FEET

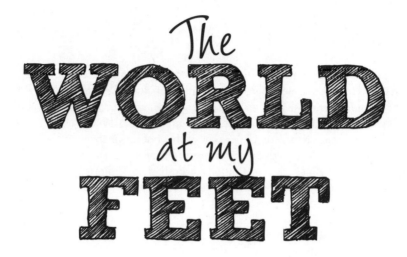

TOM DENNISS

ALLEN&UNWIN
SYDNEY・MELBOURNE・AUCKLAND・LONDON

First published in 2015
Copyright © Tom Denniss 2015

Allen & Unwin
83 Alexander Street
Crows Nest NSW 2065
Australia
Phone: (61 2) 8425 0100
Email: info@allenandunwin.com
Web: www.allenandunwin.com

Cataloguing-in-Publication details are available
from the National Library of Australia
www.trove.nla.gov.au

ISBN 978 1 76011 209 7

Internal design by Luke Causby/Blue Cork
Photographs by Carmel Denniss
Maps by MAPgraphics
Set in 12/18 pt Sabon by Midland Typesetters, Australia
Printed and bound in Australia by Griffin Press

10 9 8 7 6 5 4 3 2 1

The paper in this book is FSC® certified.
FSC® promotes environmentally responsible,
socially beneficial and economically viable
management of the world's forests.

CONTENTS

FOREWORD

Peter FitzSimons

Most people consider a marathon to be the pinnacle of endurance events. And getting through a 42-kilometre run is usually followed by weeks of rest and recovery. In fact, as impressive as that is, it is really only running in the lower foothills of the Himalayas.

Everest, I reckon, is running the equivalent of 622 marathons in 622 days.

I first heard about Tom Denniss and his astounding odyssey in early 2012. Here was a bloke who was circumnavigating the Earth on Shanks's pony—on foot. Could there be any better way to see the world?

Floods, snow, hail, searing heat, rattlesnakes, komodo dragons, vicious dogs, deadly cliffs of ice and gun-toting rednecks—Tom faced them all in his travels, at the same time experiencing the geography, history, and culture of the regions through which he ran.

This is an epic story of an ordinary Australian on an extraordinary journey, told from the ground up—quite simply, a ripping yarn of heroic proportions. And throughout the journey Tom raised money for Oxfam, helping Third World and impoverished communities to become self-sufficient.

So, sit back and enjoy this amazing read—the story of the fastest-ever run around the planet—a true 'world' record.

March 2015

MAPS

North and South

AMERICA

Gra
Detroit Lak

South Dakota

Rapid City
Black Hills
The Badlands
Wall

Minneap
Pierre

Wyoming

Alliance

Cheyenne
Fort Collins
Boulder
Denver
Fairplay
Salida
Colorado Springs

Nebraska

California

San Francisco

Carmel

Big Sur
San Simeon
Pismo Beach
Santa Barbara
Los Angeles
Palm Springs
Salton City
Brawley

Utah

Monument Valley

Grand Canyon

Prescott
Wickenburg
Quartzite
Phoenix

Blythe

Cortez

Colorado

Cuba

Taos
Santa Fe
Albuquerque

UNITED ST

New Mexico

Arizona

MEXICO

ARGENTINA

Portillo
Uspallata

Los Andes
Quillota
Valparaiso

Mendoza

San Luis

Vicuña Mackenna

Buenos Aires

CHILE

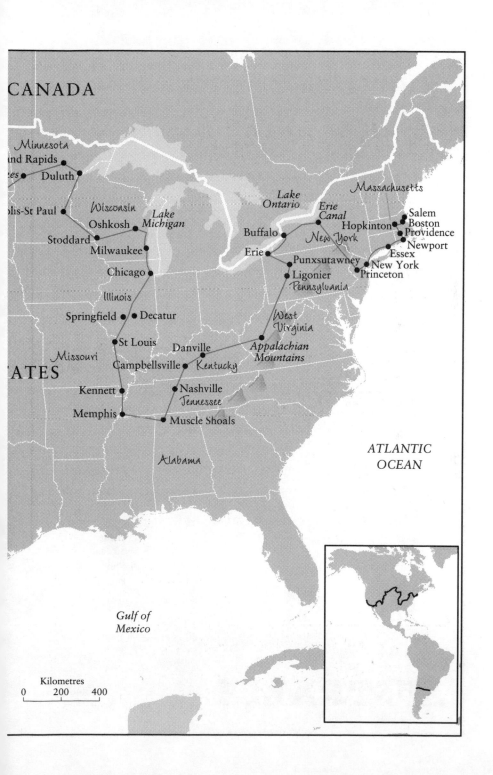

CANADA

Minnesota
nd Rapids
es
Duluth
olis-St Paul
Wisconsin
Oshkosh
Stoddard
Milwaukee
Chicago
Illinois
Springfield • Decatur
St Louis
Missouri
TES
Kennett
Memphis
Lake
Michigan

Lake
Ontario
Buffalo
Erie

Danville
Campbellsville • Kentucky
Nashville
Tennessee
Muscle Shoals

Alabama

Massachusetts
Salem
Erie   Boston
Canal   Hopkinton Providence
New York   Newport
Punxsutawney   Essex
Ligonier   New York
Pennsylvania Princeton

West
Virginia
Appalachian
Mountains

ATLANTIC
OCEAN

Gulf of
Mexico

Kilometres
0   200   400

South
China
Sea

●Kuala Lumpur

Malacca● ●Muar
Batu Pahat ●Pontian

INDIAN
OCEAN

Kilometres
0   150   300

MALAYSIA

Western Australia

South Aust

Kalgoorlie●
Southern Cross● ●Coolgardie
Merredin ●Yellowdine
Cottlesloe● ●Meckering ●Norseman
Beach   Cocklebiddy●   ●Eucla
                                 ●Madura   Fowlers Bay●   ●Cedur
              Balladonia   Caiguna   Streaky Bay●
              Road
              House   Great
                                 Australian
                                 Bight

AUSTRALIA

Kilometres
0   150   300

NEW ZEALAND

Auckland
Hamilton
Tauranga
Rotorua
Lake Taupo
Mount Ruapehu

Tasman
Sea

Wellington
Marlborough
Kaikoura
Christchurch

PACIFIC
OCEAN

Queenstown
Central Otago
Oamaru
Dunedin

Kilometres
0   150   300

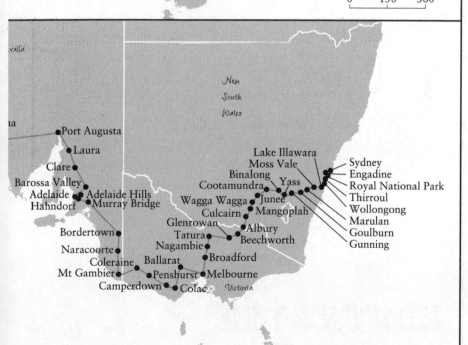

Australia

New
South
Wales

Port Augusta
Laura
Clare
Barossa Valley
Adelaide
Hahndorf
Adelaide Hills
Murray Bridge
Bordertown
Naracoorte
Coleraine
Mt Gambier
Penshurst
Camperdown
Colac
Ballarat
Broadford
Melbourne
Nagambie
Tatura
Glenrowan
Beechworth
Albury
Culcairn
Wagga Wagga
Junee
Mangoplah
Cootamundra
Binalong
Yass
Moss Vale
Lake Illawara
Sydney
Engadine
Royal National Park
Thirroul
Wollongong
Marulan
Goulburn
Gunning

Victoria

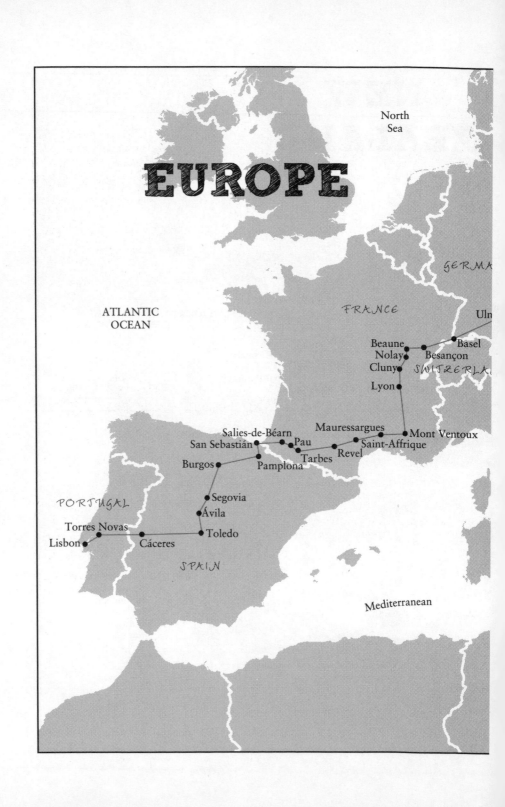

PROLOGUE

Late on the morning of 7 November 2012, I reached the top of the biggest hill I'd ever attempted to scale. It had taken me just a day and a half to run from the base of the Andes mountain range to the summit of the Cristo Redentor Pass, almost 4000 metres higher. The sky was a deep blue and the air was clear and crisp; it was also unusually warm for this altitude and I felt comfortable in my shorts and T-shirt. This was a breathtaking moment for any runner, but the serenity of the occasion belied the danger ahead.

Running is not a dangerous sport. In contrast to the head collisions, broken bones and torn ligaments of football, the horrific crashes of cycling and motor sports, or the facing up to a rock-hard cricket ball travelling at 150 kilometres per hour, running is a positively sedate pastime. Or so I thought.

But there are rare occasions when running can be decidedly hazardous to one's health; times when it can provide just as much danger and drama as any high-risk sport. And running at the top of the mighty Andes was one of those times.

Running over the Andes was always going to be one of the highlights of my run around the world. The natural beauty of the mountains, coupled with the extreme challenge of relentlessly running uphill to this lofty elevation of 4000 metres was a match made in heaven for any serious 'journey runner'—the name by which runners like me have come to be known. I'd anticipated this day for three years, ever since my decision to include the Andes in my itinerary. But I hadn't anticipated the drama that would unfold in these stunningly spectacular mountains.

The Andes is the second highest mountain range in the world. Extending thousands of kilometres, from tropical Columbia in the north to the quasi-polar regions of Argentina and Chile in the south, these mountains form a natural physical barrier between the east and west of continental South America. This was the same barrier I was now attempting to conquer on foot. And it was going very wrong.

I found myself balanced on a narrow ledge, teetering precariously over the edge of a near vertical slope of ice. Desperately trying to retain my footing on the slippery surface, I was acutely aware that there was nothing but a 1000-metre drop to the valley floor below. With my back to the wall of ice and my feet poised on the 10-centimetre wide snowy ledge, I gravely surveyed my predicament.

Having run to the top of one of the world's highest mountain passes, I was now staring over the side of this cliff and into potential oblivion. This was, by far, the most dangerous situation in which I'd ever found myself. I had to stay calm, as a rash move would almost certainly claim my life. I needed to somehow make my way back along this cliff of ice and snow to the dirt road I was on just minutes earlier.

Extreme danger focuses the mind. And this was precisely the case now. I was relieved to find myself thinking incredibly clearly, with an almost surreal feeling of heightened awareness. This was definitely not the time to be lacking in concentration.

Fond memories of running halfway around the world during the previous ten months were relegated to the backburner of my mind. My only consideration at that moment was surviving this extremely dire situation of my own making. Alone, and with no hope of external rescue, I kept admonishing myself for my silliness. I was in an awfully perilous position. The term 'life and death' is bandied around too freely to describe moments of danger, but this was truly a life and death situation.

Ever since the decision to run around the world, I had dreamt of that very location at the top of the Cristo Redentor Pass, higher than any point I had ever been on Earth. I had meticulously researched the ascent and descent on Google Earth and knew all about the eighty or so hairpin bends I needed to round. The pass forms the natural border between Chile and Argentina, and at the top you're only 16 kilometres in a direct line from the majestic summit of Aconcagua.

This peak, reaching almost 7000 metres into the sky, is the highest mountain in the world outside of the Himalayas. Catching a glimpse of Aconcagua had been on my list of priorities for the world run. Perversely, Aconcagua was now directly in my field of vision, but I couldn't have cared less. I had much more important things to fix my eyes upon—such as prospective footholds in the ice that might support my weight and save my life.

The day had begun far less dramatically. It was the middle of spring and the morning had dawned without a cloud in the sky; just like every day in Chile since I'd arrived. I had spent the previous day running from the town of Los Andes, at the base of the mountains, to the ski resort of Portillo at 3000 metres above sea level. Portillo is the only place in the Southern Hemisphere to have hosted the World Skiing Championships and, with its stunningly beautiful outlook, it's easy to see why it was chosen.

My wife Carmel had driven the support vehicle ahead that day and booked us into a room in the resort. The hotel is situated spectacularly on the edge of a glacial lake, and our room had a balcony that overlooked the lake itself. The ski season was over, and the hotel was relatively empty, but we were made to feel most welcome by a senior staff member, Elena.

I had run strongly that day and was feeling great—a day that included more than 50 kilometres laterally and almost 2500 metres of vertical ascent. Despite concluding the day's running at 3000 metres elevation, I was not short of breath and I was suffering no ill-effects from the altitude.

So, in the morning, and with a sumptuous resort breakfast under my belt, I started my run and headed up past the Chilean border control checkpoint, constantly being passed in both directions by cars, trucks, semitrailers and tour buses. After all, this is the main thoroughfare for vehicles travelling across South

America between the Pacific and Atlantic oceans. Leaving Chile requires no customs or immigration checks, though I sensed several border guards considered me a curiosity as I ran by.

These days, there is a modern tunnel linking Chile and Argentina, channelling 3 kilometres right through the mountain at an altitude of 3200 metres. However, there is also an old dirt road that winds its way to the top of the pass, reaching nearly 4000 metres. This trail has been used since colonial times, including in 1817 by the local army of liberation as part of the campaign to free Chile from the Spanish. In fact, the high point of the road is also known as El Paso Los Libertadores—the Pass of the Liberators.

As I looked up at the constant stream of switchbacks, forcibly bending the road back and forth as it wound its way into the sky, I could only wonder at how difficult this ascent must have been for an army to scale two centuries ago while carrying all its equipment. It's now a breeze for vehicles, with the bitumen-sealed highway extending all the way across the Andes, including in the tunnel that burrows its way through the steepest and highest part of the mountain range.

However, the authorities do not allow the tunnel to be used by pedestrians and cyclists, so I had to follow in the footsteps of those ancient travellers and take the 200-year-old high road.

Eventually reaching the turn I needed to make, I left the bitumen highway for this rough dirt road that snaked its way up the side of the steep slope. Carmel was following me in the car, but after about ten hairpin bends, we started to strike problems. I was constantly clearing the road of small boulders so that the car could pass by.

And then the road deteriorated to the point that the car became bogged. Unable to make further forward progress, we decided the prudent option was for Carmel to take the car back down the mountain and drive through the tunnel, meeting me on the other side where the two roads joined up again.

So I waved goodbye to my wife—and only support crew—watching the car descend into the valley far below me. It seemed to take an eternity for Carmel to reach the main highway, with the vehicle disappearing around one bend before eventually reappearing at the next.

The situation was complicated by the fact that mobile phone reception is non-existent that high in the Andes. The forbidding cost of constructing phone towers in such a remote region clearly isn't warranted by the relatively sparse demand. I knew that things could go wrong, but I had no choice. If I didn't run over the mountain pass, the world run would come to a premature end.

It immediately became evident that we'd made the right decision to send the car back and through the tunnel. As I ran higher up the mountain, the dirt road became a quagmire, with melting snow forming a boggy river along the gravel surface. This resulted in a mix of ankle-deep mud, ice and snow.

I was slipping and sliding, and was often reduced to plodding along at a slow pace. I passed two bulldozers on the way. They were the only types of vehicles that could traverse such a road, and they were there to repair the surface after the winter snows. In effect, the road didn't really exist beyond the point at which the bulldozers were working. The bulldozer drivers looked at me with a quizzical mix of surprise and amazement as I ran by.

I finally made it to the top, and felt it was worth the trouble. The view from that altitude, the highest point I'd ever been on Earth, was truly awe-inspiring. I looked back from where

I'd run. The road meandered its way down the mountain like a crooked ribbon.

I was at the border of Chile and Argentina, albeit devoid of any human activity—both countries now house their customs facilities further down the mountain on their respective sides. The former military post at the top was unmanned for a simple reason—it was impossible to reach in winter.

While there is officially a road down the other side, the snow had completely obliterated it. As is standard practice with mountain roads, its construction involved 'cutting' into the hillside, but the snow had now reclaimed the mountain. In place of the road was an extremely steep cliff of snow and ice. I could see the road re-emerging about 100 metres further on. I somehow needed to get there to continue my run.

And then the real trouble started.

I crawled out along the precipice with its drop of nearly 1000 metres below. I soon realised this was suicidal when I watched fragments of snow and ice tumble away and disappear out of sight far below. I'd covered about 20 metres when I started slipping toward the edge and, for a brief moment, was stuck in no-man's-land. One false move and, it was clear, I'd begin a slide that would end with my lifeless body on the rocks far below.

And I did slide. When a protrusion of ice broke off under my foot, I began to slip uncontrollably. I felt myself completely lose traction and I urgently plonked my body into an icy crevice that was, thankfully, just below me on the slope. If that crevice had not been there, I would not be here to tell this story.

So there I sat, contemplating my grim predicament, with the very view I had come here for, Aconcagua, looming high before me.

I rested a moment, my butt quickly getting cold. Despite the altitude, the air temperature was well above what I had expected and so I was wearing just a T-shirt and shorts. But the ice was, well, the temperature of ice—zero degrees Celsius—and it was rapidly chilling every part of me that came in contact with it. I knew I couldn't sit there for long.

Looking at my options, I could see that ahead of me there were numerous crevices along the mountainside—large grooves in the ice—randomly situated along the slope, a natural consequence of the snow melt. I was more than pleased to see them; they, like the one I was sitting in, might save me if I slipped again.

But immediately before me, the slope dropped away, getting ever steeper, to such a degree that it simply disappeared out of sight. The slope to my left also steepened and I could see I had no chance of making it to the point where the dirt road continued. My only option was to go back the way I had come.

Strangely, I found myself estimating the probability of my survival. I calculated I had a 50 per cent chance of making it. Even Russian roulette offers its protagonists much better odds. My greatest concern was that my hands would become too cold to grasp the ice and snow. I had experienced this feeling while cycling in the French Alps, unable to discern if I was applying pressure to the brake levers on the descent. Without functioning hands I stood virtually no chance of clinging to the mountainside.

I began to dig footholds, one at a time, and tested each before placing the toes of my shoes as far into these holes as I could manage. I considered taking my shoes off so that my toes could get a better grip in the ice, but decided this might result in a loss of feeling in my feet. If I were to lose the ability to feel with my hands, I would need my feet more than ever.

Forming holes in the snow for my hands to grip as best they could, I slowly began to make my way back to the dirt road. It was only 20 metres, but it felt like the proverbial mile. I would dig my hands hard into the snow every time I felt myself starting to slip down the icy white cliff. It was touch and go; life and death. I decided not to look down, reserving all my concentration for the task at hand.

I eventually reached firm ground, and with it came the greatest sense of relief I've ever experienced. I still had some significant problems to overcome, like how to get off this mountain, but at least I was going to live another day.

The next task was to survey my alternatives. I decided the only thing to do was to continue over the top of the local high point. Going off-road, I crawled even higher up the mountain slope to where it flattened out a little, then climbed, slipping and sliding, to a point directly above where the road reappeared about 20 metres below me. Now I just had to get down to that road. So I gingerly began my descent, at least knowing that the furthest I could fall was only as far as the road below.

And that's exactly what happened. I slipped and went into an uncontrolled slide, partly on my hands and partly on my backside. Don't let anyone tell you that old snow is soft. It's very hard and sharp. I landed on the dirt roadway, bruised and bleeding, but at least I hadn't fallen all the way down the mountain to my death. I could now continue running around the world.

Welcome as it was, the dirt track was very badly maintained which meant my resumed pace wasn't much faster than the motion of the nearby glaciers. As I slipped and slid through the mud and snow, I could see the main highway 1000 metres below. Carmel had been waiting for me for three hours by the time I reached that road. She had been desperately worried, and was very relieved when I had finally appeared as a speck on the mountainside above.

By the time I reached the car I'd had enough for the day, and so had a tearful Carmel. We were both mentally and emotionally exhausted. We decided that, instead of me running for hours to the next hotel, it made more sense to call it a day. I would get in the car and we'd drive back the 10 or so kilometres through the tunnel to the Hotel Portillo. We would return the next day and I would restart where I had stopped on the Argentinian side of the border. That was the plan.

However, after passing back through the tunnel another problem presented itself. I hadn't actually reached the Argentinian border checkpoint, which is some distance down the mountain toward Mendoza. I had not, therefore, officially set foot outside of Chile. But the Chilean officials didn't know this. They thought we were trying to enter Chile from Argentina. The Chilean border authorities are not the least bit interested in you as you leave the country, but they are very rigid and meticulous about you entering. Apparently no-one runs from Chile over the Cristo Redentor Pass and then drives back through the tunnel to the border check. Funny that!

Luckily, some of the officials had observed the highly unusual spectacle of me running past the checkpoint that morning. I was able to explain the situation in very broken Spanish, and we were allowed to pass through after ten minutes of cursory paperwork.

Finally back at the Hotel Portillo, we found Elena and explained what had happened. Amid great sympathy from the other staff, she checked us into the same hotel room with the amazing balcony view. I promptly flopped onto the couch and spent the next several hours calming down while watching coverage of Barack Obama being returned as President in the 2012 US elections.

The next day I continued my run around the world with a refreshing new perspective and a renewed appreciation of what I had achieved so far. I also had a better understanding of just how dangerous running can be at times.

My start at the Sydney Opera House had taken place almost a year earlier, and so many cherished memories had been generated since then. I was now already halfway around the world. More importantly, I was still alive.

CHAPTER 1

The journey begins

I began my run around the world at the Sydney Opera House on 31 December 2011—New Year's Eve. Having appeared on Channel 9's *Today Show* that morning, I spent the next few hours making last-minute preparations before heading to the Opera House by train with my family and several friends.

The Sydney Opera House is one of the world's foremost locations for New Year's Eve celebrations, with a fireworks display that is second to none. I knew that more than a million people cram the foreshore of Sydney Harbour to watch these fireworks. But I hadn't realised just how early they turn up for the occasion.

In hindsight, it wasn't a great time to start a run around the world from the Opera House. It was almost impossible to move as the crowds of revellers swelled ever larger under the warm sunny skies of early afternoon.

About thirty of my family and friends gathered to see me off. Some took quite a while to find the start point—thank goodness for mobile phones. Final group photographs were no easy feat as we struggled to find space among the milling thousands.

One of my oldest and dearest running mates—Greg Hudson, also known as The Hud—had agreed to accompany me that day to my destination at Bondi Beach. The Hud had trained and run with me during my first marathon in 1983, so it was fitting that he joined me for the first day of my run around the world.

It was to be just a short prologue stage, finishing at the waters of the Pacific Ocean. I'd aimed to start at 2 p.m. but the goodbyes resulted in a slight delay to the plans. Farewells to family and friends can take long enough, but heading off for the best part of two years to circumnavigate the globe on foot takes the goodbye process to a whole new level.

Officially, I started running at 2.23 p.m., though the first few hundred metres were mostly covered at a walking pace as The Hud and I threaded our way through the masses. After an eternity of preparation, my odyssey was finally underway. I was now officially running around the world.

It doesn't take a rocket scientist to realise that running around the world requires a lot of planning. The logistics are mind-boggling, and so it seemed to me when I started to plan for this challenge. Previous events in my running life had always been single-day affairs, the planning for which was a breeze. But this event was going to take the best part of two years.

Until 2008 I had never run further than a marathon: 42.195 kilometres. My fastest marathon time of 2 hours 49 minutes was run in 1987, more than twenty years earlier. I now had no hope of ever running that fast again, so I decided to up the ante with a new challenge—was I capable of running 100 kilometres?

The ideal testing ground was the 2008 Sutherland Relay for Life, a cancer research fundraising event that was organised by a long-time friend of mine, Rod Coy. I ran 250 laps of the Sylvania Athletic Field that day in 9 hours 26 minutes. With a lunch stop of more than forty minutes, my actual running time was 8 hours 45 minutes for the 100 kilometres. I was pleased with that.

I had proved to myself that running 100 kilometres was achievable, so what next? The following year I was determined to go to another level—I would attempt to run 1000 kilometres between Melbourne and Sydney. For the first time, logistics and planning became an issue. Organising myself for a one-day 100-kilometre event had been easy. But 1000 kilometres was going to take at least two and half weeks to run. It would also involve multiple considerations I'd never previously had to contemplate for any running event.

Running from Melbourne to Sydney in 2009 was a fantastic experience, and I learned so much—not just in coming to terms with the logistics but also in understanding the injuries and physical pitfalls that are endemic in a multi-stage running event. The differences between ultra-long multi-day runs and shorter single-day events are numerous. Single-day events feel like races. The underlying tone of such events has, at least to me, always been about speed—how soon could I get to the end?

On the other hand, journey running—the odyssey of traversing large distances between towns, states and even countries—simply didn't feel like a race to me. Speed was irrelevant. The pace was whatever felt comfortable. Journey running felt like an adventure and a holiday rolled into one.

Because I was running at such a leisurely pace, the physical effort required in the Melbourne to Sydney run was less than for any shorter race in which I'd been involved. The same was true of the training—slow, easy running, albeit lots of it. No heavy breathing, no chest feeling like it was about to explode, no oxygen debt. This was comfort running.

I completed the 1000 kilometres in eighteen and a half days. As easy as this run was on my lungs, my tendons probably weren't as prepared for it as they could have been. I was in quite a bit of pain from tendonitis for much of the run, learning valuable lessons that would ultimately hold me in good stead for the future.

But at the mental level I was totally inspired. How could I get more of this? What would be the next challenge? I immediately began to think about the answer to those questions.

I considered running eight marathons in eight days in the eight Australian states and territories but, to my mind, the cost of the flights for the support crew and myself outweighed the positives that might accrue. What about running across or around Australia? This had been done before several times, but that wasn't what mattered. If I did run across Australia, I would, without doubt, want to go to the next level after that—a run around the world. And this would require me finishing with a traverse of Australia anyway. Why not just go straight to running around the world and kill two birds with the one stone?

I would not be the first to run around the world. Jesper Olsen from Denmark had already achieved a documented version of this feat in 2005. And he was, at that very time, late in 2009, involved in his second lap of the Earth; on this occasion a north–south transit which he had begun in mid-2008. Tony Mangan from Ireland was to attempt a world run too, starting his adventure in 2010. Tony's was to be the longest single run around the world, totalling approximately 50,000 kilometres and taking four years. An English woman, Rosie Swale-Pope, had circumnavigated the northern hemisphere a few years earlier as well.

The fact that this handful of people had conquered similar challenges to what I was envisaging was comforting. If successful, I wouldn't be the first to run around the world, but I would be joining a very elite club.

I tossed the idea around in my head for a couple of months. I was daunted by the logistical aspects, but the logistics weren't going to be the deal breaker. I had a family, and I wasn't prepared to simply take off for the best part of two years on my own. If I was going to run around the world, then my wife Carmel was going to have to buy into it too.

If you have a family, a time-consuming undertaking like running around the world can only be embarked upon at certain times during one's life. The period between the birth of one's children and those same children reaching adulthood is effectively ruled out of contention. That's roughly two decades of life in which it's inappropriate to even contemplate this sort of thing—too much responsibility. And, of course, there's the first two decades of one's own life—too young. Needless to say, the last few decades of life are hardly conducive to such a physical challenge either—too old.

The reality is, teenagers don't run around the world—they have to attend school and have no money to fund such a run. A 35-year-old with two kids and an emerging career doesn't run around the world for reasons of duty. And a 75-year-old is likely to be too elderly to be successful in such an endeavour. In fact, there are very few windows of opportunity in life for a person with a family to run around the world. But there are some!

And I had actually just reached one of these rare windows. My children, Hannah and Grace, were now in their early twenties and I finally had enough savings in my bank account to cover the expected cost of such a gruelling undertaking. I was also in adequate physical shape for this sort of challenge. If Carmel was up for it, then it was 'all systems go'. If she wasn't, the idea would die a natural death.

Uyen is an inviting Vietnamese restaurant in Charing Cross, just a few hundred metres from our house. Its authentic food and flavours make it a favourite with many residents of the area. The dishes, with their simple English translations such as Unique Beef Salad and Squids in Ginger, are exquisite and exotic taste sensations. Carmel and I are big fans, having frequented the restaurant for many years. So much so, we've become good friends with the proprietors. On one of our regular visits, in October 2009, accompanied by our close friend Libby, the conversation was appropriate for me to bring up the topic of running around the world.

To my surprise, not only did Carmel react extremely positively to the idea, but so did Libby. By the end of the night, both of them were hooked on the idea. Carmel was going to accompany me the whole way, and Libby was keen to be involved as much as she could.

Carmel is an excellent photographer and loves nothing better than travelling to new and exotic locations in which to indulge her passion. Besides that, she also simply loves travelling. In hindsight, these facts, coupled with her belief that running around the world was a great personal project for me to embark upon, meant that my wife was always going to look favourably upon the idea. And for me, it simply couldn't happen without Carmel. In my mind, running around the world became a reality that night in Uyen.

From that day on, I was constantly thinking about the run. However, each time I found myself imagining being out on the road, running along the rim of the Grand Canyon or across the Nullarbor, I would remind myself it wasn't going to happen unless I spent my spare time in preparation instead of daydreaming. I made a list of everything I thought I would need to do in the planning stage. This list itself took a full week to prepare.

The items to address were seemingly endless. Sponsorship and funding, arranging support vehicles for each country, visas, choosing a charity and gaining its imprimatur as their representative, obtaining GPS systems and tracking devices, organising phones and communications, having a website designed and tailored to my needs, taking care of personal finances such as credit cards, health insurance, in-absentia payment of recurring bills and a myriad of other small tasks all had to be attended to before I could leave. Not to mention arranging to be away from my job for two years.

Work for me involved developing a technology to convert the energy in ocean waves into electricity. With a PhD in Mathematics and Oceanography, I decided a while ago to put my knowledge to use, so I invented a system that does just that. In the 1990s I founded a company to commercialise this technology. I handed over the reins in 2005, but I've continued to be involved ever since in the further development of the technology and the associated business side.

Not long after making the decision to run around the world, I talked about it with the company CEO. He was sympathetic to my desire, so we started making arrangements for me to have minimal input for two years, starting in 2012. I would remain associated with the company but on a nominal basis, working remotely 'from the road' if needed, until I had finished the run.

The acquisition of sponsorship also proved to be challenging in the early days of the planning. I approached all the obvious candidates—companies who made running shoes, sports drinks, sports clothing—all to no avail. In most cases I didn't even receive a response. I have since learned that most running-shoe companies have no interest in having their products associated with someone who might not achieve the success for which they're striving. For such companies, there is more downside to a failure than upside to a success.

However, I finally found a major sponsor in Next Digital, a young e-commerce company with its headquarters in Melbourne (which has since become part of a larger entity called Asia Pacific Digital). My good friend Roger Sharp was the chairman of the company, but he wanted to stay at arm's length and not influence any decision regarding sponsorship, so he facilitated a get-together with the boss for me.

An ensuing meeting in August 2011 with CEO Andy Burke sealed the deal. He loved the concept of sponsoring my run. He had confidence in me from the start and was determined to stick by me. I had almost been resigned to embarking on my adventure without a major sponsor. Now that I had these guys on-board, I couldn't have been happier.

Choosing a charity to support was an easier affair. I had been donating to Oxfam for years and had also participated in one of the organisation's 100-kilometre Trailwalker events. Oxfam helps to empower third-world and other needy communities to become self-sufficient. 'Challenge Poverty' is one of Oxfam's mantras. This worthwhile charity also had a history of raising funds through events that involved covering long distances on foot, making it a perfect fit for me. Oxfam management agreed, and the organisation thereby became the official charity of my run around the world.

One of the most time-consuming tasks of all, however, was the planning of the route. It's not possible, of course, to design a route around the world in the most microscopic of detail, but I needed to have a macroscopic view of where I would be running and when. My philosophy was simple—pass through certain key points in the world at predetermined times of the year and make the rest up as I went.

So I started by listing my broad objectives in regard to the course. Many of these had to be discarded. For example,

I really wanted to run across Russia, Kazakhstan and China, but Australians must enter these countries within three months of obtaining a visa. I could not possibly reach Russia from Australia within three months of beginning my run, so any visa would have been invalid by the time I presented myself at the border of the country. Appeals to the Russian Embassy in Australia fell on deaf ears, putting an end to Russia as a country on my route and, likewise, Kazakhstan and China.

I mentally debated as to which direction I should head—east to west, or vice versa—with a keen eye on the seasons. Direction was easy, as west to east meant I'd encounter more tailwinds than headwinds. Not that wind direction is anywhere near as critical to a runner as it is to a cyclist, but tailwinds are still preferable.

The seasons, however, were a more crucial consideration. No one wants to be running across the Nullarbor in summer or across the Andes in winter. In fact, the weather was perhaps the most important constraint of the whole route-planning stage. It is simply impossible to cross the Andes on foot during winter, as the road over the Cristo Redentor Pass, later to be the scene of my dramatic close-call, is completely closed and impossible to cross on foot.

As I found, even in late spring the road is obliterated by snow in places—it simply doesn't exist. In winter there are kilometres of the road like this that are impassable, not just the 100 metres that I would eventually encounter. I had to ensure the snows had adequately melted before I reached this segment of the run or I stood no chance of crossing the Andes. As it transpired, I only just achieved this by arriving in late spring. I certainly wouldn't have been successful in crossing the mountains had I been there a few weeks earlier.

I also needed to consider the definition of a 'run around the world'. There had been no official definition until recent years but I had decided to base my run on the only fully documented previous world run in history—that of Jesper Olsen of Denmark, which he achieved in 2004–05.

Jesper had completed his run by covering more than 26,000 kilometres and crossing four continents contiguously from west to east, taking 662 days to do so. His was a run of epic proportions including running across Siberia (he had managed to enter Russia within three months of starting his run in London). Jesper had set the standard and I could find no better precedent for my run.

After an exhaustive iterative approach, I finally settled on a broad outline of my route, satisfying all the seasonal and other requirements, as well as emulating the general guidelines inherent in Jesper's run around the world. My run would see me start and finish at the Sydney Opera House, cover at least 26,000 kilometres, cross four continents contiguously from one major ocean to another, and run via antipodal points (points opposite each other on the Earth's surface).

Midway through 2011 I had decided on a plan; one whose route and timing would serve me well on all these levels, not least of which was the desire to run in interesting locations and among spectacular scenery. With a minimum of mandatory course rules to adhere to, supplemented by a few locations I personally considered 'compulsory', the route was otherwise flexible and at my whim. My philosophy was simple: 'So long as I have a pair of shoes, I can head in any direction I choose.'

The plan entailed kicking off with a short first leg from the Opera House to Bondi Beach. This was followed by running the length of New Zealand, across North America, across South

America, across Europe, part of Asia, and then finishing by running across Australia.

And the run was to be as much an exotic extended holiday as an athletic endeavour.

All these components of the planning phase were very important but, without doubt, the most vital aspect of the preparation for a challenge like this is the training. The Melbourne to Sydney run had demonstrated to me that the tendons in my feet and legs needed 'more miles in them'. If I was going to fail, this was the part of my body that was most likely to let me down.

My plan was simple—to run as much as possible before I started the world run. Every opportunity I had, I would run. I'd run early in the morning, I'd run to the train station on my way to work, I'd run back from the train station, and I would throw in a long walk each lunchtime. I even ran along the platform while waiting for my train to arrive.

People who lived in my suburb were used to seeing me out on the road, perhaps thinking I was a little crazy. Now they were sure of it.

Winter wasn't a problem, but on summer mornings I found I could only run for intermittent periods to the train station in my work attire. I needed to include regular walking breaks to ensure I didn't start sweating too much. Yes, personal hygiene suffered a little during the warmer months. I hope my work-mates didn't notice too much.

During 2011 I averaged 20 kilometres per day—more than 7000 kilometres for the year. In early December of that year

I passed the 100,000 kilometre mark in total, the overall distance I'd amassed since I started logging my mileage back in 1983. When asked how many miles I'd invested into training for the world run, I would jokingly quote this 100,000 kilometres.

In some ways, though, it wasn't a joke. I'm sure the sheer volume of distance ultimately contributed to my making it to the starting line of the world run. And just as important was the consistency.

For more than seven years prior to beginning the world run, I had not missed a single day of training—more specifically, this equated to 2684 consecutive days of running in the lead-up to the start on New Year's Eve 2011 (this sequence has since been extended and remains unbroken at more than ten years at the time of writing).

And during those seven-plus years I had averaged nearly 14 kilometres per day. Some days were longer, of course, and some were very short. But at least I had compelled myself to run on every one of those 2684 days.

I wasn't sure if the volume and consistency of my training was going to be enough to get me to the finish line of a run around the world, but at least I'd given it the best shot I could muster. If my body was going to break down, so be it. But I wasn't going to die wondering.

As The Hud and I left the Sydney Opera House behind us and made our way through, thankfully, diminishing crowds, the pace began to quicken. Feeling fresh, this small prologue leg would perhaps be the fastest section of the whole world run.

We wound our way through the Eastern Suburbs of Sydney, finally arriving at Bondi Beach after a relatively short 16.77 kilometres—a distance that would later take on some significance. I dipped my toes in the Pacific Ocean before heading off to indulge in some restrained New Year's Eve celebrations at the nearby Clovelly Hotel.

The next day I would continue my run around the world—in New Zealand.

CHAPTER 2

New Zealand

Leaving home for nearly two years is an emotional experience, especially when you're leaving part of your family behind. Very early on New Year's Day 2012, Carmel and I walked out our front door, not knowing when we would next walk back through it. Our daughters, Hannah and Grace, despite the festivities of the previous night, were there to see us off. Tears flowed freely. At least they were happy tears, but they were also tinged with the sadness of an extended absence.

At Sydney Airport, we were met by Libby. A couple of her sisters and several other close friends had come to see us off. There were more goodbyes, more tears, more happiness and then we were winging our way to Queenstown in the south of New Zealand.

Queenstown is an outstandingly picturesque town in a spectacular part of the world. Serene freshwater lakes separate majestic mountain ranges, with rugged yet beautiful topography reigning supreme. The dusty peaks of summer, at the time of our arrival, give way to snow caps in winter (and sometimes even in the warm seasons as well). The local economy relies heavily on action sports and the outdoors, with skiing, jet boating, bungee jumping and white-water rafting all popular, and it's easy to see why.

We were met at the airport in the early afternoon by my good friend Roger Sharp. Roger and his wife Christine have a holiday house just out of Queenstown and had invited us all to stay our first two nights in New Zealand with them. Roger, as Chairman of Next Digital (now Asia Pacific Digital), had played a key role in facilitating my sponsorship for the run, and both he and Christine were to make further appearances as I ran around the world.

Another friend, Roger Evans, a.k.a. Chook, had offered us the use of a car for the New Zealand leg. Chook lives in Hamilton on the North Island, but keeps a car—a Honda CRV— garaged in Queenstown for when he goes there to ski. Since it was summer, he wouldn't be requiring the car for another few months. Chook's generosity was greatly appreciated; car hire, as Carmel and I soon learned, would be an expensive component of my world run. And, like the Sharps, Chook was to make several more appearances during the world run and play a major role in its success.

After picking up the vehicle from Chook's holiday unit and getting all our gear comfortably packed into it, I quietly slipped into my running shoes and shorts. The second stage of the world run was about to begin. Finally, here in Queenstown, it felt as if my adventure was truly underway. It was such a pleasure to be on the road in earnest, running through the idyllic New Zealand countryside and thinking of the adventures to come.

As it was already mid-afternoon, I only ran 25 kilometres that day, eastwards toward the Central Otago region of the South Island. Three hours later I stopped for the day just past the Kawarau Gorge, where the world's first commercial bungee-jumping business originated, and watched a few daredevils take the plunge.

The girls picked me up and we headed back to Roger and Christine's place, celebrating with some fine red wines that evening. A year earlier Roger had searched for a fifty-year-old bottle of wine for my impending fiftieth birthday, but couldn't find one. Instead he presented me with two twenty-five-year-old bottles, quipping 'Anyhow, two twenty-five-year-olds are better than one fifty-year-old'. We drank one of those twenty-five-year-old bottles of red that night, toasting the adventure that lay ahead.

The next few days were as perfect for running as is possible. The Central Otago region used to have a network of railway lines, but the main track has since been converted to a bicycle path called the Otago Central Rail Trail. Passing through towns such as Clyde, Lauder, Ranfurly and Middlemarch, I couldn't have hoped for a more tranquil path on which to run—approximately 150 kilometres of it. Roger and Christine and their two children accompanied me for two days on bicycles, staying with us at night and making up a support crew of six. Christine also ran a few kilometres with me, becoming the second person of many to do so over the next two years.

The preparation for such a massive run had been a long and extensive, but mostly positive, experience. It didn't, however, go entirely without a hitch. I had expected to be running each day in custom-made T-shirts with my run logo emblazoned across the front. I'd organised and paid for these well in advance of the start. But the company responsible for the screen printing had informed me the shirts would not be ready until a few days before Christmas 2011. This made me nervous.

I was instructed to arrive at the company's office in the Sydney suburb of Ultimo on the afternoon of Friday 23 December to collect the shirts. I decided to phone early that morning to co-ordinate the pick-up. The response was a recorded message which horrified me. The company had closed down for Christmas and would not be returning until mid-January. Despite being fully aware of my reason for ordering the shirts and the important role the company was playing in my adventure, the management, clearly intent on departing for their Christmas break a day early, had quietly 'snuck away' without even providing me the courtesy of a chance to come in early and take delivery of the merchandise.

I would have been happy to pick up the shirts at whatever time was convenient for the company, but I was never given that opportunity. I had no option but to depart for New Zealand without my personalised shirts, instead running the first few months of the odyssey in nondescript generic jogging clothing. Eventually my sponsor, Next Digital, came to the rescue with new official shirts tailored to the run. However, I wasted nearly $1000 on those original shirts. I tried not to let that sour my running experience. Thankfully, the stunning New Zealand scenery and the thrill of a new adventure made it impossible to be sour.

After a week of running—which included the most southerly point of my world run, 46 degrees south of the Equator—I eventually reached the Pacific Ocean at Dunedin. Once the largest city in New Zealand, Dunedin was founded by Scottish settlers in 1848, with a rich history ensuing. Today, the city is a microcosm of Scotland; it's so Scottish, it's often referred to as 'Edinburgh of the South'. The architecture reflects its Northern Hemisphere cousin, with many ornate stone buildings, as do the city's street and place names. Dunedin can also claim the world's steepest residential street, Baldwin Street, part of which has a gradient of 35 per cent. I wasn't going to run up that street, but I did have to contend with several of the city's other very steep streets.

I also discovered they know how to make meat pies in Dunedin. For lunch that day I enjoyed what was perhaps the best pie of my life. Seriously, it was that good!

The hospitality on the South Island was amazing. Upon hearing about the run, people we didn't know offered to help us. And strangers would make their homes available to the three of us with barely a moment's notice.

One such person, Andrew Sloan, went on to help us immeasurably throughout the run with his superior IT skills, particularly at converting videos into the required web format. Carmel would email Andrew the troublesome video, and Andrew would email it back in a workable form. Without him, so many of the videos that featured on the website during the run would not have seen the light of day. Andrew, an accomplished runner and multi-sport athlete in his own right, also ran 14 kilometres with me to the town of Palmerston.

As I made my way up the coast of the South Island, I managed to find lots of back roads that paralleled the highway, reaching the seaside town of Oamaru a couple of days later. The region has a long Maori history. It also displays great European-style architecture, with some original buildings from the 1800s still in near-perfect condition.

That night we were offered accommodation at a stunning guesthouse called Pen-y-bryn Lodge, run by a couple of guys from New York City who had moved to Oamaru to pursue a more relaxed lifestyle. That was possibly the most luxurious accommodation of the whole world run. And right up there with it was a similar guesthouse the next night near the town of Hook. I had imagined a somewhat Spartan existence during this run; instead, we were being royally pampered by a bunch of lovely people.

Within two weeks I had managed to run more than 700 kilometres to Christchurch, halfway up the South Island. The city had recently been devastated by an ongoing sequence of earth tremors, sporadically punctuated by fully fledged earthquakes. We'd again been offered free accommodation that weekend. Demonstrating an amazing level of trust, the owners of the house, who were away for the weekend, had made arrangements for Carmel and Libby to pick up the key from a nearby relative. We had the house to ourselves, despite not having ever met its owners, Rebekah and Steve.

That night I experienced my first earthquake. I had slept through a minor earthquake as a kid in 1973 but there was no way I could have slept through this one. Measuring more than 6 on the Richter scale, it felt like the house was going to implode. I can only imagine what it feels like to be in a really big earthquake of, say, 8 on the Richter scale.

Luckily for us, Rebekah and Steve had already 'proofed' their house against these quakes—any glasses and plates that remained after the first earthquakes were stored so that they couldn't fall out of cupboards. Thankfully, there was minimal damage that we had to clean up.

Running through the downtown region of Christchurch the next day, I soon came to realise the magnitude of the disaster that had been wreaked on the city by the two big earthquakes of the preceding year. The first, in February 2011, despite registering only 6.3 on the Richter scale, had killed 185 people. Six months later, a more powerful 7.1 magnitude quake further devastated the city, though did not result in any direct fatalities. So many of the city's buildings had been damaged to the point they had to be demolished. The quakes had destabilised the ground to such a degree that future building in some locations is now untenable. The whole city has had to undergo a complete rethink as to its future. It will take many years to recover and the city will never again be as it was.

After a filming and interview session with New Zealand National Television, I was picked up by the girls that afternoon about 30 kilometres north of Christchurch. We headed back to the borrowed house, finally meeting Rebekah and Steve who had returned from their weekend away.

Over dinner that evening at a local pub, there were further regular tremors. We were disturbed, but the locals hardly even noticed it. After all, there'd been thousands of these tremors since the geological activity had begun many months before. I guess it's possible to get used to anything. (Funnily enough, I never felt a tremor while I was running, yet they occurred regularly when I was inside buildings. This was not coincidental—artificial structures exacerbate the effect, making an earthquake much more noticeable.)

The next week was spent running in more remote regions, along the north-east coast of the South Island. Kaikoura was a highlight, with its seafood beach market and seal colonies to the north of the town. By the end of Week 3, I had run the length of the island, culminating in a delightful day in the Marlborough wine region, running on roads lined with extensive vineyards of sauvignon blanc. I had also chalked up more than 1000 kilometres.

Prior to starting the run, I was determined to be extremely vigilant and self-disciplined in regard to prospective injuries. Any ache or pain was to be taken seriously and I was going to limit my daily distance to the low side of expectations for the first couple of months. There was no point in going out hard, only to suffer for it later. It's one thing to hang on for a week or two with an injury. It's a completely different challenge to try to bear that same excruciating pain for seven hours every day for two years.

However, by the time I reached Picton in the far north of the South Island, I realised I was handling the physical aspects far better than anticipated. I had no injuries and no aches that weren't to be expected. I had averaged 53 kilometres per day and was well ahead of where I had thought I'd be at this stage. As we crossed the Cook Strait by ferry to Wellington on the North Island, I truly believed for the first time that I might actually be capable of completing this epic adventure in good shape, both physically and mentally.

We stayed two nights in Wellington with a colleague and friend of mine, John Huckerby, and his wife Liz. I've travelled to various parts of the world with John in the past as part of our work in furthering ocean renewable energy—Spain, Norway, Mexico and even Wellington itself. Now I was his guest, and what wonderful hosts the Huckerbys were.

Wellington is somewhat of a hidden gem when it comes to international capitals. There are few cities that are so visually stunning and the social scene is vibrant too. Restaurants and bars abound. The downtown area is nestled in among the lower reaches of land that border the harbour and is overlooked by the impressive peaks that surround the city. The downside is the weather, with wind and rain a constant companion of Wellingtonians. And the omnipresent potential for earthquakes is also a negative.

Lying on the boundary of the Pacific and Australian plates, the city is no stranger to seismic activity. The earthquake of 1855, measuring 8.2 on the Richter scale, permanently heaved many parts of the surrounding harbour up above sea level. In fact, the international cricket venue known as the Basin Reserve was once part of the sea—it really was an ocean basin prior to 1855.

After a terrific dinner at a restaurant in the city, I ran a short day and commuted back by train to the Huckerbys' place, allowing the girls a free day to enjoy Wellington. That afternoon we even caught the latest *Mission Impossible* movie at the local cinema, followed by a sumptuous baked dinner at John and Liz's that night. And after two relatively short days on the road, I was feeling alive and full of running.

Making my way north entailed some memorable countryside but it was also a significant moment of my round-the-world route. This part of New Zealand is on the opposite side of the Earth to the region around Madrid in Spain. These two regions were to qualify as the antipodal points I needed to satisfy the technical requirements for running around the world. If I were to theoretically drill a hole directly through the centre of the Earth from where I was running in the North Island of New Zealand, I'd emerge near Madrid. As I ran along the quiet back road, I contemplated the fact that in roughly a year's time I would be running upside-down relative to my current orientation.

One morning I passed a driveway that led to a farmhouse about half a mile off the road. Tied to the front gate on short leads were two friendly but distressed dogs. I don't know why they were there but they were desperate for attention and fretting terribly. I felt very sorry for these animals and wondered why working dogs had to be treated in this way. Here, on such a large and fully fenced property, why couldn't the farmer give his dogs better living conditions?

This lack of awareness of the psychological needs of animals was to become a common theme as I ran around the world, particularly in regard to dogs. In the rural regions of the United States, as well as in many other developed countries, I was to see countless dogs in small cages or on very short chains that were clearly suffering from what I can only describe as 'psychological abuse'. They were obviously considered by their owners to be no different to any other farm machinery—simply an asset to be made use of, just like a tractor or plough. I understand these animals have a function but I can only hope that one day attitudes may change and a more compassionate treatment of working dogs and animals in general may ensue.

As if in response to this situation, or perhaps due to me spending so much time alone on the road, I found myself talking to the animals that I passed throughout my world run. Herds of cows and sheep, horses and, of course, dogs were the most common recipients of a 'conversation'. The dogs and horses were generally up for a chat of sorts, and the cows in New Zealand would often race up to the fence to check out the unusual sight of me passing by. The sheep, however, were much more, well, sheepish, usually scampering in the opposite direction.

— 🏃 —

I gained my first glimpse of Mount Ruapehu on 25 January but didn't actually reach the majestic volcano for another three days. It's so prominent on the landscape that the 2800-metre giant's snow-capped peak can be seen from any local high point for hundreds of miles. It was not on my agenda to run to the top.

However, the mountain brought back memories of another regal summit I actually had scaled—Haleakala is a 3000-metre-high volcano on the Hawaiian island of Maui, where I participated in the Run to Sun in 2009. A 58-kilometre race from sea level to the top of the peak, this was my first and only (so far) official ultra-marathon event and I was elated to finish 9th overall.

But the Run to the Sun was not without its difficulties. Though the weather conditions at the start of the race were close to ideal, a cold snap hit by the time the competitors passed an altitude of 2000 metres. Ice and snow caused the police to ban support vehicles and my crew—two friends from Sydney—could not reach me. I was, however, unaware of this fact and constantly cursed their absence every time I rounded a bend and found they weren't there. In shorts and T-shirt, I was shivering uncontrollably in temperatures as low as minus 18 degrees Celsius, while the wafts of snow and sleet further sapped my heat reserves.

Thankfully, I just made the finish line before capitulating completely. I was rushed into a heated van, covered with blankets and fed warm drinks, but it still took a couple of hours before I felt warm again. After that experience I never again underestimated the dangers of running on or near snow-covered volcanoes. And, for that reason, I wasn't going to risk venturing up Ruapehu this time.

As I made my way up the North Island I came to appreciate the tumultuous geology of the region. A volcano like Mount Ruapehu is an impressive sentinel but it would pale against the super-volcano that once stood where Lake Taupo is now located.

Running along the highway from Ruapehu to the lake, I noticed charred logs sticking out of the earth, exposed when the road-building process had cut through the hillside. It was clear the trees had been a casualty of an intense inferno, combined with a massive mudslide—the hallmarks of a major volcanic eruption.

On investigation, I later learned this occurred about 1800 years ago, during what was the biggest eruption on Earth of the past 5000 years—much larger than Krakatoa. It enlarged Lake Taupo, which itself was formed in a super-volcano eruption some 26,500 years ago, that being the largest eruption on Earth during the past 70,000 years. My run around the world was providing an unexpected benefit—in a hands-on way I was coming to appreciate and learn a lot about geology.

Had it not been for volcanic and other geological activity, all the land on Earth would have long ago eroded into the sea, resulting in a fairly uniform depth of ocean covering the whole planet. Instead, the Earth's crust has constantly been renewed over billions of years as magma from below covered old rock and pushed it deeper down. Evidence of this phenomenon was to become all too obvious to me the following month when I was running across North America.

More geological peculiarities were revealed a couple of days later when I ran into Rotorua. Famous for its steaming geysers and mineral baths, the city has a perpetual smell of hydrogen sulphide hanging in the air. It's a bit off-putting to visitors, though the locals have gotten used to the odour of rotten-egg gas.

It was here I suggested Carmel and Libby avail themselves of the array of spa and health treatments on offer while I ran on towards Tauranga the next day. I often managed through the day without their support by relying on shops and petrol stations in the numerous small towns I passed through. This was to be another of those occasions. Sometimes, however, things don't work out the way you intend.

After I headed off for the day, the girls sought out some of the pleasures of Rotorua, on the understanding that I'd call if I needed anything. Unfortunately, there were no shops of any sort along the road that day—and no mobile phone reception either. I had no alternative but to keep running without food or drink.

As I approached the outskirts of Tauranga, I finally came upon some phone reception. The girls quickly hurried to me, but by the time they arrived I'd already run more than 40 kilometres under the New Zealand summer sun without a drink or food. Strangely, I felt fine and was not suffering unduly at all. It felt like my body was becoming accustomed to getting by on minimal fluid intake. This apparent adjustment was to become even more pronounced as the world run continued. As big a distance as 40 kilometres is to run without supplies, it turned out not to constitute a record for my world run.

By this time I was a month into my run around the world and I'd settled into something of a daily routine. Though no two days were identical, a semblance of regularity was creeping in. I would awaken around 7.30 in the morning, take my time to get dressed while I indulged in whatever was on offer for breakfast. This ranged from cereal and muesli to toast and honey or perhaps scrambled eggs.

One constant with which I'd start the day, however, was the large 'chocolate milkshake' that Carmel prepared for me each morning—actually, it was Nesquik in milk. Despite nearly two years of the same thing, I never tired of this breakfast ritual.

I would generally find myself on the road between 8.30 and 9 a.m. each day, carefully ensuring I was in the precise location at which I'd finished the afternoon before. Stretching was unnecessary—the pace was simply too slow to need it. I'd click on my GPS watch and check that it was working properly before heading off. Proper documentation was of the highest priority for me.

The running itself was much slower than I'd been used to during the past thirty years. For decades I'd been used to training at a pace between four and five minutes per kilometre. Now I was running at seven minutes per kilometre, and this was to slow even more in the coming months.

But because it was so slow, I was feeling fine all day long. Most runners are used to pushing themselves hard over a relatively short distance. It's the most time-efficient way to conduct an exercise regime. But it also means the running involves a level of pain. It's exactly that pain—shortness of breath and a pounding heart—that deters many people from taking up running.

But journey running is completely different. I was running at a pace that precluded any shortness of breath. Nor did it raise my heart rate unduly. It was simply comfortable. Many people professed amazement that I could talk without any apparent effort while running. My response was, if I was breathing heavily then I was running too fast. And running too fast is lethal when you're aiming to cover 26,000 kilometres.

I would take breaks whenever I felt like it—toilet stops, talking to cows, examining some interesting object by the road or to have a drink or something to eat. It was leisurely running and I was thoroughly enjoying the constantly changing landscape.

The days passed quickly and I wasn't struggling at all to cope mentally. I didn't listen to music or use any other form of distraction—I simply relied on a combination of the ever-changing panorama and my own thoughts to get by. There was no particularly tough period of any day. I generally felt pretty much the same at the end as I felt at the start—perhaps just a little wearier but nothing of which I was overtly aware.

However, I did enjoy completing each day of running. Carmel would prepare another chocolate milkshake (a litre in the morning, a litre in the afternoon) and I'd put my feet up as I stretched out on the bed and attended to my documentation and blog post. The most critical aspect was the uploading of the GPS data from my watch to the Garmin website. Sometimes this did not go smoothly, especially when the internet connection was tenuous.

This post-run 'work' took anything from half an hour to a couple of hours, depending on the speed or slowness of the internet. A slow connection often drove me crazy, particularly if I'd written my blog post then lost it into cyberspace. On those rare occasions I'd have to quickly try to replicate the missive before I forgot what I'd written.

And then it was time for a little celebration to mark the end of the day. If our place of abode that evening included a bath, I'd relax in the warm water for half an hour while reading and sipping a beer. Then we'd head to dinner, which always included a couple of glasses of red wine.

It was just like being on an unusual and long holiday, with all the associated feelings of excitement and contentment. Bedtime was typically between 10 and 10.30 p.m. And then I'd enjoy a fantastic night of sleep, waking fresh in the morning to do it all again.

— 🏃 —

In Tauranga we were put up for the night by Scott, the coach of the local school's cross-country team, who also joined us for an inspiring visit and barbecue. I pushed on over the next few days to Hamilton, the milk capital of New Zealand, where I was met by Chook and several members of the Hamilton Road Runners Club, accompanying me for the final 20 kilometres into the city. The club arranged a function in a local pub that evening, where we got to meet, among many others, Chook's brother Don. A larger-than-life character, Don was later to become an important supporter of the world run.

We stayed in Auckland with some of Chook's friends while I finally concluded the New Zealand leg of the world run, reaching Auckland Airport on 7 February 2012. I had covered 1894 kilometres in thirty-eight days, and I was in much better shape than anyone had expected, including myself.

It was now time to run across North America.

CHAPTER 3

California

The run across North America began in San Francisco with a support crew of three. Carmel's good friend and fellow teacher Jenny had decided to join us for five weeks and we were thrilled to have her along.

After a brief stopover in Honolulu, we arrived in San Francisco late in the evening the day before Jenny's birthday. A night at an airport hotel was convenient then it was time to begin preparations for the longest leg of the world run.

Chook had come to the rescue again with a support vehicle. He and brother Don were co-owners of a car, a maroon-coloured Suzuki 7 (a large seven-seater), which they garaged in Denver at the home of another brother, Peter. Neither expected to be using the car until the end of the year, and they offered it to us for the duration of the North American leg. Chook even had a friend fly to Denver and drive the car to San Francisco, dropping it off at the airport for us to pick up. What great blokes!

We took possession of the car and drove into the city, spending a couple of days sightseeing and getting set up for the long journey ahead. We were very pleased to acquire SIM cards from T-Mobile that offered amazing value. For $60 per month, I was able to make unlimited calls to any phone in the US, unlimited calls to any landline anywhere in the world and there were no limits on text messages and data either. Incoming calls from anywhere in the world were free too. Given the importance of communication during the run, not to mention the need for data (maps, internet, tracking devices etc.), these SIMs proved to be just what we needed. (By the way, T-Mobile did not sponsor my run and I have received no financial or other gain for the sentiments expressed above.)

After celebrating Jenny's birthday at Fisherman's Wharf on the city waterfront—an interesting experience in itself when a patron at a nearby table who'd had too much to drink vomited all over the floor next to us—I commenced my run across North America on 12 February 2012—my mother's birthday. Leaving from out the front of our hotel, I ran down to the nearby harbour and along the waters of San Francisco, gazing out at Alcatraz in the distance.

My route across North America was flexible. I only had a handful of interim destinations I considered compulsory. I wanted to run down the Californian coast, through Los Angeles and Phoenix via the Grand Canyon and Monument Valley, up through the Black Hills of Dakota, across to Chicago, past Niagara Falls and on to the finish in Boston via New York City. I also wanted to get close to both the Mexican and

Canadian borders and to pass through some of the southern states if possible. How and when I got to these destinations, though, was pretty much left to fall into place.

It was, however, important for me to be running in the north of the continent during the middle of the summer. I certainly didn't want to be suffering the heat of the deserts or southern states during the hottest time of the year. That was the plan but I had to be willing to roll with the punches, should they be thrown.

The first couple of weeks of North America were some of the finest of the whole world run. Passing through the towns of Santa Cruz, Monterrey and Carmel, I basked in sunny winter conditions as I ran leisurely through the central Californian coastal farming belt. Crops of strawberries and artichokes abounded and I regularly encountered farm workers speaking Spanish as they toiled in the fields.

Carmel was particularly taken by the quaintness of Carmel, but of course it was the name that really captured her attention. Once lorded over by Clint Eastwood as mayor, the town is still home to many celebrities and the nearby Pebble Beach has often been the venue for major US golfing tournaments.

Throughout New Zealand, Carmel, Libby and I had been enjoying a bottle or two of red wine each evening between us. In the Land of the Long White Cloud, it was predominantly the pinot noirs that are produced so admirably by the winemakers. In California we were finding merlots and zinfandels to be the popular variety.

I'd had correspondence from several friends, known to enjoy a drop themselves, who were interested in my views on the red wines of each region of the world through which I ran. I thought about this for a while, dubious that my less-than-expert opinion on the subject would be appreciated. How could I offer a more objective assessment instead?

Then I hit upon a quantitative proposition. What if I rated red wines by their relative value, according to price? I came up with a simple formula to compare wines based on their drinkability versus the cost of the bottle. I coined this measure the Red Wine Value Quotient, or RWVQ, thereafter publishing updates on my blog whenever a new wine surpassed the previous record-holder for value.

But the best-laid plans can quickly come unstuck. A few days after I finalised the details for this global adventure in wine tasting, Carmel and the girls brought back to the motel room a bottle of local merlot. I only rated it a 5.5 out of 10, which normally would not be expected to feature as a great value wine.

It was not great but it was a decent quaffing wine. However, they'd bought this bottle for just US$1.79. My formula normalised the cost into Australian dollars, and the exchange rate at the time resulted in a conversion to about A$1.65. It's very hard to beat a wine for value when it's going so cheaply—unless, of course, it's absolute rubbish, which this one wasn't.

The bottle's RWVQ score worked out at just over 100 and I never found another red wine during the whole run around the world that surpassed this Californian merlot in terms of its RWVQ score. And so the RWVQ competition fizzled out almost before it began.

Of course, I experienced better red wines on an absolute scale but their higher prices ruled them out of contention for the title of Best Valued Bottle. For the next year and a half, I still enjoyed the nightly testing of new reds, living in hope of finding an even better value bottle. The quest turned out to be forlorn but, as they say, it's the journey that matters, not the destination.

Immediately after the town of Carmel, I began the 150-kilometre trek along the bit of coastline known as Big Sur. Considering it's such a beautiful stretch of coast and is centrally located between San Francisco and Los Angeles, and in a state with more than 50 million inhabitants, I found it amazing that the highway through the Big Sur region was so sparsely populated with traffic.

There are no towns, just small accommodation options here and there, which makes the area feel even more remote. It took me three days to run from Carmel to San Simeon, enjoying all the twists and turns, ups and downs, bridges and canyons, and the spectacular views from high above the North Pacific.

San Simeon is home to the nearby Hearst Castle. Built for newspaper tycoon William Randolph Hearst between 1919 and 1947, the castle housed many famous guests over the years, including entertainers Charlie Chaplin, Bob Hope, the Marx Brothers, Clark Gable, Joan Crawford and politicians Calvin Coolidge, Franklin Roosevelt and Winston Churchill. I only got to admire the castle from the highway as I ran by but Carmel, Libby and Jenny enjoyed most of the day visiting the monumental edifice as part of an organised tour. I did get to see a colony of sea lions, though—hundreds of them lazing in the sun just metres from the roadside. There were so many that some were even engaging in turf wars, rearing up and clashing their bodies against each other until the issue of real estate was settled. Most, however, were content to lie peacefully on their small patch of sand.

A couple of days later, just past the town of San Luis Obispo, I came upon a somewhat surreal sight. Right in the middle of the road, covering the parallel yellow dividing lines, was a dead skunk. This was literally the Dead Skunk in the Middle of the Road, as brought to prominence by the Loudon Wainwright III hit song of the early 70s.

That same day I also ran close to the nearby Pismo Beach. This is the location of the Nipomo Dunes, expansive mounds of sand where many movies have been filmed, especially those requiring a Saharan-like panorama such as the original 1923 version of *The Ten Commandments* by Cecil B. DeMille. Many of these movie sets now lie buried under the dunes.

But my memory of the name Pismo Beach comes from a much less lofty piece of cinema—*The Bugs Bunny Show*. Pismo Beach was where Bugs and Daffy were heading (via a long rabbit burrow) to eat the famous local clams when, upon emerging in Ali Baba's cave, Bugs declared he knew they should have 'taken that left turn at Albuquerque'. One of the real pleasures of running around the world is stumbling upon icons of popular culture like Pismo Beach.

Continuing in a southerly direction for the next two days, I passed the Vandenberg Air Force Base just before the town of Lompoc. Many satellites have been launched from Vandenberg and it is still home to intercontinental ballistic missiles (ICBMs) or nuclear missiles. It was also groomed as a launch and landing site for the space shuttle, though no shuttle ever did leave from or land there. I was hoping to fluke a launch of some sort as I ran by (a satellite, that is, not a missile), but I was out of luck.

I had settled in nicely to running in California. The roads were quieter than I had expected and when they were busy there was a good shoulder on which to run. I was churning out around 50 kilometres per day without a problem and I was enjoying novel countryside I'd never before set eyes upon. I couldn't have been happier with the way the world run was going.

My pace had plateaued at around 7 minutes 30 seconds per kilometre and, with rest stops here and there, that pace translated to about 7 to 8 kilometres per hour. My 50-kilometre days were taking about seven to eight hours, roughly the length of a normal working day—appropriate, I thought, as this was now my day job.

The slight reduction in my pace over the first 2500 kilometres was initially very worrying—what if the trend continued throughout? I'd have ended up slower than walking pace. But the trend didn't persist. The speed plateau I'd reached at this stage of the run turned out to be sustainable.

It wasn't lost on me that I'd settled into a pace that was around half my best marathon pace. It was even slower when compared to my shorter-course personal bests. I was now covering 10 kilometres in around 80 to 90 minutes with stops, or around 75 minutes excluding stops. This paled in comparison to my 10-kilometre personal best (PB) of 33 minutes 50 seconds. I comforted myself with the fact the running I was doing now was easy and painless; covering 10 kilometres in 33:50 was never easy, and certainly not painless.

I had never before celebrated my birthday outside of Australia, but on 24 February 2012 I did so for the first time. I awoke on a warm sunny morning in the town of Solvang to gifts from all three girls.

Solvang, a few hours' drive west of Los Angeles, was founded by Danish settlers around a hundred years earlier. The town now looks like a mini Danish village and much of the local economy is based around tourists visiting for the Denmark experience. Solvang is even referred to as the 'Danish capital of America'. For me, it was a suitably unusual place to wake up on my first overseas birthday.

That morning, as I passed Lake Cachuma and began a long ascent up the Chumash Highway to the top of the San Marcos Pass, I received a call from *The Ellen DeGeneres Show*. Libby had let the program know what I was doing and the phone call was about a possible appearance as a guest on the show. I spoke with a staffer from the production division for a while and she especially liked the support-crew angle; three women in their fifties. My appearing seemed likely—until we discussed dates. I would be passing through Burbank, where the program is filmed, on what happened to be Justin Bieber's eighteenth birthday and therefore the show had no spare spots for me that day. Justin Bieber's birthday was far more important than someone running around the world.

I finished a short day in Santa Barbara, where we were to stay with Libby's nephew James and his young family. The evening was worthy of a birthday. After a lovely meal at a Mexican restaurant, washed down with several Margaritas, we went to a bar that was featuring a live band—my favourite way to celebrate a birthday.

The 2 a.m. finish wasn't sustainable on a daily basis but a one-off wasn't going to hurt and I had already planned a short 25 kilometres the next day, running as far as James's office. From there he drove me back to Santa Barbara where the birthday after-party consisted of a delicious lunch on the waterfront—local seafood, of course.

The next morning I started my run into Los Angeles. After a stint on the Ventura Highway, I ran the coastal stretch through Malibu, right past Charlie Harper's house. We stayed that night in Calabasas, which Libby informed us was the hometown of the Kardashians (something I didn't particularly care to know).

The girls had visited a cafe the previous afternoon, their Australian-ness not going unnoticed by the proprietor who was quick to inform them that her establishment was once the favourite haunt of a famous Australian who had spent some time living and working in the vicinity. When the mystery Aussie turned out to be Jimmy Barnes, I was dubious of the support crew's story but wrong to doubt it—the next morning I was pleasantly surprised to find that Jimmy was now a follower of my Twitter account. Wow!

From there it was on past the Santa Monica Pier and down to Venice Beach, where I would see the Pacific Ocean for the last time on the world run—we would not meet again until I was just a few days from finishing in Sydney.

Moments like these really brought home the enormity of the challenge. Comprehending that I was leaving this vast ocean behind, running around the Earth for the next year and a half, to come up behind it again on the other side, was as daunting and emotional as any realisation I'd had or was to have during the entire run around the world.

Turning my back on the Pacific, I headed inland to Hollywood, where we caught up with an old student of Carmel's that evening. Valeria was in Carmel's kindergarten class in 1981 and Year 6 class in 1987. As an adult she had moved to California to take up an acting career, including a speaking part in *Sister Act 2* with Whoopi Goldberg. Valeria was now 37, married and living close to Hollywood—I still remembered her well from her primary-school days when I used to help Carmel in the classroom. We all enjoyed the evening together and even made some calls back to Sydney to Valeria's other teachers from the 1980s, courtesy of our cheap SIM cards.

The next day I ran over the Hollywood Hills, conducting my own private tour of the celebrity mansions. I took in its famous streets such as Sunset Boulevard, passing iconic locations like the Chateau Marmont, scene of John Belushi's death in 1982. I cruised through Laurel Canyon, home of luminaries of popular music and culture over the years, including Jim Morrison, Frank Zappa, Joni Mitchell and even Harry Houdini before them. The short day was finished in Pasadena on Colorado Boulevard—the street has been referenced on an episode of *The Big Bang Theory* as the location of the main characters' apartment block. Unfortunately, I saw no sign of Sheldon.

After a little trouble finding a cab—it's Hollywood, after all—I returned to our motel and even managed a short nap in the girls' absence (they hadn't yet returned from a tour of Paramount Studios).

That evening I caught up with an old friend, Peter Mensah, who was working in Hollywood at the time. I had been introduced to Peter several years back in Hawaii by Cynthia, my great colleague from the wave energy industry. In the early days of the organisation, Cynthia had helped me develop the wave energy company into a world-leading player. We had been in Hawaii on business at a time when Peter was filming *Tears of the Sun* on Oahu with Bruce Willis. Peter has since appeared many times on the big and small screens, including roles in *Avatar*, *Hidalgo*, *300*, *The Incredible Hulk* and the *Spartacus* series. We enjoyed a meal at one of Peter's favourite Hollywood restaurants while marvelling at how different our lifestyles currently were.

I started running the next day in Pasadena under typically clear southern Californian skies. As I forged my way east, the Californian landscape became more and more dry. The wind also picked up. One morning it was so fierce it blew my cap off. Nothing unusual about that—but this time the cap flew down the street so fast that I stood no chance of catching up with it. I waved goodbye to that cap and turned back into the wind, running against it but only progressing at a slow walking pace.

Past Mount Baldy, scene of one of the toughest climbs in the Tour of California cycle race, I eventually crested a gentle pass and headed down into a desert valley toward Palm Springs. Wind turbines abounded, many from the early days of the industry.

I finished my run that day in Palm Springs in the dark, having covered 68.8 kilometres. This was to remain the biggest single daily distance of the world run until I reached the Nullarbor Plain, almost eighteen months later.

Palm Springs is an unusual place. Completely dependent on irrigation water, it's an artificial oasis in an extremely dry desert.

It's also popular with both the gay and retiree communities and as I ran through the main street early that Saturday evening the town's hub of restaurants and bars was already bustling.

The next day was a short one to the town of Indio. This place was of critical importance to me, because from here there was only one road heading east for the next 150 kilometres and that was the Christopher Columbus Transcontinental Highway—the number one highway across North America and a road that's in the upper echelons of importance when it comes to freeways. I was aware I might not be allowed to run on this highway and a quick visit to the local Highway Patrol office confirmed this to be the case.

The CHiPs policeman was very helpful, though, and we worked out an alternative route. I had to run south, almost to the Mexican border, then swing around through a remote desert region before joining up with the highway again at Blythe, just before the Arizona border. As tough as this was going to be, at least I was comfortable knowing there was no other option. It also afforded me the opportunity to achieve one of my pre-run aims: making it close to the Mexican border.

My new course took me along the western shores of the Salton Sea and on to the town of Brawley. This was fascinating running territory. The Salton Sea is the largest lake in California and its surface is 69 metres below sea level. In fact, the deepest part of the lake is less than 2 metres higher than the low point of Death Valley, making it one of the lowest places on Earth. The body of water itself lies directly over the San Andreas Fault, which is why it's so low—the Earth is essentially being parted along the fault line. The only reason the area hasn't been inundated by the Pacific Ocean is because thousands of years of sediment build-up from the Colorado River has effectively dammed off the region from the Sea of Cortez.

The Salton Sea was a dry lake bed until 1905, when flooding in the Colorado River overwhelmed an irrigation canal. A small inland waterfall, flowing from the higher Colorado River to the Salton Valley, quickly grew in size until it was 25 metres in height. There was little the authorities of the day could do to stop it and the river continued to rush in until the whole area was full of water. Initially a freshwater lake, the Salton Sea is now hyper-saline due to evaporation and low rainfall and many of the bird and fish species are dying or leaving the lake.

I certainly found the desert around the Salton Sea to be one of the driest regions I've ever run through. Sweat doesn't even appear on your skin, such is the evaporation rate. But with the dry air literally sucking the moisture out of your body, you certainly know about the aridity soon enough when thirst starts to kick in.

Late on the afternoon of 5 March I passed the 3000-kilometre mark of the world run and finished the day on the outskirts of Salton City, a virtual ghost town. The town was built for water sports when the lake was fresh but the super-salty water ruined the plans of the developers and land in the town now sells at incredibly cheap rates—less than $1000 per acre in many cases. As well as being set in one of the driest and most geologically unstable parts of the Earth, Salton City is also prone to a cataclysmic flash flood, should the sill between the lake and the Sea of Cortez ever be breached by an earthquake—not exactly a great selling point.

It took me two days to reach Brawley, with its fertile farmland tended by Mexican workers from just across the border, only 40 kilometres to the south. From Brawley, I needed to run nearly

150 kilometres through an even more desolate region to Blythe. Not one town existed in the interim, so the support vehicle was working overtime for the three days it took me to complete this section, commuting me back to Brawley one afternoon and on to Blythe the next.

The Glamis sand dunes were a highlight of this stretch, providing a Saharan-style backdrop for my run, but they were made even more interesting when, in the middle of the sandy nowhere, I met an Australian geologist, Todor. He was conducting scientific tests on a new sensing instrument in the desert sands about 50 metres from the road. Todor and his fellow scientist, Joe, provided me with a welcome stop and drink of water. Then, on the spur of the moment, the Aussie decided to take time off from his duties to run with me for a few miles; he was picked up down the road by his colleague in their car.

Reaching Blythe, I took the opportunity to visit the nearby 'desert giants', or intaglios as they are known. Similar to the Nazca giants of South America, these were 'drawn' by the ancient inhabitants of the area many centuries earlier by scraping away the surface layer of the ground. The largest human figure is 52 metres long. Not discovered by Europeans until an aeroplane pilot noticed them in 1930, these geoglyphs are difficult to date. Some experts estimate they could even be up to 12,000 years old.

As interested as I am in this sort of history, I had a special reason to visit these particular geoglyphs. As a child I had been a keen reader of the Hardy Boys series of books and the *Mystery of the Desert Giant* was the first Hardy Boys book I ever read. It was set around the town of Blythe, with Frank, Joe and Chet spending time at these desert giants and boating down the nearby Colorado River.

It was an unusual interlude for me that day, though this type of unique tourism is exactly what a run around the world so often facilitates. I'm sure few tourists from Australia have ever thought to travel to Blythe and visit these prehistoric desert wonders.

On 10 March I ran across the Colorado River and into Arizona, having covered more than 1300 kilometres on foot through California in just 26 days. As I was crossing the river, I imagined the Hardy Boys pushing off from the shore on the Californian side in their hired boat. These flashbacks to the stories of my childhood made me consider the sequence of circumstances that led to me becoming a runner—one who was now treading a path around the world. As a child I had read about the land of the desert giants, now I was running through it. The realm of the imagined had become a reality. How had this come about?

CHAPTER 4

The running child

Woolgarlo is a tiny village on the shores of Lake Burrinjuck in central New South Wales. In fact, a village is too grand a word to describe what is essentially a boat ramp facility for those fishing the lake. The lake itself exists solely as a consequence of the Burrinjuck Dam on the Murrumbidgee River. In times of drought, when the Murrumbidgee shrinks to a trickle, fishing boats need to be backed much further down the ramp to access the lake—a lake that is speckled with countless drowned trees, ghosts from the pre-dam past.

To reach Woolgarlo, one needs to travel about 6 kilometres down a dusty unsealed road, through rolling sparse hills that form part of the lower slopes of Australia's Great Dividing Range. Lined sporadically with eucalypts, the road and its surroundings are quintessential Australian countryside. At the age of twelve, I ran this same 6 kilometres of dirt track, from the town to the intersection with the sealed road that snakes its way from the Hume Highway to Burrinjuck Dam.

Why? Well, partly because I was bored by the lack of fish being caught by my keen angling family. I've always been too impatient for fishing. Instead, I asked my mother if I could run back towards the farm at which we were staying, to be picked up somewhere along the road by the family car after they'd finished fishing for the day.

There are two photographs still in existence, taken by my mother, with me in blue track pants and no shirt, jogging along this brown ribbon of dirt with a backdrop comprised of dry grassy sheep paddocks and the occasional eucalypt tree. There was nothing else in sight. Even then, in 1973, I had a strong urge to make my way across the rural countryside under my own steam, feeling the sense of accomplishment that comes from covering distances that most people consider to be the domain of automobiles.

In my mid-twenties I was co-founder of a cycling group, which has since come to be known as the Tour de Bois. Based on nothing more than a bunch of likeminded friends wanting to ride through the Australian 'bush', the Tour de Bois has risen to minor legendary status, at least in the eyes of those making the annual pilgrimage.

The tour comprises a week of cycling through bucolic Australian farming land and forests, staying in rustic country pubs and generally having a rollicking good time. Since its inception in 1988, the Tour de Bois has enjoyed an unbroken sequence of yearly rides. I have missed just one—during which I was running around the world.

The essence of the Tour de Bois is identical to my motivation as a twelve-year-old for running the Woolgarlo road—it's the feeling of accomplishment we derive from covering long distances through the countryside using only the power of our own bodies. Oh, and the après-cycling shenanigans play a big part in the Tour de Bois too, with many a cold beer consumed while getting to know local farmers, shearers and that special breed, the outback publican. But that's another story.

Simply put, I love being out in the countryside and I love running (and cycling). What better way to combine the two than to run around the world. But countless people enjoy being in the countryside, yet most enjoy it in a more sedate manner than I do. Why do I like to run through the countryside? And an even more basic question than this—why do I like to run at all?

The short answer is that I really don't know. I guess I couldn't give a more succinct explanation than that of Forrest Gump when he was asked why he was running back and forth across the USA. In his slow southern drawl, his response was breathtakingly simple: 'I just felt like running.' And so it is with me.

But there must be deeper reasons than this and uncovering them requires a little history. What factors led to my fascination with being out on the road; a fascination that would ultimately lead to me circumnavigating the Earth on foot?

Like many a young boy, it was sport that first captured my imagination. And the sport that interested me the most as a child happened to rely heavily on running.

Previous generations of my family were not sports people. I recall virtually nothing from my parents, grandparents, aunties or uncles about any of them participating in sporting activities.

My mother played a year of basketball when she was fifteen and won a trophy, and an uncle had played a bit of cricket, but that was about the sum of it. If my family of generations past had participated in sport, they certainly weren't overt in recounting it. While some kids of my generation were explicitly expected to play soccer or rugby league on the weekends, there was no push from within my family for me to be involved in any form of sport at all.

It was on the suggestion of a school friend that I decided to play soccer when I was seven years old. Soccer at that age is not much more than a chaotic scrum involving every player on the field other than the goalkeepers—and sometimes them too—trying to kick the ball at the same time. That said, I enjoyed the game a lot but after two seasons I was yearning for a different challenge. As great a game as it is, soccer was not *the game* where I came from.

That game was rugby league, otherwise known in the local lexicon as 'footy'. It was the sport that commanded all the attention in the back pages of the newspapers, on the radio and during Saturday afternoons on the television. It was the game all the coolest kids seemed to play, and I wanted to give it a go.

Early in 1970, another friend from school suggested I join him playing rugby league for Windang. The club's home ground was located just across the bridge that spans the entrance to Lake Illawarra, about 2 kilometres from my home. I jumped at the opportunity. I was going to play my first game of footy.

Junior sport is often a bastion of nepotism and the situation was no different at Windang. Most boys in the team had fathers who drank together at the local pub. These boys were assured of being in the run-on team. As one of the only team members whose father was not part of that clique, it was my role to sit on the sideline in case of injury to one of the main team.

And sit on the sideline I did. As a nine-year-old, I would turn up to every game, always hopeful of getting some time on the field. The best weeks were when I got to put on one of the reserve jerseys. I would proudly wear the white top with black V while I watched the game, yearning to get on to the field.

Some weeks, though, I was consigned to the reserve reserves bench, where I wasn't even given a jersey to wear. Either way, I'd head home after each game, hopeful of getting a run the next week. I wanted so much to feel the sensation of playing the game, but halfway through the season this had not happened.

And then another opportunity arose. Our school was entered in the Nowra Knockout. As the name suggests, a winning team advances through the draw like a tennis player in a major tournament, with a losing team bowing out of the competition. In 1970, the competition was based on weight, and my team's cut-off was the imperial measure of 4 stone 7 pounds.

As we turned up to the ground, I was beside myself with expectation at playing my first-ever game of footy. However, before gaining the stamp on the wrist that allowed one to play, each player had to be officially weighed. I stepped onto the old-style scales and my heart sank when I saw the weigh-master shaking his head—I tipped the scales at 4 stone 9 pounds.

It's not easy for a nine-year-old to lose two pounds in an hour but that's what I tried to do. I jogged around the field, went to the toilet several times and even stripped down to my underwear for another public weigh-in just minutes before the game. By this stage a small crowd of adults had assembled, hoping to see this little boy who had gone to so much trouble and effort to 'make the weight' actually make it on to the field. They could sense how much it meant to me. I even heard one woman whisper to another that she was going to cry if I didn't make the weight.

It's hard to describe the disappointment I felt when I was told I was still an ounce over weight—a mere ounce! I don't know whether that woman cried but I do know that I was not allowed to play. I was told, however, that if our team won, and I lost just a little more weight, I might be able to play in the subsequent game.

But our team didn't win and with that loss went the opportunity to play my first game of footy that day.

But there was still hope, as there were several games remaining in the season with Windang. I had not given up thinking that the coach might feel it was worth taking a risk on me. To be fair, I had no idea if I had any ability at the game at all, so there was no way he could know either. It was simply more convenient to leave me on the sideline, just in case I was a complete disaster. And the sideline is where I stayed, right up until the last game of the season.

By the time this last game came around my eternal optimism had waned somewhat. A season of sitting on the sideline does that, even to an ever-hopeful child. And it appeared my sagging sentiments were warranted. Sadly, as the jerseys were handed out, I was told once again to take my place on the sideline.

This week was a little different, though, as our team had not made the finals. It appears this infused our coach with an unusual level of risk-taking. It's difficult to relate my exhilaration when, late in the game, I was told to replace one of our players. It came as a complete surprise to me and the excitement I felt outweighed even the thrill of a Christmas morning—I was actually about to play in a game of footy.

It didn't really matter so much to me if I was good, bad or average. That's not how kids think about sport. I just wanted to be part of a game. I proudly ran on to the field, excited like never before. However, there were now only three minutes remaining on the clock.

Our team had possession for most of this time. I chased the play around from ruck to ruck, trying hard to involve myself. I was desperate to touch the ball and have a run, just as I'd seen others do and had daydreamed of doing myself. Until I touched that ball or made a tackle, though, I couldn't really consider myself to have played a game. But no-one passed me the ball.

When the referee blew the whistle for the final time that day, it marked the end of my first season of footy—a season that comprised just three minutes on the field.

One whole year and I had not made a tackle nor touched the ball.

I made an important decision early the next year. If I were to play for Windang again, I would likely spend another season warming the reserve bench. Instead, I decided I would play for Warilla. This was the suburb I lived in, the playing fields were closer to home and it was the club at which many of the boys at my school were members. What did I have to lose?

Warilla was also a more popular club, with five grades in the ten-year-old age bracket. The A team essentially picked itself. These were the guys who were known to be able to play the game and this was the team in which every other boy aspired to play. For the rest of us, there were the trials.

The word went around that prospective new players were expected to be at the ground in their shorts and boots the Saturday morning before the season proper commenced. I could hardly believe it—all I had to do was turn up and I'd be given a game, even if it wasn't a proper competition match. I'd dreamed about playing for so long and the reality was about to materialise. It didn't matter to me that it was only a trial.

A large group of hopefuls assembled early that morning in bright sunshine. Once again, the thrill of pulling on a football jersey was palpable—this time it was the blue and gold of the Warilla Gorillas. To me there was something magical about football boots and jerseys.

Two groups of thirteen boys were randomly thrown together and told to head out on to the field as opposing teams for the ten-year-old age-group trial. I had no idea what position to play in, nor did I know where to stand for the kick-off as I'd never started a game before.

So I went to the spot that was closest to the ball; 10 metres from halfway in the centre of the ground. This put me right in front of the opposition player who was about to initiate play by booting the ball towards our team. And so began the game.

The opposition kicker was remarkably accurate for a ten-year-old. His kick was as straight as any kick could hope to be. It came directly at me, hitting me in the middle of the chest before ricocheting straight up into the air. It was my first touch of the ball in a game and it looked like it would also be my first mistake.

But I watched the ball carefully—it rose to a height of 5 metres or so then came right back down into my arms. Okay, so I'd made a small error in not taking the ball cleanly, but I had recovered. Now I had the ball and I knew the aim was to place the ball over the opposition's try line, so that's the direction in which I headed.

The next ten seconds is still clearly etched in my memory as one of the greatest highlights of my life. I ran and I ran and I ran. I sidestepped, weaved and swerved around the players from the other team. When there were no more players left to beat, I ran the remaining metres to the try line and placed the ball under the uprights. I had scored a try from the kick-off with my first ever touch of the ball and not a finger had been laid upon me.

This was the first time I realised I could run. All children love to run. One only has to observe a child placed in a playground with other kids—the first thing that child will do is run. It's the most natural activity there is. But children are not conscious of running as sport. It's just fun. Being a good or bad runner is not a concept that enters a child's mind—until they become involved in a sport that relies crucially on running.

And so it was with me. Running around the school playground playing tag was one thing. All the kids could do that. This was different. This type of running produced a rush like I'd never felt before.

As I picked up the ball and started to walk back toward halfway, all four coaches of the lower grades for that year— the 10B, 10C, 10D and 10E teams—came running on to the field from their various vantage points, brandishing notebooks and pens.

As it transpired, the 10B coach reached me first. 'What's your name, son?' he asked. I replied and he quickly jotted down my details. But then he added, 'You can go off now.'

'Why?' I asked, horrified that my game was over.

'You're in the team,' he said. 'You'll be playing for the 10Bs this year. We'll give another kid a chance now.'

After spending just three minutes on the field the previous year, I had now managed a measly ten seconds. But at least I was subbed off for the best of reasons. I was in the team, and I would ultimately get to play every minute of every competition game that year.

— 🏃 —

Later that year I received further confirmation that running was an activity for which I had some proclivity. Ten years of age was the first opportunity to race over 100 metres in the school athletics carnival at Warilla North Public School. I placed third in my age group and made the Junior Boys 4 x 100m Relay team. I was certainly not the fastest kid going round but ours was a special year of students when it came to running.

Our relay team went on to win the State Championships, setting a new state record which stood for more than twenty years. We repeated this feat three more times by the time we reached the age of fifteen. Yes, I could run, and so could several of my school mates.

I wasn't a great runner—after all, I was only the third fastest in my year at Warilla North—but I now had a taste of running in a competitive environment and it was enough to motivate me to want more.

At that same state carnival in 1971, I happened upon an athletics handbook which outlined every world record for every running event for every age group from ten years up. I was intrigued, but not just by the sprint records.

The marathon particularly fascinated me. All the other races were on the track but here was an event which was run on the road, often in the countryside. I'd been on holidays in the countryside and it seemed such a noble and beautiful place to run a race as long as the marathon.

I immediately set myself a challenge. Each year I would run the same number of miles (in a single run) as my age in years. I had my father measure the distance around our block with the car's odometer and I then calculated how many laps I needed to run to reach 10 miles (in 1971 Australia was still a year away from adopting the metric system).

The local kids in the neighbourhood saw me as a novelty for the first couple of laps but by the final few circuits I had become the focus of a concerted campaign of light-hearted heckling and jeering. At least they didn't take to throwing rocks at me, which was one of the more usual punishments for maverick behaviour in those days.

I finished my 10 miles in good shape, much to the amazement of everyone, including my parents. This was prior to the running boom that took hold in the Western world after Frank Shorter won the 1972 Munich Olympic Marathon. There were no road runners in my neighbourhood in 1971, especially not young kids.

By the end of that year, at the age of ten years and ten months, I was both a sprinter and a long-distance runner. I was far from elite at either of these disparate and seemingly mutually exclusive ends of the running spectrum but I enjoyed them equally, regardless. More importantly, I already had plans to one day run a marathon. Little did I know at the time, the ambition would not stop there—one day I would also run around the Earth.

CHAPTER 5

Arizona

Arizona is a desert state. It is hot and dry in summer, and mild and dry in winter. Rainfall is minimal. Having crossed the bridge over the Colorado River from California to Arizona, my map was showing a service road running alongside the Christopher Columbus Transcontinental Freeway, so I chose this option. But maps can be misleading.

The road was nothing more than a very dusty track that seemed to be used only by dune buggies and trail and quad bikes. I was running over dry creek beds, through sand and gravel and alongside a never-ending array of cacti. Despite vaguely following the freeway, the track wound through remote countryside and I only saw a few people riding in or on the aforementioned style of vehicles. And then the road disappeared completely.

Luckily, I was still quite close to the freeway. I did some cross-country running, scrambled up an embankment, climbed over the barrier and was on the Transcontinental Highway. I hadn't checked with the Arizonan officials but I suspected it was also illegal to be a pedestrian on their stretch of this road. I ran a bit faster, hoping to reach the next off-ramp before a policeman came along. A few kilometres on, at the top of a hill, I finally reached a road that veered off toward the town of Quartzite.

Quartzite is one of the most eccentric towns in the whole of the US. Its summer population, when the temperature is unbearably hot, numbers just a few thousand. But in the very comfortable winter months it swells to more than a million inhabitants, most of them in campervans.

Quartzite is widely considered the campervan and mobile home capital of the world. The relatively warm temperatures and dry conditions attract a demographic known as 'the snow birds'—mainly retired couples from the snowbound north of the continent, intent on escaping the harsh winter. There is also a thriving gemstone trading industry during these months, operating from a makeshift business district of tents and trailers.

By the time I ran into town in early March, the vast majority of the snow birds had flown north again to return to their jobs and normal lives, something for which I was grateful. Accommodation was easy to find, as was a meal at a local restaurant. I doubt this would have been the case had I arrived two months earlier.

Quartzite's other main claim to fame is that Wyatt Earp was supposedly the town's sheriff for a brief period in the 1880s, following his infamous role in the Gunfight at the O.K. Corral, which took place at Tombstone in the south-east of the state. Wyatt would struggle to recognise the town these days during its snowbird months.

For several days I was engrossed in classic desert running. Long flat straights were the order of the day, with only the occasional cactus to add a third dimension to the landscape. Entries to ranches were commonplace along the road, with their simple construction of two posts with a wooden plinth across the top, usually adorned with some quirky ornament like a sheep's skull or a fancy-looking hub cap. The homesteads themselves, however, always seemed to be too far away to be visible, hidden in the distant foothills or in gullies below the horizon. And omnipresent in the background were the towering mountain ranges, coloured brown, black, red, purple or whatever the going hue was for that time of the day. In the desert, the variations of light are amazing.

We stayed a night in the small town of Salome at an eccentric and highly interesting establishment called the Westward Motel. The proprietor, Rande (pronounced Randy), was a career roadie, having worked on tour nationally and internationally with some of the world's biggest bands—The Rolling Stones (three times), The Police, Pink Floyd, The Grateful Dead, Deep Purple, Ted Nugent, The Moody Blues, The Allman Brothers, Kenny Rogers, Rush, Genesis, John Mellencamp, Dolly Parton and Heart. What a resume! And he was a great guy to talk with over a few red wines.

Air force training was an obvious activity in this remote region. On the road the next day I heard the unmistakable roar of jets overhead, looking up to see two of them firing missiles of some sort. The missiles flew rapidly, trailing a smoky plume behind their fiery exhaust, before exploding a few kilometres up in the sky. The jets then flew off again at high speed, having completed their practice manoeuvres. With this sort of display going on it was hard to get bored on these dead-straight and flat desert roads.

The four of us stayed in Burro Jim's Motel that night, eating at the adjacent Coyote Flats Bar and Café. Both these classic establishments had supposedly been featured in movies. The girls befriended an old guy in the bar at Coyote Flats. He even invited them to a rodeo the following day in Wickenburg, the next town I was to run through.

This was the Real Wild West, complete with cowboys and all. Carmel, Libby and Jenny donned their best 'yee ha' clothes and had a great time watching the bareback riding. (They assured me no animal was harmed.)

I, on the other hand, spent another day on the desert road, passing a landmark from the pioneering days. About 8 kilometres out of Wickenburg, I stopped at an historical marker, indicating this was the site of an Apache ambush of the Wickenburg to Ehrenburg stagecoach in 1871. Five men and a woman were killed in the tragedy. Looking around at the dry, dusty, cactus-filled landscape, it was easy to imagine that event as a scene from a movie. Unfortunately for the stagecoach occupants, it was all too real.

The following day, on the road to Phoenix, I noticed there were no cars approaching me on my side of the highway. I even started running down the middle of the north-bound side of the divided road. A few kilometres later I realised why. There was a serious road accident ahead and the police had blocked all traffic in that direction. I noticed helicopters departing just before I reached the accident.

I eventually passed the scene—a car and an RV had collided head on and the RV had rolled. I ran on ahead for about a

100 metres to the point where the police had stopped the traffic. The Highway Patrol guys informed me there had been a fatality and several serious injuries. They told me the injured had been airlifted to hospital and an investigation was underway. They expected to re-open one lane 'soon'.

I continued running past all the stationary cars and trucks stranded on the highway. People were milling around, standing, sitting and even lying down. It reminded me of REM's video clip for 'Everybody Hurts'. And suddenly I had become 'the messenger'. I spent the next few kilometres stopping frequently and filling people in on what had occurred. Many of them were too far back to even know that it was an accident. The queue was about 3 kilometres long. This was one of the times it paid to be on foot—I was the only person who didn't get held up by the roadblock.

I'd had innumerable discussions in the months leading up to my world run, with a common theme being the unusual nature of the undertaking. The majority of people were supportive but there was often a derisive undertone of 'this is not natural'. Running all day long just seemed so abnormal in most peoples' minds, so entrenched has our modern sedentary lifestyle become.

Wrong! Running long distances is actually quite natural. The human race has, in fact, evolved doing exactly that. Prior to the agrarian revolution approximately 10,000 years ago, attrition hunting was the norm.

Human beings can't run fast enough to catch an antelope or deer when it is fresh and full of energy; attrition hunters, however, gradually chase down the animal over a period of hours or even days. This practice involved one or more members of a tribe and the runners would simply wear down their prey.

The pace was slow and the technique methodical. The chasers would get near, perhaps throwing in an ambit sprint in the hope of reaching the animal. The creature would then run off again. This process would be repeated over and over until the intended victim would eventually succumb to exhaustion. The hunters, who had been jogging for hours, would then move in for the kill with a final sprint. Even today, some pockets of humanity, such as the Kalahari Bushmen, still practise attrition hunting on occasions.

Hundreds of thousands of years of evolution have dictated what is truly natural to modern humans, including in the realm of running. Long-distance slow jogging for hours is the norm, perhaps interspersed with a little walking and occasional short sprints. Running 10 kilometres at top pace is actually more unnatural than running all day long at a very slow but manageable speed. And sitting around for eight hours in front of a computer screen is definitely not natural, evidenced by the increasing prevalence of lower back and pelvic problems in those who do this daily.

On 14 March 2012, at the end of another of these long and slow but entirely natural days of running, I ambled into the suburbs of Phoenix. A late starter as far as its history goes, Phoenix is now the sixth largest city in the US and one of the largest state capitals in the country. It's an interesting place to

visit but I'd included it in my itinerary for another reason—to see my old friend Walter.

For more than a decade, Walter had been heading his venture-capital fund's investment in wave energy and had spent several stints as a board member of our company. He was a regular visitor to Australia. I had caught up with Walter in some unconventional locations in the past as part of our jobs—besides Sydney and Zurich, we'd had meetings in the village of Grindelwald at the base of the majestic Eiger in the Swiss Alps and in an historic pre-Revolutionary War town in Connecticut. Now I was on his home turf.

Though he grew up in Switzerland, Walter was living in Phoenix with his wife. They invited all of us for dinner, along with their daughter, her husband and two kids. Walter's daughter was running her first marathon later that year and he wanted her to meet me. The hospitality was really laid on, with some of the finest food of the whole world run served that night, including spectacular homemade bread.

The next day's run was a short one, spent traversing Phoenix from one side to the other. That afternoon provided one of the more humorous episodes of the entire adventure. I was invited to one of the major television stations for a live interview. The three girls came along as well and we found ourselves in the 'green room', waiting for my appearance.

There was another guy in the room too, who was due on before me. We introduced ourselves and exchanged small talk. Carmel then approached the guy with her camera, asking 'would you mind', expecting him to take a photo of our group. He said 'sure' and promptly assumed a standard photograph pose, before quickly realising his mistake, much to his embarrassment.

We were soon to learn he was Joe Nicholls, one of the biggest country music stars in the US, and an artist who has been nominated for four Grammy Awards. His mistake was understandable, as he gets asked to have photos taken with fans all the time. Joe is a very likeable and polite guy but we, in our ignorance, had never heard of him. We all had a good laugh, with his manager jokingly declaring, 'It'll do him good.'

The next day was a sad one, with Jenny leaving early in the morning. She had to get back to Australia after five weeks with us on the road through California and Arizona. We were all sorry to see her go. I headed off in a northerly direction and by mid-morning I had left Phoenix behind me. Jenny had done the same by bus a few hours earlier. Carmel and Libby, once again reduced to a crew of two in the ever-faithful support car, were the last to hit the road that morning.

Arizona is something of a two-tiered state. The south, around Phoenix, is relatively low in elevation. The north of the state is much higher, sitting on a plateau at around 2000 metres in altitude. The next two days, therefore, involved a lot of uphill running.

After wonderful mild to warm weather to this point, I awoke one morning in the Arizona high country to snow. I was quite thrilled to be able to do some white weather running but I hadn't anticipated the snow getting heavier. I didn't have any long running pants, so I spent the day in shorts in temperatures of minus 8 degrees Celsius.

The reaction of locals was one of incredulity. They clearly thought I was weird and when I ducked into a Burger King to get a warm drink, several patrons gave me a wide berth, not wanting to tangle with someone who appeared strange enough in his actions to be potentially unstable in mind. I finished the day in Prescott, with wet and freezing feet and a body that was shaking uncontrollably.

Pulling the curtains aside the next morning, I was greeted by the sight of the support vehicle buried in snow. Carmel and Libby expected me to call a lay day but I was determined to get on the road. I went to the front desk of the motel, borrowed a shovel and proceeded to dig the car out.

An hour later the car was free and I headed off in sunshine and still conditions, even if the countryside was under a blanket of metre-deep snow. The temperature increased quite rapidly and by early afternoon much of the snow had disappeared. I even experienced the privilege that day of running past a seconds-old calf, still attached to its placenta, with its mother licking the shiny membrane from its body.

As I ran I continued to climb gradually until I was 2230 metres high, roughly level with the highest point in Australia, Mount Kosciuszko. Heading north from the town of Williams one morning, I was virtually alone on the road. Barely any traffic passed me and the long flat straights made the road seem even lonelier.

Then ahead in the distance I caught a glimpse of another individual on foot. This was most unusual! I slowly caught up with him and noticed he was walking with a pole and a backpack. My greeting startled him as my running style had become so efficient that I made little noise as each footfall touched the road and he hadn't heard me coming.

Jeremy Bolam was an Englishman who was walking the trails across Arizona from south to north. Unfortunately, the unseasonal snows had obliterated the trails and forced him to do a few days on the roads. I stopped and walked with Jeremy for a couple of miles, exchanging stories and contact details and reflecting on why we were doing what we were doing. Jeremy is an adventurer from way back and this was merely the latest in his retinue. Writing books about his exploits is not new to Jeremy either.

I called the girls and made sure they were aware of Jeremy, suggesting they stop to say hello when they passed him later that morning on their way to meet me. Feeling invigorated by this chance encounter with a like-minded soul, I started to run again, occasionally looking back—on these long straight roads it took an eternity before Jeremy was out of sight.

Late on the same day I came upon one of the most memorable panoramas of the whole world run and one that would take anyone's breath away. The flat open sections through which I had been running had given way to forests and rolling hills, with the road bending to and fro with the contours of the land. I ran up a slope covered in trees, knowing I was close, and then, suddenly, out of nowhere it appeared in front of me—the most massive slice through the Earth's surface I'd ever set eyes upon: the mile-deep Grand Canyon!

Everyone knows about this wonder of the natural world but pre-existing knowledge of something can often lead to a let-down when one actually encounters the thing itself. But the Grand Canyon is different. It doesn't disappoint.

The Grand Canyon is simply so spectacular you cannot help but be in awe of it. And, thankfully, there is no uncontrolled development either. In fact, the official park buildings and motels are all quite old and, to my pleasant surprise, virtually invisible until you are within a stone's throw of them.

Like any desert feature, the colours of the Grand Canyon vary dramatically throughout the day, especially around sunrise and sunset. I had arrived just before sunset and was treated to one of these displays of subtly changing light, with the opposite walls of the canyon exhibiting a golden glow. It was truly one of the most memorable experiences, not just of the world run, but of my life so far.

As I'd learned during my time running through New Zealand, the Earth's surface has never been static. The crust has been constantly replenishing itself over the more than four billion years of the planet's existence. Time and time again, volcanic lava, ash, mud and other sediments cover the Earth's surface and harden, only to be covered in turn by the next geologic event.

The Grand Canyon, cut into the earth by the flow of the Colorado River, is only about six million years old. It was initially much like any other watercourse. However, as the river sliced deeper and deeper into the underlying rock, it exposed the earlier layers that had been buried for aeons. So much so, that the rock in certain places at the bottom of the canyon—the layer known as the Vishnu Schist—is nearly two billion years old, almost half the life of the Earth itself, and has lain buried since its formation.

Even though the rim of the Grand Canyon is now 2 kilometres above sea level, the whole region actually lay under the sea when the Vishnu Schist rock was formed. Such is the dynamic nature of the Earth's crust. I was in awe of not only the beauty of the place but also of its unfathomably long history.

The next day, 23 March, was just as memorable. Carmel and I took a helicopter flight over the canyon early in the morning. I then got to run along the southern rim for the rest of the day. That particular experience has to be high on the agenda for any serious runner—a 40-kilometre run along the rim of the Grand Canyon!

The girls picked me up that afternoon and we commuted back to the main village where we had Champagne and canapés on the edge of the canyon as the sun went down. It doesn't get much better than that.

On I ran to the east, past amazingly rugged gorges and rocky hilltop peaks devoid of vegetation. Further downstream these gorges would eventually become the Grand Canyon, which was now, sadly, behind me. In the distance I could see the Painted Desert. Fluffy pink clouds sat suspended in the sky, with equally brilliant colours emanating from the land itself.

We overnighted in towns including Cameron, a former Navajo trading post that now houses a motel, restaurant and the usual shops selling indigenous American trinkets. And I passed the 4000-kilometre mark on 25 March outside Tuba City, another Navajo town of which I have no idea where it got its name. Several days later I reached the border with Utah—and the famous Monument Valley.

CHAPTER 6

Into the Rockies

Monument Valley is every bit as visually spectacular as the Grand Canyon. Consisting of ancient mesas and buttes projecting vertically into the sky, the valley is part of the Colorado Plateau that sits at more than 1600 metres above sea level. The region was once the site of massive rivers that have eroded much of the higher ground and deposited it on the valley floor.

Monument Valley has also been the location of many movie scenes over the years, the most famous being the *Forrest Gump* segment where Forrest, trailed by his numerous disciples, decides to call it a day and end his odyssey with the line, 'I'm pretty tired. I think I'll go home now.'

Carmel and Libby, knowing for some time that I'd be running through this iconic region, decided they'd dress me up as Forrest Gump for a few photos and videos. Weeks earlier they had bought a wig and fake beard and were itching to reach the exact place on the road where Forrest had stopped. They drove ahead that morning and prepared themselves.

The straight section of road featured in the film is very long and I could see them up ahead for nearly an hour before I reached the site. I donned the wig and beard and we all had a good laugh as I acted out the scene, minus the entourage of followers, of course. A few other carloads of people stopped at the same place to pay homage to Forrest, though none went to our extravagant detail.

After all, I was actually running this road, just like Forrest did.

Several times that morning I passed cattle on the side of the road that were not fenced in. Fencing must be impractical here, as the livestock need to graze over much greater distances in order to survive. A lot of these were bulls and I had to run within metres of these giants.

The experience put an entirely different slant on the term 'running with the bulls'. There's a common belief that bulls charge the colour red. If true, it's a good thing I wasn't wearing red that day but I was wary of the beasts all the same. Luckily, none of the bulls charged, though they didn't shy away from me either. They merely eyed me suspiciously, continuing to chew dry grass as I nervously sauntered by.

Around lunchtime I reached the unusually named town of Mexican Hat. I soon realised where the name had come from, with a rock formation on the hill above the town that was a perfect replica of a sitting person wearing a large sombrero.

During the warm sunny afternoon I ran through some of the most arid yet beautiful countryside imaginable, climbing higher and higher. By the end of the day I was able to look behind me and see the Monument Valley 'monuments', sublimely perched in the valley far below.

I had been in regular email contact with Tony Mangan in the months before I began my run. Tony had already embarked on his own world run some fourteen months earlier. His experience, and willingness to share it, was a boon for me.

One of the many pieces of advice Tony had provided me was to monitor the symmetry of my leg strength. Put more simply, he recommended I check the circumference of my thighs on a consistent basis. One leg being thicker than the other implied an imbalance.

Such an asymmetry can be initiated by a variety of causes. An initially minor and imperceptible injury can result in the favouring of one leg, with the other leg doing more of the work and, hence, getting larger. Alternatively, continually running on the same side of the road can lead to one thigh increasing in diameter due to the constant camber. The bottom line is, asymmetric muscle strength is likely to ultimately lead to problems. It's better to identify and correct the underlying problem in the early stages.

Taking Tony's advice, I measured my thigh circumference on a weekly basis in the early months of my world run, one occasion being just after my foray through Monument Valley. My lack of injuries and insistence on varying the camber by swapping the side of the road I was running on were clearly paying off. I never did detect any difference in the thickness of my thighs.

I interpreted this as confirmation I was well balanced. Physically, at least—some may have argued the balance didn't extend to the mental domain.

Utah is not your average US state. With a high proportion of the population being Mormon, various towns are 'dry'. This did not appear to be state law but with some entire municipalities consisting of teetotallers there wasn't any commercial sense in setting up a store to sell beer, wine or spirits.

It made it difficult at times to enjoy what had become my standard treat of two or three glasses of red wine at night. Not that this inconvenience mattered too much as my route, which 'cut the corner' of the state, only had me in Utah for three days before crossing into Colorado.

After a difficult day running into a howling headwind, the first night in Colorado provided an insight into the lives of the people living in this far south-west corner of the state and, I assume, in many other parts of the rural United Sates too.

Across the road from our motel in the small town of Dove Creek was a cute bar where we chose to have a pre-dinner drink. We were the only customers and were served by a young woman whose four-year-old son was watching TV in the corner. She was very interested in where we were from and what we were doing there. Tourists were clearly rare in town.

As part of the conversation I asked whether she had travelled much. 'Not much,' she replied, 'but I once went to Arizona.' The border with Arizona was barely 100 kilometres from her home and that was the furthest she had ever been in her life.

The conversation brought home to me how lucky I was to have travelled so much in comparison and, contrary to the case of this particular woman, how much easier it now is to travel compared to yesteryear. Running around the world was not always so readily achievable.

Just inside the front door of my home hangs a framed montage of old photographs. Several of these images are of my mother's father. The photos in which Grandad features range from 1906, when he was three years old, through to his fifties.

One thing that strikes me about these photos is that every one of them was taken within a 60-kilometre radius of each other. I have seen numerous photographs of my grandfather, as well as many of my other three grandparents, yet the geographical range in which all these images were captured hardly varies more than this same 60 or so kilometres.

The basic fact is, the generation of my grandparents simply didn't travel very far. I don't think my grandfather ever left the state of New South Wales. Overseas travel was far too exotic to even contemplate. Even his daughter, my mother, has only ventured beyond the state's borders on a few occasions, and not by much. Like my grandfather, she has never held a passport.

In contrast, the same framed montage shows a couple of photographs of me, at the ages of two and seven. These were taken some 400 kilometres apart. My grandfather didn't venture much further from home than this in his whole life. In more recent times I had visited more than 50 countries and I was now circumnavigating the world on foot—this would have been unimaginable in Grandad's day.

Although the case of my grandfather and me is but one example, few would argue that current generations are much more mobile than their predecessors. My grandfather's most likely chance at international travel was by going to war. Luckily for him (although I believe he considered himself unlucky), he was too young at eleven years old for World War I.

By the time Australia followed Britain into World War II, Grandad was a 36-year-old with a limp, courtesy of an accident in his younger days involving a Tarzan swing, a submerged tree stump and his shin bone. While others died on foreign shores, my grandfather was confined to manning an observation post on the Australian east coast, just a couple of miles from his home.

His job was to look out for Japanese submarines and ships. In almost six years, none appeared. The only incident of any note was when a merchant vessel failed to identify itself, prompting a shell to be fired across its bow. Grandad always claimed this period was the most boring time of his life, on a par with the hundredth occasion he had to watch the whole four-hour length of the movie *Gone with the Wind* (he was also a movie theatre projectionist). Instead of heading off to Kokoda, Borneo or Singapore, his one great chance to see the world was spent doing crosswords in a concrete bunker, then driving home for dinner each night.

The reasons for the drastic increase in travel by generations subsequent to my grandparents are multi-fold. International travel is certainly a lot cheaper now in real terms and it is also faster and easier. The internet makes it simple to research a destination in detail. Google Earth even allows us to view real images of exactly where we intend to go. Foreign exchange is as simple as withdrawing cash in the local currency from any ATM in that country—no need for travellers' cheques anymore.

In my grandfather's day, a trip to the UK, for example, would have required him to make currency arrangements before leaving Australia, followed by a three-day flight with many stopovers or perhaps a cruise lasting several weeks. If he wanted to venture on to the European continent, he would have needed to take phrase books for the languages of the countries he intended to visit—no iPhone apps for him, with their translation facilities at the touch of a screen. All in all, it was a much bigger deal to travel in bygone days, and considerably more expensive.

So, would my grandfather have been able to run around the world 60 years ago, had he the desire to do so and two good legs that were up to the journey? a moot question, but I doubt very much that I would have been capable of such a feat if I had lived in his generation. The physical aspects of such a run are only part of the equation. For me, in 2012–13, the logistics were just as formidable as the daily toll on my body. But in the 1950s, the logistics would have dwarfed the physical challenges.

In fact, until the advent of Google Maps and smart-phones in the early part of this century, I would have struggled to accomplish the feat of running around the world for logistical reasons alone. On innumerable occasions during my run I found myself in situations where a paper map would have been insufficient. I often needed to zoom in to Google Maps to view the streets and intersections in greater detail before I could work out whether I needed to make a turn. Without this ability, I would have run the wrong way too many times to count, wasting precious kilometres and even more precious physical and mental stamina.

Carmel was to be my support crew the entire way around the world but there was no way Carmel and I would be able to stay in touch throughout the day, particularly in busy cities, without mobile phones. Before the mid-1990s and the advent of the mobile phone network, running around the world with a support crew would have been practically out of the question.

It's not that it's impossible to run around the world on your own, or without these modern conveniences—it's just that to do so would require enormous effort at the planning stage, as well as a whole lot more mental toughness. I am lucky to be living at a time when the task has been made much easier than it once was, and it will get easier still for those who choose to take on similar adventures in the future.

The efforts of those who went before me, such as Jesper Olsen, Rosie Swale-Pope and Tony Mangan, are all the more amazing, given what I had come to know about the logistics and practicalities of running around the world.

Without a doubt, running around the world is much easier now than at any time in the past, just as international travel is so much easier and more common than it used to be. That said, it turned out to be quite common in the rural regions of the US to meet locals, such as our Dove Creek girl, who had rarely ventured across their own county lines.

The next morning was a case of déjà vu when I pulled back the curtains of the motel room in Dove Creek. Like my experience in Arizona, the ground was once again covered in snow and I still didn't have any long pants in which to run. I spent a cold day running in the open countryside, whipped by icy winds as I made my way on foot to the town of Cortez.

Running in shorts in sub-zero temperatures is not as difficult as some might think. As long as I was wearing plenty of warm clothes on my top half, I was reasonably comfortable. I didn't find my bare legs suffered too much. The physical effort of running created enough internal warmth to keep my legs from feeling uncomfortable.

There was one downside, however. With just a thin piece of material between my genitalia and the bitingly cold wind, I did have concerns the region might suffer from frostbite. It certainly did feel different down there, particularly at the extremity, which was aching incessantly. I stopped for sporadic checks and each time, thankfully, all parts were intact.

Cortez, in the south-western corner of Colorado, was an interesting place. It was easy to imagine the town a century ago, with a wild-west style main street frequented by gunslingers. We availed ourselves of a great micro-brewery, wine bar and restaurant on this same main street, the Main Street Brewery, enjoying a long and friendly discussion with the proprietor to boot.

After a 24-hour respite from the weather, the snow finally arrived again the next day in the late afternoon. But by this time I was much higher in the Rockies and the snow was a lot heavier than the day before. A long run of more than 60 kilometres finished amid a freezing blizzard with ice and snow lining my eyebrows. It was an extra special pleasure that night to have a long hot shower in our motel room in the town of Durango, followed by a lovely home-cooked meal, courtesy of Libby.

From Durango I turned south and headed for New Mexico, passing an emu farm along the way. Just as with crops, the farming of animals these days is an international affair. Emus are very curious animals and the whole flock ran up to the fence to greet me. Although I was aware of this inquisitive trait, I instead chose to imagine the emus' interest in me was due to our common homeland.

By 4 April, after just three days in the south-west corner of Colorado, I reached New Mexico. It wouldn't be long, however, before I was back in the mountain state.

At the state border I stopped at a petrol station for a drink. In front of me in the queue was one of the heaviest people I have ever seen. The guy must have weighed close to 300 kilograms. He was buying a dozen large 3-litre bottles of Coca-Cola and the attendant jokingly asked him if he was having a party. The response was astounding—no, they were all his own supplies, to drink that day while he was driving his truck. It wasn't hard to see how he'd become so large.

The next few days were a bit monotonous, with little in the way of towns or other evidence of civilisation to break up the desert landscape. The highlight was cresting the dividing range. This is an imaginary ridge line that winds its way along the length of the Rocky Mountain Range, separating the western Rockies from the eastern Rockies. Until I passed that point in northern New Mexico, all rainfall had ultimately flowed toward the west and the Pacific Ocean. Now all rainfall would end up flowing toward the Gulf of Mexico and the Atlantic Ocean.

The lowlight was the sad occasion I passed a roadside tribute to a mother and her five children; all had died in a car accident. Monuments to victims of the road were a common theme throughout my run, but never had I seen six from the one tragedy. Even worse, never had so many been children. I won't forget those six crosses in the middle of nowhere.

I finished the day of 7 April in bright sunshine in the town of Cuba. If ever there was a cue for a song, it was here. Carmel and Libby met me at the signpost that heralded the town and handed me my guitar, which I had been travelling with thus far. On the side of the road I belted out a verse and chorus from the song 'April Sun in Cuba' by 70s band Dragon.

Quirky little events like this were an important component of my run around the world, allowing me to remain mentally fresh. That evening we enjoyed delicious Mexican food, based heavily around fresh avocados and tomatoes, preceded by a few margaritas at a terrific little restaurant in town.

Each morning I would invariably reach a mental milestone when I passed the 16.77-kilometre mark. This unusual distance was only significant because it was how far I ran on the first day of the world run, from the Sydney Opera House to Bondi Beach, with the legend known as The Hud.

Every day henceforth, via the odometer function of my Garmin watch, I would be conscious of reaching the

16.77-kilometre mark of that day's run. It's a completely arbitrary distance but it had become a milestone I looked forward to attaining each and every day. Interim milestones such as these were an important way to break up the day of running.

I decided to christen the distance of 16.77 kilometres a 'Deci-Hud'. It took me a while to finalise the name, as The Hud is renowned for his toughness on the road and I considered a mere 16.77 kilometres to be too short a distance with which to honour him. But ten times that distance might be appropriate. So, instead, I defined the distance of 167.7 kilometres as a 'Hud'. And that's how the 16.77-kilometre milestone I passed each day came to be known as a Deci-Hud.

Assigning a name to a subjective distance is not without precedent in running. In a similar fashion, the arbitrary distance of 42.195 kilometres is now known as a marathon. Perhaps one day we'll see the Hud become an Olympic distance for ultrarunners, complementing the shorter marathon distance. It's a little further than 100 miles, which is only fitting as The Hud always goes that little bit further.

Regular days of 50 kilometres or more were eventually punctuated with a short run into Albuquerque, along the banks of the Rio Grande. I never managed to work out which left turn it was that Bugs Bunny should have taken in this city, but I knew I had to make a left in order to head eastwards again.

After a period of relatively flat running, I faced plenty of uphill as I made my way towards the small mountain town of Madrid. Taking its name from its much larger Spanish counterpart, Madrid is a delightfully unusual and eclectic place which needs to be visited to be fully appreciated.

The town is where a major part of the movie *Wild Hogs* was filmed, starring John Travolta, Tim Allen, William H. Macy and Martin Lawrence. We learned this fact from the locals who had their town commandeered for some weeks during the filming. And we ate that night in the same cafe that featured in one of the main scenes.

Although the nature of the landscape was mostly unvarying, I was still enjoying the daily running. It was still vastly different to almost all the other scenery I had spent my life running through. So the day after our stay in Madrid I was quite content to run through what appeared to be exactly the same countryside as I'd been seeing for weeks, on another very long straight desert road. This road, however, had a 'must see' ending—the city of Santa Fe.

Santa Fe has a long history, with the region being occupied over the years by indigenous Americans, Spanish conquerors and finally colonial settlers and ranchers. Nowadays Santa Fe is a hotbed of creativity at so many levels, attracting all manner of people looking to 'break the mould'. That night we had dinner with Patty, a friend of my former colleague Cynthia. Patty took us to a great little restaurant in the old part of town—great restaurants seem to be the norm rather than the exception in trendy and upbeat Santa Fe. The place was buzzing and the food was innovative and delicious.

The next day, a short one of running, I dropped in to see some friends of Walter's in their impressive home in the hills above town. The architecture and building styles of Santa Fe are as unique and interesting as the other aspects of the city and this one was no exception with its ornate touches and interestingly designed outdoor lap pool. As I left the house to run down the hill to town, three deer bounded over a clump of bushes and almost collided with me. This city was full of surprises.

Running through the centre of town shortly after, I experienced one of those unique occasions where 'world run meets moment from history'. Completely out of the blue, I noticed a plaque on a wall as I jogged through an old part of the city. I love to learn about the history of the places I run through, so I stopped to read what the plaque had to say. It turned out this was the jail where Billy the Kid had been held for some time after being captured by Pat Garrett. It's amazing what you stumble upon when running around the world.

We had dinner again that evening with Patty at a very popular North African restaurant. The food was superb, the atmosphere terrific and the owner a delight to talk with during the meal.

Sante Fe had been a revelation at many levels.

The northern part of New Mexico, centred on Santa Fe and the surrounding towns, is unique in more ways than one. But perhaps the most distinctive feature of the area has nothing to do with the landscape itself. As it transpires, this is one of the greatest hotspots of intellectual thought and research on the planet, especially in the fields of physics and mathematics.

The Santa Fe Institute attracts all manner of leading thinkers in their respective fields, exploring diverse subjects ranging from non-linear chaos theory and weather prediction to statistical fluctuations in the stock market. Just north of Santa Fe is the small town of Tesuque, which I had been told was the home of Murray Gell-Mann.

Murray is the man who discovered and named the sub-nuclear particles known as quarks, the fundamental building blocks that make up protons and neutrons. I actually ran right through the main street of Tesuque, hoping to catch a glimpse of Murray but, alas, he was nowhere to be seen that morning.

Just a little further up the dry and dusty highway is the turn-off to Los Alamos, where most of the work on the Manhattan Project took place during World War II. Located up in the hills, Los Alamos was temporarily home to, or was visited by, many of the giants of twentieth-century physics, including Albert Einstein, Richard Feynman and Enrico Fermi. As terrifying a weapon as the atomic bomb was, and still is, this is the place where it was developed (although it was tested some distance away in the south of New Mexico).

So many of the heavyweights of science and other associated disciplines have plied their trade in this region of New Mexico over the past seven or so decades, yet you'd never have known by simply running through the landscape. Covering this physically barren but intellectually rich terrain on foot was quite humbling, knowing it had been the location of so many Eureka moments over the years.

And to juxtapose the cerebral high with the physical, I passed the 5000-kilometre mark of my run around the Earth that same afternoon of 14 April.

About this time I really started to feel like I was in the Rocky Mountains. The Sangre de Christo Mountains, part of the

Rockies, loomed on my right as I ran up through a long canyon to the town of Taos. Taos is where, according to the locals, Julia Roberts owns a nearby property. The same locals claim she is somewhat reclusive. I certainly didn't see Julia either, as I ran through town on my way north.

A couple of days later I crossed into Colorado again, this time with snow-capped peaks visible in every direction. This was journey running at its best.

I spent several days running through the region known as the High Plateau. This is a desert plain sitting at 2500 metres above sea level, surrounded by peaks of 4500 metres. It was picture-postcard stuff and exactly what I had envisaged as the perfect running terrain. Despite being up so high in the Rockies, the ground was almost dead flat. In fact, most of the main roads in the Rockies are not steep at all, making it an easy place to run or cycle. There are some mountain passes but even these tend to be relatively gentle to climb on foot.

Finally running out of the High Plateau valley one Saturday afternoon, I finished the day on the crest of the 2700-metre-high Poncha Pass. This was the highest elevation I'd reached so far on the world run. By this stage I was so accustomed to the altitude that I was breathing no differently to how I did at sea level.

In a beautifully quaint restaurant overhanging a babbling mountain stream in the town of Salida, I celebrated that night with the largest margarita I've ever laid eyes upon. It was the equivalent of between six and eight standard margaritas. Carmel and Libby both chose to decline, which was probably a wise decision on their part. I was a bit dusty the next morning but my supercharged metabolism did a fine job of processing that giant margarita right out of my system.

In fact, such was my metabolic rate, whatever I ate or drank was processed and passed through me within hours. My Garmin watch was telling me that each day's running used up about 6000 calories (25,116 kilojoules). This was on top of the 2500 or so calories (10,465 kilojoules) needed to maintain normal biological functions, such as stabilising body temperature at 37 degrees Celsius. So I guess I was consuming around 8500 calories (35,581 kilojoules) per day.

I would always try to eat some healthy food each day but it's impractical to maintain a perfect diet on the road. The bulk of my intake was ultimately junk calories. It's possible to get away with this type of diet when you're using up so much energy. Eating 8500 mainly junk calories daily might work during a world run but it would be a recipe for disaster for the average adult.

Despite my less-than-perfect diet, including the margaritas, I was feeling fine and I was running effortlessly through the Rockies. All was well with the world run.

CHAPTER 7

Out of the Rockies

The next big pass I had to climb in the Rockies was that of Trout Creek. This was a little steeper but a 5 per cent gradient is very manageable when running slowly uphill in minimal traffic. The 2880-metre summit was again a new high point for the world run. After a brief descent, I spent the afternoon in a vast dry valley, gradually making my way upwards again towards an array of snow-capped peaks. Colorado has something like 50 peaks of 4300 metres or more, though none surpass that elevation by much.

By the end of the day, 23 April, I'd reached the town of Fairplay, nestled under towering peaks at the far side of the valley, and a new record altitude maximum for the world run—just over 3000 metres.

It had been a long and hilly run of nearly 60 kilometres and the battery in my Garmin GPS watch was almost empty. The watch battery always seemed to drain more quickly if it was cold or when I was at altitude. The typical charge life of between six and eight hours meant I was always in danger of losing the data from the final moments of each day. This potentially placed me in the unenviable position of having missing data. To avoid the problem I often had to run the last few miles at a faster pace than was ideal. On this occasion I actually needed to sprint to the finish of the day before the watch battery died.

Then I had one of those moments of discovery again. It didn't take long to learn that Fairplay is the town on which the television series *South Park* is based. In fact, the whole valley is part of South Park County.

All through town there are murals and signs dedicated to the series, with images of the four boys abounding. Eric Cartman, in particular, features prominently among the officially sanctioned graffiti. We were also told by a local resident that the town is the childhood home of the creators of the series, though others claimed they grew up closer to Denver. Yet again, running around the world was providing me with a classic experience in pop culture.

I finally emerged from the Rockies a few days later, on 26 April, but not before a bizarre encounter one morning in a campground with a middle-aged couple from Georgia. This husband and wife were on a motorbike, touring the Rockies. With a southern drawl identical to that of Cletus from *The Simpsons*, they happily chatted over breakfast while smoking four bongs each, their speech slowing after each. By the time they'd finished, their eyes were slits and they could scarcely talk at all. Scarily, the duo then sluggishly mounted their Harley, the wife seated behind, and headed off down the highway. It was a safe assumption this routine was repeated on a daily basis.

The fact they hadn't had an accident to that point was mildly comforting. Still, I couldn't help feeling this was a ticking bomb. A tragedy was only a matter of time.

After running for nearly 100 kilometres in the shadow of one of Colorado's most famous mountains, Pike's Peak, I eventually cruised down a long and sometimes very narrow canyon into the city of Colorado Springs—but not before an interlude through the Garden of the Gods.

The Garden of the Gods is a small park area with a plethora of spectacular rocky landforms poking up towards the sky. It's like a smaller version of Monument Valley, only the rock formations are even more obtusely shaped. Running in novel places like this was always a highlight for me.

Colorado Springs itself is the venue for a lot of elite performance athletic training. Sports of all kinds use the city as a base for high-altitude training camps, including many of the US Olympic squads, and fit-looking individuals wearing sports shoes are a common sight. This prompted me to consider my own experiences with sports shoes—one I wouldn't have guessed at just a few years earlier.

From 1983, when I first started logging my running mileage, until 2010, I had been a heel-striker. This is a term given to those whose outside heel first touches the ground during each foot strike. Heel-strikers have been the most common form of runner until now, and probably still are.

A heel-striker requires shoes with lots of support, especially to guard against over-pronation, where the arch of the foot rolls inward excessively. I had always worn shoes with this sort of support—heavy, thick-soled, stiff shoes that never felt flexible enough in my view. I had always argued against stiff shoes, as the natural motion of a foot is to bend easily and flexibly just under the ball of the forefoot.

Then I discovered an ultra-light and super-flexible running shoe in a sports shop. This shoe had no support at all and I wondered how anyone could run long distances in such a thing. I tried on a pair and found them to be the most comfortable running shoe I'd ever donned. Wouldn't it be wonderful if they could somehow be supportive as well? The shoes were inexpensive, so I decided to give them a try.

When I went for my first run in these shoes, I found it virtually impossible to land on my heels. My feet would roll in and I knew I'd end up injured. So I decided to try landing on my mid-foot; this helped greatly. Although the style felt awkward at first, I found I was landing lightly and the over-pronation disappeared immediately.

I persevered with this new forefoot running style—with me it was actually somewhere between the forefoot and mid-foot that was striking the ground first—and it gradually started to feel more normal. It probably took me about three months before forefoot running felt completely natural and by this time I found it very unnatural when I tried running in my old supportive-style shoes. I'd made the conversion and there was no going back.

A mid-foot or forefoot style allows the force generated when striking the ground to be dissipated over a longer period of time, as the weight of the descending body (which is many times the stationary body weight) is absorbed gradually. This period of force absorption is still short—tenths of a second—but it is a much longer time period than is afforded the more impulsive heel-striking style.

With heel-striking the same force is absorbed within hundreds of a second as it's transferred as an impulse up the leg, through the knee and into the hips. In theory, injuries should be far less prevalent when employing a forefoot running style, since the bones, ligaments and tendons of the foot and ankle do much of the work in evening out and dissipating the force of each foot strike.

When I ran from Melbourne to Sydney in 2009, I suffered some overuse injuries while wearing stiff supportive shoes. I wasn't sure whether such injuries would still occur during my world run, regardless of the shoes I was wearing—were injuries simply a function of covering large distances?

Once I got past my first 1000 kilometres of the world run without any sign of an injury, it was obvious to me that the new running style had made the difference. The actual shoes I was wearing were somewhat irrelevant—when one strikes first with their fore- or mid-foot, it doesn't really matter what sort of shoes you wear; support is no longer critical, so the more comfortable the shoe the better.

Having just run the length of New Zealand, down the Californian coast, across the deserts of Arizona and New Mexico and over the Rocky Mountains—a total of nearly 6000 kilometres, yet completely devoid of injury—I was feeling very pleased that I'd changed my running style and shoes. I'd never felt more comfortable in a pair of shoes, nor had I been so free of soreness and injury.

I was so pleased that I decided to run a short day to celebrate the fact. The final descent of the Rockies and my arrival into Colorado Springs heralded a special treat; the three of us visited a movie theatre that afternoon, followed by a sumptuous dinner. Some time for relaxation was warranted.

Turning northwards again, I spent two days working my way to the suburbs of Denver. This was where the support vehicle 'lived', at the home of Peter Evans, brother of the car's owners Roger and Don. We stayed with Peter and his daughter and that evening we enjoyed a wonderful meal at a nearby steakhouse, then a long chat after dinner at home with Peter. The three of us were especially appreciative of Peter's cordiality, including the opportunity to sleep in a real house for a change. It had been a while.

On 29 April I ran through the centre of Denver itself. This was one of the easiest of the large cities I've ever traversed on foot and included a stint along a cycle path next to a river. I even passed the arena in which the Denver Broncos play their home games—Mile High Stadium. As you can guess, Denver is situated a mile above sea level. Finishing the day in the town of Golden, we appreciated from the motel room a view of the Rockies towering above us to the west.

Next was another well-known base for athletes looking to take advantage of the benefits of altitude training—the city of Boulder. I believe Rob de Castella, fellow Australian and former world champion marathon runner, used to live in Boulder for part of the year while he was in the country for the US road racing season. Perhaps better known to many as the setting for the 1970s television series *Mork and Mindy*, Boulder is also the site for a lot of environmental and Earth-based science research, such as the National Centre for Atmospheric Research (NCAR).

A couple of friends of mine from my days as Australia's representative on the International Energy Agency's Ocean Energy Systems Committee were living and working in Boulder. Now key proponents of the country's wind energy program, they met us at a bar in town that evening, along with a friend of a friend from Australia. The six of us enjoyed a balmy evening on the sidewalk, chatting over dinner and a few beers. I had wanted to visit Boulder for decades and my time there lived up to expectations. And it was made even better by good company.

Leaving Boulder, I spent another hilly day running to Estes Park at the base of the Rocky Mountain National Park. The next morning I was joined by a couple of local runners for the first 6 kilometres, followed by a day of downhill into the town of Loveland. Downhill running is much harder on the legs than uphill or flat running. I was always careful not to overdo the pace downhill, lest I contract an injury.

Having reached the 6000-kilometre mark late in the afternoon of 4 May, I celebrated by enjoying a meal and a few drinks with Carmel and Libby in a cute little restaurant in the city of Fort Collins that evening, witnessing the bizarre occurrence of a full-sized train rolling down the middle of the narrow tree-lined street—a completely normal scene on this thoroughfare. It was like seeing an ocean liner steaming up a creek.

A couple of days later, on 6 May, I crossed the Colorado state border into Wyoming, finishing the day in the capital, Cheyenne. I'd run well over 1000 kilometres in the state of Colorado alone.

Now I was in bison country and the border crossing housed a large restaurant and bar complex that featured bison burgers on the menu. However, the $16 price tag was far above my budget and I settled for more conventional fare.

Pushing on to the north, I spied an historic plaque on the outskirts of Cheyenne indicating the nearby site of the first below-ground nuclear missile silos in the US. Like at Vandenberg Air Force Base, these were also ICBMs or Intercontinental Ballistic Missiles.

By this time it was approaching mid-May and we had been in the US for nearly three months. The US has a visa waiver policy with Australia, allowing citizens to visit for three months at a time without the need to apply for a visa. I had intended to reach Canada within this timeframe, run in that country for a while and then re-enter the US for a second stint of three months.

However, as luck had it, the US changed its policy on the very day I started my world run, requiring visitors from Australia and other visa-waiver countries to now not only leave the US but to also leave the North American continent completely.

This imposition meant we could not utilise a visit to Canada, Mexico or any Caribbean island as a means of renewing my three-month visa-waiver status. We had to leave the country and travel to another continent altogether before returning a short time later. There were closer continents, of course, but I felt we may as well use this mandatory time out of the US to travel home to Australia. It was a long way to go, but so were all the other options.

And so it was that we headed back to Sydney for three days, spending time at home with family and friends, before returning to Cheyenne to take up again at the exact point at which I had stopped. As much as I was enjoying the running, the sights and the people I was meeting, it was nice to have a break. We stayed in our home those three nights, savouring the short period of normality.

It was not easy leaving to head back to the US. I'd been running from morning to late afternoon, seven days per week, since the beginning of the year, and I had been looking forward to this short stint at home. By this juncture I was 6140 kilometres into the world run. Despite having run almost daily for more than four months, averaging nearly 50 kilometres per day, I wasn't even a quarter of the way around the world yet.

CHAPTER 8

The Black Hills of Dakota

The Rocky Mountains are a classic case of the Earth's tectonic plates colliding and buckling the ground upward to form a mountain range. This process is rarely confined to just the obvious peaks. The buckles, albeit smaller, usually extend a significant distance either side of the range itself and this is the case with the Rockies.

Coming down from these 'outer Rockies', I found myself descending for the next month or so, even though the descent of this particular crease in the Earth's surface was so gradual as to be imperceptible. I only knew I was going down because the elevation reading on my Garmin watch told me so.

And this was also where the prairies began. Rolling hills of grasslands were the order of the day and trees were minimal. The undulating terrain was further evidence of the creases in the Earth's surface caused by the collision of two tectonic plates over millions of years.

It felt a little strange resuming my run just outside of Cheyenne. Three days at home in Sydney hadn't been a long break but it was long enough to create a surreal feeling as I clicked on my Garmin watch to kick off the next phase of the odyssey. Jet lag probably added to the odd feeling.

My first day back from Australia was spent on a 50-kilometre run that took me almost to the border of Wyoming and Nebraska and included the most unwelcome of stops.

Most runners will experience a particularly nasty reality of the sport at some stage in their life—the uncontrollable urge to go to the toilet while out on the road. Brought on perhaps by what was eaten the night before (chilli does it to me), maybe as a result of simply eating too much or for some completely unknown reason, the bottom line is that such an occurrence constitutes the worst of times for a runner.

It's a nightmare that I've had to deal with several times over the years, including on one very embarrassing occasion in Hyde Park in London. One can't cover more than 100,000 kilometres over half a lifetime of running without the odd case of having 'the runs on the run'.

Actually, without wanting to get too involved in the details, it's fair to say we're not talking about diarrhoea here—rather, something in between diarrhoea and what most people would consider a normal motion. In the end, that's not the critical issue—what's important is that, when your body tells you it has to go, there's not much you can do about it. This is a very real problem for a runner from time to time and it happened to me as I was about to cross the state line from Wyoming into Nebraska.

I was still in the town of Pine Bluffs, only about 1 kilometre into my run that day, 15 May, when the affliction struck.
Thankfully, there was minimal traffic on the road in this small
township and I managed to duck behind a little wooden railway
building between the road and the tracks. Unfortunately, I didn't
quite make it in time.

It wasn't pretty. I had to immediately call Carmel, who was
still back at the motel, to drive out to me with a change of
clothes. Shielded by the open car doors, front and back, I spent
the next little while cleaning up and getting myself in decent
shape to continue running for the day.

An acute attack like that is rare and, in fact, only happened
to me once more during the entire twenty or so months of the
run around the world. I know that other long-time runners will
have suffered the same ignominy and hence have sympathy for
my plight on this occasion. Running around the world entails
more than just the positive uplifting experiences. A world runner
must also cope with negative and humiliating incidents as well.

As I crossed into Nebraska I realised the countryside was now
going to be much the same for the next week, so I settled into
playing a game of my own invention.

Running around the world provides a unique perspective on
the world's drivers and one of the emerging and worrying trends
of recent times has been mobile-phone use while at the wheel.
I was not just seeing this but also experiencing it directly in the
form of texting drivers wandering off the road—or, of more
concern, into the lane of the oncoming traffic—before realising
and suddenly veering back on course.

To while away the time on the prairies of Nebraska, I decided to count the number of men and women who were using their phones while driving. I had regularly heard opinions expressed that women are more prevalent in their phone use as drivers but I felt this was anecdotal at best and I wanted to conduct my own more scientific statistical study while I was on the road. As a scientist, I've always believed that one should be able to back up opinions with facts (unlike many politicians, for whom facts simply get in the way of ideology).

So I took two different samples of 100 phone-using drivers (200 phone-using drivers in total) over a period of a few days. The first sample resulted in 52 women and 48 men observed using the phone while driving and the second 49 women and 51 men. From these results, one could not argue for a gender bias either way.

The worrying trend, however, was the overwhelming numbers of phone-using drivers of either sex traversing the same roads on which I was running. And, as if to confirm this 'fact', no sooner had I finished my impromptu study than I was startled to see a car veering off the road and straight toward me. I had to jump out of the way just in time to observe the driver suddenly look up from a phone and jerk the wheel back toward the road.

As a runner who was spending an unusually large amount of time on the roads, I was hoping I wasn't going to be a casualty of this disturbing modern trend.

As I pushed on into the panhandle region of Nebraska, the temperatures began to increase noticeably. Until now I had been pretty much running in the US winter and early spring. Now summer was getting closer and it was obvious.

We awoke one morning to brilliant warm sunshine under cloudless skies in the town of Kimball—perfect weather for Libby's birthday. Carmel had managed to find balloons and birthday banners the day before and we indulged Libby in a celebratory breakfast before I began running. This was followed up with a birthday dinner that evening in the town of Gering. It was Libby's first (and probably only) Nebraskan birthday.

That afternoon I discovered that mobile-phone use can be hazardous to a runner's health as well as that of a driver. I received a text message from Sydney, so I stopped running to read it. Rather than stand still to reply, I decided to walk a little while I typed an answer. I was well off the road on a wide shoulder and my eyes were directed down at the phone as I walked. I made that most common mistake of being distracted by the phone instead of paying attention to where I was heading.

I don't know exactly what caught my attention but I looked up to see, not 2 metres away, a large rattlesnake coiled and ready to strike. It had obviously slithered out onto the shoulder of the road some time before but the regularly passing cars were scaring it and preventing it from venturing into traffic. With my arrival the deadly reptile had found a much slower moving target at which to aim its frustration and fear.

Had I wandered a half a metre closer before noticing the snake, it almost certainly would have struck. The difference between a safe outcome and a potentially agonising death had been less than a half second of reaction time.

I quickly changed the phone from text mode to video camera and started filming the encounter. I carefully gave the poor serpent a wide berth as I moved around it. The whole time its eyes followed me unswervingly, the main part of its body coiled on the ground, rising vertically to a tensed cobra-like head.

As I made my retreat, I kept glancing back until I was too far away to see it anymore. The last I saw of the creature it had still not made a decision to cross the road, all the time feigning strikes at each and every passing vehicle. If it did try to cross the road, I doubt the attempt resulted in success.

Summer was approaching. This meant all those snakes that had been hibernating during the winter would now be out looking for food and mates. Survival on the road demanded I be acutely aware of this fact. After that little incident I was ever mindful of the existence of snakes in the grass.

A couple more days of similar terrain, running through a monotonous visage of sand hills and grassy tussocks, brought me to the town of Alliance. Here we experienced a wonderful example of hospitality toward strangers. The motel we were staying at was operated by mother and son, Arlene and Justin. They kindly invited the three of us to a barbecue in their own home that evening. Delicious food was complemented by fascinating stories of their lives.

Justin calls Arlene his mother but we later learned that he is not actually her son. They adopted each other some years back and the bond seems as strong as any equivalent blood relationship. They were very generous toward the three of us, as well as to the other motel guests, including an 82-year-old woman who rounded out the evening with an amazing display of tap dancing. I hope I'm that agile at 82.

At the opposite extreme of the world-run experience, two days later I encountered one of the most horrific instances of road kill I've ever seen. To that point I'd passed innumerable animals whose existence had been terminated by cars and trucks, from hedgehogs and skunks to coyotes and deer, but this one was extreme. A deer had been hit by a large vehicle of some sort and its limbs were scattered all over the road. The impact had literally torn the animal to pieces. I tried to look away as I passed the gruesome scene but I needed to keep my eyes on the road to avoid stepping on or tripping over body parts. It didn't smell, so its death must have been very recent. Encounters like that always left me a little less chipper for a while.

Past the town of Chadron, where a legendary 1000-mile horse race to Chicago had begun in the nineteenth century, I pushed on into South Dakota. Here I found one of the rare respites from the prairies in this part of the country—ahead of me were the Black Hills of Dakota.

Rising out of the surrounding plains, this relatively small mountain range was the refuge of local Native Americans in the 1800s after they were chased off the prairies by the advancing tide of Caucasian Americans. The new arrivals were content to leave the 'red man' in the hills—until gold was discovered there and the incumbent tribes were again chased away, this time to the far less hospitable Badlands.

The Black Hills have an array of sites to offer the tourist. The town of Hot Springs has a well-preserved architectural style based on red sandstone, the town of Custer (named after General George) is abuzz with visitors and hosts a great little wine bar that parades local produce. And the bison are aplenty—I had to be careful on one occasion when I ran within 20 metres of a large herd. They checked me out but were content to continue grazing. Given the reputation of bison for unpredictability, I was rightly relieved when the herd was out of sight.

But the real highlight of the Black Hills is the two iconic megalithic monuments—Crazy Horse and Mount Rushmore. These sculptures, carved into the mountains, are in close proximity to each other and are as impressive as I'd expected. I ran past both in the same day.

The Crazy Horse Memorial was just to the north of Custer, and I took time out with the girls to have a look around the visitor centre. At 170 metres high and nearly 200 metres long, this tribute to the legendary Lakota leader Crazy Horse is the largest mountain carving in the world. Begun in 1948, the structure is expected to take many decades yet before it is completed.

The magnificent sight of Crazy Horse atop his steed is truly impressive. A division of the Sioux nation, the Lakota tribe's second most famous citizen is Billy Mills, the 1964 Olympic 10,000-metre champion. This fact added a relevant touch of poignancy for me; as a fellow runner, I was covering these beautiful Black Hills on foot, just as Billy Mills might have done.

Running through the Black Hills was made even more enjoyable by the Mickelson Trail. The trail is an old railway line that has been converted into a cycle and walking track. I got to run more than 30 kilometres on this path, under a thick canopy of mountain conifers, and I was virtually alone. I only saw two cyclists the whole day, making it one of those magical running experiences.

A few hours later I rounded a bend on the twisting and thickly forested road to the sight of Mount Rushmore. Arguably the world's best-known mountain sculpture, this monument honours four US presidents—George Washington, Abraham Lincoln, Thomas Jefferson and Theodore Roosevelt—and was constructed between 1927 and 1941. As large as these granite carvings are at 18 metres high, all four heads could easily fit inside the head of Crazy Horse alone.

I was met at Mount Rushmore by a local television journalist from nearby Rapid City. He ran a story that night on the state news featuring an interview with Carmel, Libby and me, with Mount Rushmore as an imposing backdrop.

After descending through Rapid City a couple of days later, I left the Black Hills behind and was back on the prairies again. Treeless grasslands stretched to the horizon in every direction as I headed east. I began to notice large billboards along the highway, each and every one referring in some way to 'Wall Drug'. I had no idea what these signs meant until I finally reached the South Dakotan town of Wall.

Wall Drug was originally a drugstore, what we'd call a chemist or pharmacy in Australia, but became so successful that it branched into just about every type of merchandise and service that could be offered to locals and travellers alike. The store now takes up a large part of the town and is visited by tens of thousands of passing tourists each year.

Speaking with locals in an independent bar in town, there appears to be some animosity toward the power that Wall Drug yields, with local council decisions almost always being made with an eye to the wishes of those in charge of that particular business.

It was over dinner in Wall that a more important decision was made from the perspective of the run. Libby had been accompanying Carmel and me for five months as part of the support crew but she had her own life to conduct and a new business venture she was keen to get started. She decided it was time to head back to Sydney to begin this new chapter in her life and Carmel and I, despite our sadness at the fact, gave her our full blessing.

Libby had been a fantastic support but all good things come to an end, as they say. So, two days later, Libby caught a bus back to Rapid City to begin her journey home. Carmel and I were now on our own and, for the first time on the world run, the support crew consisted of a single individual.

CHAPTER 9

Minnesota

he town of Wall has another attraction besides its kitsch drugstore. It is also the closest settlement to the Badlands of South Dakota and draws many tourists for this reason alone. The Badlands, as the name suggests, is a region of extremely barren and inhospitable canyons and buttes, in some ways resembling a smaller version of the Grand Canyon. If ever there was an example of what erosion can do, the Badlands is it.

The Badlands was the last popular geographical location I would see for a while and, after passing by the region, the running became a lot more monotonous. The prairies continued, with rolling grassy hills as far as the eye could see. While the prairies to the east of the Dakotas are much flatter, those of the western half are very undulating. This continuous rolling visage was broken temporarily when I crossed the Missouri

River in Pierre, the capital of South Dakota. It was 30 May and I had just passed the 7000-kilometre mark that afternoon.

With a population of 13,000, Pierre is the second least populous state capital in the US. I found it to be quite a charming place of just the right size for a runner. And it was here that one of the most prolific followers of the world run first became a fan.

Lynell Asher noticed me running through town that morning without thinking too much about it. Later in the day she read a story in the local newspaper, photos and all. She logged on to the website and Facebook, began following on a daily basis and never looked back.

It was the realisation there were regular daily followers of the run—people like Lynell—that made the mental side of running around the world so much easier. With often tenuous internet connections, the nightly blog post could sometimes take me hours to finish. Knowing there were people always interested in reading my latest blog offering was a major inspiration to persevere with this nightly ritual.

I reached the eastern side of the state of South Dakota a week later, ambling into the small rural town of Clark. Throughout the US one sees thousands of 'Historic Site' plaques with short explanations of the local history and there was a particularly unique example in Clark.

Here I learned the story of a little boy of about five years of age who, in 1888, lived on a farm near the train line just outside the town. Every day the boy would wave enthusiastically to the driver of the regular train that passed by. The train driver didn't know the boy's name so, among his colleagues, he simply referred to him as the 'Little Fellow'.

This friendly ritual went on for a couple of years, with the strange anonymous relationship becoming legendary among those in the railroad fraternity. Until one day in 1890, when the Little Fellow inexplicably stopped appearing. Concerned about the sudden change in routine, the train driver began to make enquiries. He soon discovered the boy had died.

The Little Fellow was buried beside the train tracks and each year after that, on the US holiday known as Memorial Day, the same driver would stop the train and lay flowers at the boy's grave. When the train driver finally passed away, his family continued the tradition. In 1951 Rotary took on the role and the ritual continues to this day.

No one knows the boy's real name. It was probably revealed at the time of his funeral but the name Little Fellow stuck and any record of his true name has long been lost. Nowadays the laying of flowers at the grave of the Little Fellow is a public ritual that's unique to the town of Clark.

It was about this time I began to notice a pain in a tendon just under the inside of my right ankle bone—the inner tibial protrusion. It was nothing at the start but it slowly became more of a concern. I began changing my running style slightly to compensate, which is always a recipe for disaster. Pretty soon I could feel problems starting to develop with muscles in both legs—muscles that were doing work they shouldn't have been doing.

It was time to start experimenting with my shoes. I didn't have anything other than a pair of orthotics, so I substituted these for the inner soles—some relief, but not enough. I then built up the inside of each shoe with layers of carefully folded toilet paper. This seemed to help and kept the injury at bay for a while, though it didn't go away. I simply had to go on, hoping that the pain didn't get worse. But I was worried.

The landscape got flatter and I eventually crossed into North Dakota. Just a few days in this state saw me through to the border with Minnesota, which I traversed just east of the city of Fargo, dubiously made famous by a Coen Brothers movie of the same name.

After weeks on the prairies, the geography changed almost immediately. Suddenly I was running through lush forests that covered gently rolling hills and lined tranquil lakes. Our first night in this new state was less than impressive, however, when an inquisitive and fearless mouse kept making an appearance in our motel room.

Carmel is not afraid of mice but this one insisted on exploring every part of our luggage. This was too much for my wife to bear. A quick trip to the motel office resulted in us moving to the adjoining room. Thankfully, the mouse didn't follow—it seemed to be satisfied now that we'd left it to its own room.

Minnesota has more than 12,000 lakes that are 10 acres or more in size. Everywhere I looked there were lakes, including a big one next to the motel at which we stayed in the town of Detroit Lakes. This was a beautiful location, made even better by a rustic restaurant and bar right on the water. We learned this particular lake was the setting for the movie *Grumpy Old Men*, with the ice-fishing scenes taking place just offshore during the frozen winter.

A day later I found myself on the Heartland Trail, which is one of the most attractive and pleasant rail trails I've ever seen. Running here was simply breathtaking. Enclosed under a canopy of forest, I ran past untold small ponds and babbling brooks, hardly seeing a soul except for when I passed through the occasional quaint village that punctuated the track every 10 or so kilometres. The surface of the trail was impeccably smooth—absolutely perfect for cycling too. It was also Paul Bunyan territory and I spied a large statue in one of the towns of this legendary giant lumberjack, whose tree cutting exploits are the stuff of American folklore.

This routine continued for several days—fantastic trails that were completely free of cars, combined with ideal weather. I ran past one beautiful lake after another in perfectly comfortable temperatures under sunny skies. It was running at its best.

And the wildlife was amazing too. The highlight in this regard was spotting two baby beavers playing in the grass on the side of the road. They weren't afraid of me at all. I didn't want these cute things to end up as road kill, so I shooed them away from the road and toward the nearest pond—I felt like I was doing the job of their mother. The baby beavers were in no hurry but they gradually took the hint and eventually made their way to safer ground. Cute as!

Another plaque, on a bridge further down the road, informed me that the small lake I was crossing was unique. It was situated at the high point of the region and waters flowed out of the lake via creeks to the south and the north. This isn't particularly special—except that water in the south-flowing creek eventually reached the Gulf of Mexico and the water flowing to the north finally emptied into the Arctic Ocean. I'm not entirely sure but this may be the only body of water in the world that flows into two different oceans. Which means the land of the North American continent is effectively dissected by this lake and the subsequent watercourses into which it flows.

Just down the road I crossed another small creek but this was a creek with a difference—the sign read 'Mississippi River'. Yes, the origin of the mighty Mississippi was just a few kilometres upstream in Lake Winnibigoshish. I often knew something of the geography of a region I was running through ahead of time but on this occasion I had no idea I was about to cross the Mississippi at such an underwhelming point in its long and winding course.

The surprises continued for this unsuspecting runner when I reached the large town of Grand Rapids in Minnesota (not to be confused with the city of Grand Rapids in Michigan). Grand Rapids proudly boasts its most famous former citizen, Judy Garland, who was born and raised in the town.

It's very much a logging town and the mill on the main road housed the largest pile of logs I've ever set eyes upon. I tried to calculate roughly how much wood there was in those massive heaps of cut trees and came up with an estimate of around a million tons. I was pleased that none of the trees appeared to have originated from old-growth forest.

On 20 June 2012, I ran into the city of Duluth, having reached the 8000-kilometre mark the previous day. Duluth is located on the far western shores of Lake Superior, the largest of the Great Lakes. That day was the wettest of the world run so far. The rain was torrential, though not cold. I found myself ploughing through deep pools that could not escape into the drains fast enough. It was not the most enjoyable of conditions for running but my troubles paled in comparison to the damage it did to the city.

In Duluth, whole shopping centres were underwater. The torrent had cascaded down the steep slope on which much of the city is built, flowing into Lake Superior. It had completely destroyed a lot of the infrastructure. Lake Superior was a muddy brown sea and the emergency services were inundated with calls for help.

It was a pity I couldn't have seen the town under better conditions because this was a place of which I did know one important fact—it's the birthplace of and was home to Bob Dylan until he was six years old. I found myself singing Dylan songs for the next few days as I ran south towards Minneapolis.

Another rail trail of nearly 200 kilometres presented itself as I left Duluth. The weather had cleared to a brilliant sunny day but the after-effects of the rain were far from over.

It was definitely spring time, as there were baby animals everywhere. A tiny skunk came up to me on the trail, showing no fear at all. Its eyes, which had just opened, were like those of a week-old kitten. I was a little wary of the potential for being sprayed but it was too cute to ignore so I spoke to it for a moment before heading on. Perhaps baby skunks don't have the capability to emit that famous odour or maybe it simply hadn't yet learned to be scared of humans. Shortly after this I stumbled upon a deer with two young fawns. The babies were speckled with white, just like Bambi. Spring was in the air, and on the ground.

The trail was washed out in parts and I had to skirt around it or climb along fallen trees to bridge the gaps. I was happy so long as I was able to get through but my luck didn't last when I was stopped in my tracks at a torrential stream of water. The floodwaters from the unprecedented rains were starting to make their way to lower ground and the rivers and creeks were quickly becoming swollen and choked.

I managed to wade through the chest-high water to a road in a small town, whereupon I decided to continue along the flooded street. I figured if my feet could feel the road beneath, then I could visually navigate along the street via the gaps between the houses. As far as I was concerned, I had to get through.

However, a policeman had other ideas and started calling me back to dry ground. I ignored him at first but he got louder and more insistent. I didn't want to get arrested or be classified as an unknown fugitive so I turned around. In front of a gathering crowd, I explained why it was important for me to get through but the policeman was adamant I would not—and lucky for me he was.

As it eventuated, a little further up the road the bridge had been washed out. I had no way of knowing this as the waters were well above the level of the road and the bridge rails. I would have continued wading along the road in neck-deep waters until the tarmac dropped away from under me, only to be swept away by the extremely powerful torrent and over a nearby waterfall. This was not how I wanted the world run to end.

The policeman made it clear that the only way forward was to take a detour that added about 10 kilometres to my route—much better than backtracking, as backtracking always meant subtracting that distance from my total. The episode was made more traumatic because I was in an area of limited phone coverage and I could not contact Carmel.

I did manage to finally get in touch with her and we met at the next town but not before a US border official had stopped me on the road and grilled me with several pointed questions. He had heard on the grapevine about a guy with a foreign accent who was on foot and trying to wade through floodwaters to get away from the police.

Given that I was quite close to the Canadian border, I guess my appearance and actions might easily have been misconstrued as that of an illegal immigrant. I calmly explained the situation once again and the border control official finally waved me on my way.

The next few days involved similar episodes, with flood-waters creating the need for detours and the local police force being called upon to ensure the public obeyed instructions. Although the weather was fine, I often ended a day with wet feet when I couldn't avoid the inevitable puddles along the trail.

After a dramatic week, I eventually reached the biggest city in Minnesota—Minneapolis. While the neighbouring city of St Paul is the state capital, the two have long ago merged into a single large conurbation. And the Mississippi was now a wide river that flowed through both cities and I had to cross it on foot twice that day via expansive bridges.

My phone had got wet in the initial deluge in Duluth and the button at the bottom of the screen was dead—the button that brings the phone out of hibernation and performs numerous other operations, such as terminating the use of an app. I could only operate the phone by turning it off then back on each time I needed to use it.

I called into an Apple store in Minneapolis and was shown how to circumvent this problem via the Assistive Touch facility. A partial fix, but better than nothing. Phones just don't get on well with water. The only longer-term solution was a new phone but I'd have to wait for that. Buying a new phone in the US would have cost me the full price. Waiting till I next returned to Sydney allowed me to replace the phone at a much lower price.

I finished the day, 26 June, at the St Paul home of a couple we'd met in Madrid, New Mexico, where they too had been checking out the cafes and stores that had featured in the movie *Wild Hogs*. David and Sherla had been touring the desert country of the west at the time but were soon to return back east, inviting us to stay with them if my run was to take me through St Paul.

My route did indeed take me there, so we accepted the invitation. Our hosts took us to a fantastic local restaurant that evening, extending wonderful generosity to a couple of weary travellers. It was good to stay in a home after so many consecutive nights in motel rooms—every night, in fact, since arriving back in Cheyenne on 13 May.

We all sat up and talked for a while that evening, although the many long days on the road had rendered me less energetic than usual; I simply had to get to bed sooner than I'd have liked.

After another in the never-ending stream of reluctant goodbyes, the next morning I departed the city limits of Minneapolis–St Paul and embarked on a week-long jaunt along the banks of the Mississippi River.

By this stage the Mississippi had become a very wide and meandering waterway. However, it was flowing much faster than usual, mainly because it was still being called upon to dissipate the built-up floodwaters from a week earlier.

A few days were spent running along a road that paralleled the river, the Laura Ingalls Wilder Highway of *Little House on the Prairie* fame. The prairies were well to the west of the Mississippi, so Laura's appeal must have spanned a broad geographical range if they named a highway after her this far to the east.

By the Saturday of that week I relaxed at the end of the day with a beer in our hotel bar in the town of Winona while watching the highlights of the opening stage of the 2012 Tour de France. The weather remained fine but it was getting noticeably hotter. The trend was beginning to worry me. Each day seemed to be warmer than the previous one and the next day would be even hotter again. I began to suffer a little at first, then a lot.

I crossed from Minnesota on the western side of the Mississippi to Wisconsin on the eastern side that same day. I had run almost exactly 1000 kilometres in Minnesota. And there, waiting for us in Wisconsin, were two strangers, Dianne and George, who were to provide the world run with one of its unexpected highlights.

CHAPTER 10

Wisconsin and Illinois

When Jenny left the world run back in Phoenix, she didn't go straight home to Sydney. Instead, she went to the Grand Canyon. You can't visit Arizona without seeing that famous landmark and because the remaining support crew and I weren't due to get there for another week, Jenny squeezed in a one-day bus tour before she flew out of Los Angeles that night.

On that Grand Canyon bus tour, Jenny met Diane. The two hit it off immediately and Diane was fascinated by the story of the run and Jenny's adventures over the previous five weeks. She made Jenny promise to let us know that there was a bed at her place in Stoddard, Wisconsin, should I be running through the town. I had always intended to go through that general vicinity so it was easy to include Stoddard in my itinerary.

Tom (seated centre) in 1973 with the relay team that won the NSW title and set a long-standing state record. On Tom's right is Bill, who joined Tom at Streaky Bay for the Pewter Mug Day during the world run and was also at the finish in Sydney.

Above: The most southerly point of the world run, heading into Dunedin, NZ.
Below: Passing Mt Ruapehu on New Zealand's North Island.

Above: The Big Sur coastline in California.

Below: Running through the Californian desert.

Above: Jenny, Carmel, Tom and Libby in the green room in Phoenix. This photo was taken by four-time Grammy nominee, Joe Nicholls.

Below: Finishing the day in the Arizona desert.

Above: A day spent running in the snow in Arizona, north of Prescott.

Below: Carmel and Tom taking time to celebrate with champagne and canapés on the rim of the Grand Canyon.

Above: Checking out the grandeur of the Grand Canyon.

Below: Tom (cresting the hill in the background) in the Arizona desert between the Grand Canyon and Monument Valley.

Above: Carrying drinks is vital for a runner in the Arizona desert.

Below: Monument Valley, a simply spectacular place to run.

Above: Running in Monument Valley at the precise location where Forrest Gump called it quits. But Tom had no entourage of followers trailing behind him.

Below: Running in the shadow of the Colorado Rockies.

Above: Lonely running on the prairies of Nebraska.

Below: Caught in a deluge in Duluth, Minnesota, birthplace of Bob Dylan.

Above: Lost among the cornfields of Wisconsin.

Below: On this day in central Illinois the temperature hit 140 degrees Fahrenheit (60 degrees Celsius).

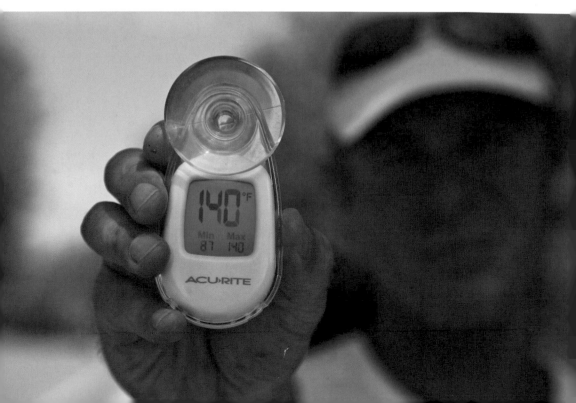

Above: Tom removing a pebble from his running shoes.

Below: Tom and Hannah patting donkeys in the state of Missouri.

Above: Trying to out-race
a giant farming vehicle in
southern Kentucky.

Left: Caught in a summer
downpour in Kentucky.

Above: Dogs loved Tom, with many choosing to join him on the road, these two in Kentucky.

Below: The quiet back roads were always Tom's preference.

Above: Tom reading an article about his world run in the *Erie Times*. Erie is a city in Pennsylvania on Lake Erie.

Below: Tom (close to camera) running by Niagara Falls in upstate New York.

Above: Enjoying a half-day interview with Jason Bennett from ESPN, near Hartford, Connecticut.

Below: The beautiful colours of autumn near Mystic, Connecticut.

Above: Running with Roger 'Chook' Evans in Massachusetts during Hurricane Sandy.

Below: Tom and Chook made the most of the unusual occasion of running through a monster hurricane.

As I crossed another of the many bridges over the Mississippi, I entered the state of Wisconsin and the small city of La Crosse, just up the road from Stoddard. Here I was met by Diane and her husband George, along with Carmel, who'd gone on ahead. Diane and George had made welcome banners and were holding them above their heads, shouting out encouragement as I approached. It was a great entry to the state.

After initial introductions I headed on toward the smaller town of Stoddard, finishing the day in the late afternoon sunshine on the eastern banks of the Mississippi River. Perched in a slightly elevated position part way up a hillside, Diane and George's home has an unimpeded view of the Mississippi, a very wide and slow-flowing river at this point. The vista is magnificent and their home is stunning.

Carmel and I were shown every bit of friendliness and generosity imaginable, from delicious local fare such as Wisconsin brats (a very tasty seasoned sausage) to drinks and spas on the veranda in the evening. We enjoyed our visit with Diane and George so much, and so immense was their hospitality, that I decided to commute back to stay another night at their house after the next day's running—and the day after that too! On the second occasion the drive back was almost 70 kilometres, but it was worth it. My usual preference was to find a motel close to where I finished running each day but staying at Diane and George's was just too much fun, warranting the extra driving there and back.

We were tempted to spend a fourth night in this wonderful abode—Diane and George certainly encouraged us to—but it would have been too far for another each-way commute by that stage. So we finally left for good on the Fourth of July. The three nights we spent in Stoddard were special and among the best of the whole run.

Diane also played a crucial role in the mechanics of the run itself. My right ankle had been slowly deteriorating and I was in constant pain much of the time when on the road. In the back of my mind I harboured a feeling of dark foreboding, half sure my ankle soreness would cause me to take an extended break from the world run.

A break like that would have been disastrous for me. Unable to make progress, I would have moped around 'like a bear with a sore head', not knowing when I might be back on the road or whether the problem would recur and ultimately stop the run entirely. This was potentially the sort of run-ending injury I had constantly dreaded.

Diane visited the drugstore and bought all manner of inserts for my shoes, from heel lifts to arch supports, as well as a tube of special putty for me to mould my own support within the shoes. I spent a couple of hours trying different formulations until I had a combination I felt best alleviated the problem. Although it didn't cure the injury completely, this helped a lot in subsequent weeks and allowed me to get through each day in relative comfort.

June had been hot but the onset of July brought with it extremes I had not witnessed thus far. Independence Day saw temperatures soar above 100 degrees Fahrenheit (38 Celsius) in the shade and every day for a week after that was either as hot or hotter. When a weather report gives us the temperature, it's always a number that's measured in the shade. However, for the most part I wasn't running in the shade. I was running in the direct sunlight and direct sunlight temperatures are usually 10 to 15 degrees Celsius above those in the shade.

The conditions I was running in were so oppressive I just had to find out how hot it really was. So we bought a thermometer from a Walmart. I started carrying the thermometer with me and that afternoon the temperature hit 58 degrees Celsius in the sunshine.

I doubted it could be that hot, so Carmel went to the Walmart again and bought a completely different style of thermometer. The next day both thermometers hit 59 degrees Celsius concurrently. It wasn't my imagination—I really was running in a furnace. And summer had only just begun.

Surviving this sort of heat while running 50 kilometres each day takes more than just determination. When the temperature gets to those levels, there is no human on Earth who can run throughout the day without artificially addressing their core temperature. It is simply too extreme for the evaporative sweating process to bring the body down to anywhere near its normal 37 degrees Celsius.

Our solution was simple. Carmel obtained a bucket of ice and a towel. Most highways in the US display a marker post every mile (1.6 km), so at each of these mile markers Carmel would pull over to the side of the road and wait for me. When I arrived, she would wrap the ice towel around my head and shoulders and I'd stand there for a few minutes until I felt comfortable enough to proceed. I would then run another mile and we'd repeat the process.

But even that wasn't enough. Every 5 or 10 kilometres I would sit in the stationary car for ten minutes with the air-conditioning on full blast. I'd then be ready for another mile. This routine went on throughout each day, for weeks.

As with most endeavours, the physical and mental aspects are inextricably entwined. Tough physical conditions create a difficult mental landscape to traverse. Waking up to another day of torture was demoralising, knowing I'd have to run through the same heat again. But the solution mentally was the same as it was physically—conquer the distance one mile at a time, slowly counting off each marker post until I'd completed my standard 31 miles (50 kilometres) for the day.

Whenever a challenge appears insurmountable, the only way to cope mentally is to break down the task into manageable segments. In this case, miles were the segments and each mile marker was a humble reward for the suffering I'd endured since the last.

And that's how I survived; one mile at a time. That was about the limit of how far I could run in this, the most extreme heat in which I'd ever attempted any form of exercise, let alone running. Thankfully, I had Carmel as my support crew. Without her I would surely have died, or at least had to postpone the run until the end of the summer.

But survival in such conditions is dependent on more than just what one does during the running phase. Hydration before and after running each day is also critical to prepare for and recover from the effort. I took a somewhat novel approach to this issue. No electrolyte drinks or supplements for me. I rehydrated with a much less high-tech option.

Before starting in the morning and after finishing in the afternoon, I would drink a litre of milk—yes, that's two litres per day. And I usually drank it in the form of a chocolate milkshake, flavoured with Nesquik (I have no affiliation with, nor have I received any financial gain from, Nesquik).

I've been drinking milk all my life but in 2009 I had been made aware of the latest sports science findings in regard to milk and rehydration. The original study tested elite athletes' performances after rehydrating on water, sports drink and milk. Milk was expected to rank a distant last. To the contrary, milk clearly came out on top.

Numerous repeat studies have confirmed this startling result, with the tests involving both elite and everyday athletes alike. As I understand it, the rationale goes something like this: the functioning of the synapses that fire the muscles is an electro-chemical reaction that depends on a particular ratio of the elements sodium, potassium, calcium and magnesium. Milk has all these minerals in almost the precise ratio that is required by the human body and likely the bodies of most other animals too.

The human body can operate reasonably well outside of this optimal ratio but performance starts to become diminished the more out-of-whack that ratio is. Too much of one—with most people it's too much sodium—and performance becomes seriously impaired, with cramps often the first obvious manifestation of the problem.

Despite running for eight hours per day, day after day, in heat pushing 60 degrees Celsius, I never once had even the faintest hint of a cramp or muscle fatigue—and I never once salted my food or took any electrolyte supplements. I even ditched the sports drinks I had been consuming during the early days of the run.

In my opinion, this aspect of my diet was one of the key components of my success in running around the planet.

And the heat didn't let up—it was just beginning. Every day brought similarly onerous conditions. Day after day, week after week, on through Wisconsin until I reached Lake Winnebago and the city of Oshkosh, where that day I passed the 9000-kilometre mark of the run. From there I ran east to the shores of Lake Michigan, turning south towards Milwaukee.

As hot as it was, the 200 kilometres or so that I ran along the shore of this Great Lake were very pleasant. The fact that the shallower parts of the lake are usually frozen solid in winter, when the temperature can reach minus 50 degrees Celsius, was not lost on me. But I would have found minus 50 easier than the plus 50 and above in which I was actually running.

I had wanted to run via Green Bay, home of Diane's beloved Green Bay Packers football team, but I had a date I needed to keep in Chicago—our daughter Hannah was meeting us there on 16 July. So I had to skip Green Bay in favour of a more direct path to Chicago. This route included a night in Milwaukee, home of the 70s TV series *Happy Days*.

The ensuing morning, as I started my run through the southern suburbs of Milwaukee, I noticed my Garmin watch wasn't working. Nothing could bring it back to life. Weeks of sweating heavily on the watch had corroded the terminals. The watch was kaput; it was cactus. And this meant I had no data recorder.

I quickly got on the phone to Carmel. I needed to ensure she started the spare Garmin outside the hotel where I began running that morning then took the same course out of the city as I did. When Carmel did reach me, I took possession of the spare device with a huge sigh of relief.

I was so pleased I'd taken the precaution of bringing a spare Garmin or I would have had a major gap in my data. It had become virtually an obsession with me to document my run with a perfect set of independent data, using a system such as that provided by Garmin GPS products coupled to the Garmin website (once again, I have no commercial affiliation at all with Garmin). All the same, the spare Garmin device was an older version and it was hand-held; not a watch. Nor did it have the same high level of functionality as more up-to-date versions. I would need to replace it at a running shop when I reached Chicago.

The shores of Lake Michigan are populated with small- to medium-sized towns that are heavily based around boating and sailing. These quaint maritime villages were always interesting to run through and especially to stay at, where we'd invariably get into a conversation with some old salt, swapping stories of my run for yarns about good and bad times on the waters of the lake.

It was summer, the days were long and the locals were in party mode, often heading straight from restaurants to post-meal live bands at the ubiquitous bars and cafes. Unfortunately, eight hours in the heat each day was taking its toll on me and I was never quite up to a long night of live music, much as I would love to have been. But perhaps the biggest deterrent was the thought of having to get through another outrageously hot day after minimal sleep and, no doubt, a few drinks more than may have been ideal.

I crossed the state line from Wisconsin into Illinois on 15 July and, after a long approach through the industrial suburbs of Chicago's north, I reached the centre of this sprawling metropolis the next day.

Running around the world provides numerous opportunities to see places through different eyes to those of the average tourist. This includes the bad as well as the good and I'd never shied away from running through areas that were usually shunned by the less adventurous.

However, I had been warned repeatedly about the area of Chicago called 'The 'Hood' and reluctantly made the decision to avoid this collection of suburbs. It is a 'no go' zone for many Chicago residents; apparently even the cops avoid the place if possible. Dire predictions that I would fail to emerge from the streets of The 'Hood finally had the desired effect and I skirted the area to the west, that afternoon eventually arriving at the home of Hannah's friends, the Ingersoll family.

Our daughter Hannah has been quite an independent traveller since she was eighteen years old and has visited Chicago several times since then on her own. The Ingersolls—the ever-friendly Carol and Bob, along with sons Bobby, Johnny and Connor—are relatives of Hannah's friends in Sydney and she has stayed at their place on previous occasions.

Carol, more popularly known as Sissy, has a link with Australia. Her mother grew up in Sydney, moving to the US when she met a soldier on leave in the city during World War II. Amazingly, Sissy's mother lived in the same street as Carmel's mother. This unlikely coincidence created a special bond between Carmel and Sissy.

Hannah had flown in the day before, so Carmel left me that morning and drove ahead to meet her. It took me a full day and 50 kilometres to run from one side of Chicago to the Ingersoll residence on the other side—and I still wasn't out of the city. Another very warm welcome was followed by a small party; something I could enjoy more fully because I was about to have my first rest day in two months—a planned day off for Carmel's birthday.

That morning, after the exchange of presents and the usual congratulations and well wishes, we relaxed for the first time in a while. It was a welcome change to break the daily routine and not have to race to get on the road. Both families enjoyed a Chinese smorgasbord meal together just around the corner. Carmel and I then found a local running shop where I purchased a new Garmin watch, albeit a more basic model than the deluxe version I'd had.

An afternoon nap was a pleasant luxury and then it was into the city for the three of us to watch a baseball game between the Chicago Cubs and Miami at Wrigley Field—Hannah had given Carmel tickets for her birthday. It was a novel experience, despite the home team losing easily. And I went within a metre of catching a home-run ball.

The next day was just a short one out of the city to the south, for our time at the Ingersoll household wasn't over. Carmel and Hannah picked me up and we returned to an occasion where we were showered with more special attention. After an interview with one of the major nightly news programs on Chicago television, we were the guests of honour at a party thrown by Sissy and Bob.

Many of the Ingersolls' friends and neighbours were in attendance. The young ones—Hannah, Bobby and Johnny—left around 11 p.m. for a nightclub in the city and were very surprised to see the party still going when they returned at 2 a.m. Sissy had coaxed me to get my guitar out and an impromptu singalong had commenced. Many old favourites were belted out—luckily the neighbours had been invited too. By 1 a.m. I had already decided to declare the following day to be an unplanned rest day. My foot had not recovered properly over the previous month, so I reasoned another day off would do it some good. Well, that was my justification for the apparent lack of discipline.

The night ended at 3.30 a.m. and we all spent a very lazy ensuing day. Carmel, Hannah and I visited the Chinese restaurant again for lunch, then we all tucked into a Chicago favourite of deep-dish pizzas for dinner.

After four nights at the Ingersolls' home, Carmel and I finally said our goodbyes the morning of 20 July and commuted back to where I'd finished running two days earlier. Hannah stayed on another day in Chicago. She was to meet us in St Louis in nine days. Sissy, Bob and the boys were amazing hosts and we were deeply grateful for our time there. I'm glad we stayed that extra day, as my ankle was much improved when I recommenced my run toward the southern states.

Firstly, however, I had to run the length of Illinois from north to south—and in the unrelenting extreme heat. A few days after leaving Chicago, the two thermometers registered a new record high of 60 degrees Celsius. I was stopped by a policeman who was incredulous that anyone would be out running in the middle of the day in such conditions. A quick explanation of what I was doing and he realised that I was probably already crazy before this day and he waved me on my way.

I was running through corn country and mile after mile of crops lined each side of the road. After a bumper start to the season, however, the heat and lack of rain were now starting to take their toll. An old saying in these parts, representative of a good crop, is the adage 'knee high by the Fourth of July'. This year the corn crop was head high by the Fourth of July and well beyond expectations. But the unrelenting weather was now taking back what it had given.

As July wore on without rain, the corn started to wither and die. It was evident to me that many crops in southern Illinois and elsewhere would yield nothing that year. Partially matured heads of corn were brown and shrivelled on the stalks. By late July I was seeing no corn or soybean crops that would be of any use to anyone. It turned out to be the hottest summer ever recorded in the US and one of the worst for crop failures, with repercussions for world markets for these and flow-on commodities.

While running in central Illinois, I passed quite close to the city of Springfield. As everyone who has watched the TV show knows, the Simpsons live in a city called Springfield—but which one is it? Or did the creators of the show invent an entirely fictitious Springfield? One particular episode includes a scene where the hometown of the Simpsons is pointed to on a map of the US, but Bart's head conveniently obscures the location at just that moment. The creators clearly wanted it to be kept a mystery.

There are many cities and towns in the US named Springfield, the largest two being in Massachusetts and Illinois. I couldn't help but wonder about the Springfield I was so near to at that time. Was there any other evidence that might suggest this city was the inspiration for the hometown of the famous cartoon family?

The first hint came when I passed a nuclear power plant. I thought, Homer Simpson works at a nuclear power plant! Could this be Homer's workplace? It was within easy commuting distance of the city. The evidence was mounting but not conclusive.

And then I spied what I considered irrefutable proof—a road sign pointing to the town of Shelbyville. Yes, just down the road from the real town of Springfield in Illinois is the real town of Shelbyville. For those who are familiar with the television series, Shelbyville is the arch rival of Springfield, especially when it comes to sporting endeavours. And, if that's not enough proof, there's even a Moe's Bar in Springfield (though, to be fair, that may have been established after *The Simpsons* brought the town to significance).

I now firmly believe that the creators of *The Simpsons* had Springfield, Illinois, in mind. How many Springfields can there be with a nuclear power plant and a Shelbyville in close proximity? Yes, I had stumbled upon the home of Homer.

It was about this time I estimate my weight dropped to its lowest—not just the lowest of the whole world run but the lowest it has been since I was fifteen years old. I didn't weigh myself at any stage during the run but the photos posted on the website elicited untold comments from friends, noting how they'd never seen me so skinny and gaunt. By my reckoning I was probably around 70 or 71 kilograms.

This prompted me to consider a topic I find particularly annoying—the body mass index, or BMI. As light as I was at that time, I would barely have made the acceptable range according to BMI. In fact, I may still have been touching on the overweight category.

The reason is that the BMI formula is fundamentally flawed in its logic. I don't know who the incompetent individual was that came up with the idea but it's a classic case of a worthy technical concept being tainted by ineptitude—in this case, whoever defined BMI had NFI.

Dividing weight by the square of height would be fine if humans were two-dimensional creatures but we're not cardboard cut-outs; we're three-dimensional. A correct definition of BMI would acknowledge weight as being proportional to the cube of our height, not the square.

Instead, we have health practitioners espousing this false notion of BMI, where a very short yet plump person will register a BMI result that's lower than a tall skinny person. There must be many tall people out there despairing at their inability to reach a mid-range BMI.

Hopefully, the fallacy of the BMI will one day be generally recognised and subsequently corrected.

On 24 July I skirted to the west of the large town of Decatur. Home to one of the biggest agricultural companies in the world, as well as a manufacturing base for Caterpillar, Decatur is an

important city in the region. But I was about to discover something I thought was much more interesting.

Sighting another of the ubiquitous historical plaques just off the road, I decided to take a look. As far as such historic sites go, this was the gold standard. Directed by the signage, I wandered up a trail that was nothing more than two tyre tracks, reaching a small monument nestled in a clearing surrounded on all sides by a thicket of trees.

There, in the bush, was the unassuming site of Abraham Lincoln's first home in Illinois in 1830. Lincoln was just 21 at the time. The house is no longer in existence but the monument stands on the exact spot that was formerly occupied by the house. I enjoyed knowing that Lincoln had trod this same ground on countless occasions as he went about his daily rural life.

As significant as the location is, there was no indication of another living soul anywhere nearby. I doubt the place gets visited often at all. This fact made the experience feel all the more special, as I stood there for a few minutes imagining what it was like in Lincoln's day.

As hot as it was, I had acclimatised somewhat and was able to get by for longer distances without the need for Carmel to be there with ice buckets. I was carrying two large drink containers with me in a pouch and these normally afforded me roughly 10 to 15 kilometres in a single stretch.

Towns were often closer than that and I was able to buy drinks at petrol stations and shops, so I was usually managing most of the day on my own, although we often met up for lunch.

There was the occasional hiccough in those rare places where the phone reception cut out but things were otherwise going smoothly for me and my support crew of one.

As I had in New Mexico and Arizona, I was now running regularly on the old Route 66. At one time the most popular road in the US, Route 66 was established as part of the official US Highway System in 1926. Popularised by the song of the same name, particularly when it was covered by the Rolling Stones, the highway meanders its way some 2000 miles across the nation from Chicago to Los Angeles.

Much of the highway has now been made redundant by the freeway system. This fact makes Route 66 much quieter and better for running. I enjoyed many days on that iconic road, noting the plaques explaining the history at relevant places.

I was especially taken by the Soulsby's Service Station in the mid-western town of Mount Olive. Opened on Route 66 as a response to the inauguration of the road in 1926, Soulsby's was owned and operated by the same proprietor until 1991, all that time selling only Shell fuel. The petrol station is something of a museum now and the original Shell pumps are still in fine condition.

By 27 July I was just a day away from the Mississippi River again, this time where it formed the border of the states of Illinois and Missouri. That evening we watched the Opening Ceremony of the 2012 London Olympic Games on television in our motel room in Edwardsville while eating takeaway from a local Asian restaurant.

The next day I crossed the mighty river and ran into St Louis, having spent a few hours jogging along the top of the levee banks. That morning I even caught sight of the confluence of the Mississippi and Missouri—where the two mighty rivers merge.

This area, and in regions further to the south, is where the Mississippi has flooded badly over the aeons. Levees have been developed gradually over the past century to cope with the flooding. These floods were the inspiration for the song 'When the Levee Breaks', which Led Zeppelin covered so well. It had originally been written in 1929 by Memphis Minnie and Kansas Joe McCoy in response to the catastrophic Mississippi floods of 1927. I hummed the song to myself incessantly as the river flowed by.

That afternoon I finished running at our motel in St Louis. This was a special end to the day, for we were reunited with Hannah once more after nine days. On this occasion, however, she was going to travel with us all the way to Memphis.

CHAPTER 11

The Deep South

It was a pleasant change to have Hannah with us on the road. Besides having an extra person there to provide support during and after the running, I always found it easier knowing Carmel had someone to talk with during the day. A bit of solitude is not a bad thing but some company doesn't go astray either. As with many things in life, variety is the key.

A celebratory night at a restaurant in St Louis was followed by another day of hot and humid weather. In contrast to the desert, where the lack of vegetation results in a very dry heat, the forests and lush farmland of the US mid-west create an extremely humid environment. Admittedly, it wasn't on a par with the middle of the Amazon (which is by far the most oppressively humid place I've ever been, easily outstripping other humid locations like Singapore and Bangkok) but it was far stickier than I had imagined.

Prior to beginning my run around the world, I had a skin check. The specialist expressed grave concern that being on the road all day, every day, for nearly two years, in many cases under the same hot summer sun I was now encountering, would be disastrous for my skin. He felt it was likely to result in all manner of skin cancers. It was a concern for me too.

I really had just two methods to protect myself—a hat and sunscreen. I'd never been a big user of either in the past but the cumulative damage of that policy (or lack of) was starting to show. However, from the first day of the world run, on 31 December 2011, I applied sunscreen with religious zeal each morning and reapplied it during the day. I also wore a cap that shaded my face throughout the day, only taking it off after the sun had set. If I hadn't adopted this practice, I'm sure my face would have looked like a prune by the time I finished the run.

My route over the next week essentially tracked the western side of the Mississippi as I wound my way through the south-east of Missouri. As expected, Carmel was enjoying having Hannah in the car and I was elated to have her on the road, even if it was for just the 5 kilometres she ran with me on a quiet gravel lane one morning. During that time we stopped to pat a litter of young kittens, as well as two donkeys that were inquisitive enough to rush to the fence as we passed by.

The girls also put together a banner and balloons for the occasion of me reaching the 10,000-kilometre milestone on 31 July. That same evening we were entertained by the motel cat, which Hannah had nicknamed Dribbling Puss. It was ultra-friendly but had the habit of dribbling when it was patted.

A few days later I ran into my last stopover in Missouri—the city of Kennett, hometown of Sheryl Crow. Kennett is a large rural town situated on the flat plains of south-eastern Missouri. As usual, there were plenty of fast food chains to be seen and no shortage of patrons to keep them in business.

Hannah had severe stomach pains during that night and we were concerned she may have needed hospitalisation. Thankfully, the following day she was a little better and then back to normal by the next evening. She had obviously eaten something that didn't agree with her but her strong constitution was able to get the better of it, as evidenced by her rapid recovery.

Around lunchtime the next day I crossed the border and into the fourteenth US state of the run: Arkansas. That night we enjoyed a meal in an air-conditioned restaurant—mandatory in this weather—in the town of Blytheville. This was the Deep South, though, and the laws unfortunately still allowed smoking in restaurants. We ate and left immediately to escape the smoky interior, retiring to our air-conditioned motel room across the car park. I don't know how we'd have survived the nights without the luxury of air-conditioning, with the minimum temperatures only descending to a humid 32 degrees Celsius.

August 5 was another of those days when the best-laid plans go awry. I had noted a town on the map where I intended to get a drink, thereby allowing Carmel and Hannah to do other things during the morning. They dropped me off and went shopping in the bigger establishment of Blytheville, the town in which we'd stayed the previous night.

However, when I ran through the smaller village of Luxora, nothing was open. It was very hot and humid and I'd run out of water long ago. I had no alternative but to continue without supplies as the phone reception was again temporarily down and I was unable to contact the girls.

By the time I made it to the next town of Osceola, some 25 kilometres or so into the day, I was seriously hanging out for a drink—one of the rare times on the whole run that I felt desperately thirsty.

After endless miles of flat farmland of corn and soybeans, I reached Marion in Arkansas the next day, just to the west of the Mississippi. Awaiting me on the other side of the river was Memphis. By this time Carmel and I had been in the US for nearly three months straight and our visa-waiver conditions were about to expire again. It was time for another quick trip back to Sydney.

After marking my stopping point, we drove to Memphis Airport but not before a visit to Graceland to see the world's premier Elvis tourism site. His home for many years, Graceland is swamped by visitors all year round and this day was no exception.

At the airport we checked in for our respective flights—Carmel and I to Sydney and Hannah to Edinburgh. Meeting up with us was just part of a big five-month world trip and Edinburgh was her next stop. Hannah told the airport staff about my run and several of them asked to have photos taken with me. Unfortunately we didn't get an upgrade.

And all too suddenly, as we rushed to board the flight, Hannah's time with us was at an end. It was early August and we wouldn't see our daughter again until December.

Having just spent another three months in a foreign land and now more than seven months into my run around the world, returning home for a few days was eagerly awaited. Carmel and I were both looking forward to catching up with family and friends. And it was also my chance to acquire a new phone to replace the one damaged during the Duluth floods.

I even arranged a bit of a 'sting' on the Tour de Bois. Each year the guys meet at a pub in East Sydney for the Annual General Meeting. I had emailed that I would be joining the meeting briefly via video link-up from the US.

At the appointed time, when everyone was watching the big screen and expecting me to appear larger than life, I quietly slipped into the back of the room. I stood behind them and casually asked, 'What are all you guys looking at?' Mouths were agape as they turned in unison. Of course, a memorable evening ensued.

Brief home visits during the world run proved to be a double-edged sword. Seeing our loved ones only made it more difficult when it came to departing again. By this stage I had already been on the road for more than seven months, having covered more than 10,000 kilometres. But that wasn't even halfway. As long as this period had been, I knew I still had more than a year in front of me and some 16,000 kilometres to go.

It was a daunting thought. A good deal of homesickness had already set in and now we had to head off again with an even longer stint on the road in front of me. It was times like these—resuming after a break—that were mentally the most difficult. The running itself was a breeze in comparison.

By mid-August I was back on the road again in Arkansas and my first day was interesting on several levels. Firstly, Google Maps led me astray. On the world run this was a vital service that was rarely wrong but when there was a problem the incorrect information could create annoying diversions.

Luckily, on this occasion I had only run a kilometre before reaching a private gate that Google Maps indicated was a public road. I had to backtrack and subtract that distance from my Garmin data.

Shortly after I came upon the main road, intending to make good use of it. But it turned out to be an elevated freeway with no shoulder at all—much too dangerous to try to run the necessary 3 kilometres to where alternative roads emerged; and illegal to boot.

So I decided to run underneath the freeway. This was a section of ground that was covered in long grass, weeds, reeds and all sorts of strange vegetation. It was wild swampy terrain, with plants that were often up to my shoulders and even head high. Obviously no human had been there since the construction of the roadway above. But other creatures had. The worst thing was the knowledge that poisonous snakes were likely to be slithering all through this waist-high grassland.

I grabbed a stick and beat the grass ahead of me before taking each step but this was no guarantee. I almost freaked out when a large lizard bolted off to the side. For a split-second I was sure it was a snake. If I'd had an alternative to this cross-country route, I would have taken it, but none existed.

Thankfully I made it to where the elevated section of the freeway finished and was able to dash on to a side road, unscathed this time. It was a scary experience and I didn't want to have to do anything like that again.

I crossed the Mississippi River once again, knowing this would be for the last time, eventually running on into Memphis and the state of Tennessee. A few weeks prior I had been contacted by a guy from the local running club in Memphis, Matt. He was following my progress and wanted to know if Memphis was part of my agenda. It was, and he subsequently informed me accommodation would be provided for the two of us and a dinner function arranged too.

It sounded nice enough. And it turned out to be a great evening, meeting many of the members of the club, having a few beers and enjoying dinner at the club's favourite watering hole. I gave a short speech then several of us headed down to Beale Street, lined with the famous bars and music venues where all the top artists play. We listened to a few live bands before Carmel and I finally returned to our hotel room around midnight.

In the morning, 21 August, I ran east through the suburbs of Memphis, stopping at Breakaway Running—the best running shop in the state. The store is owned and operated by a local runner, Barry, who had paid for our accommodation the previous night and had also donated several running shirts of top-notch quality for me to wear during my run. Again, I was most appreciative of the generosity and I wore these shirts regularly after that. (I even have one on right now as I write these words.)

Just a bit further down Union Avenue I experienced another of those little surprises that a world run provides from time to time. I passed a small nondescript commercial building and a sign just happened to catch my eye. I was tempted to ignore it and keep going. I'm glad I stopped; on closer investigation I discovered this was Sun Studio—the birthplace of rock'n'roll.

It is widely considered that the first rock'n'roll single was recorded at Sun Studio in 1950; 'Rocket 88' by the Delta Cats, of which Ike Turner was a band member. Many others followed later in the 1950s, including Johnny Cash, Jerry Lee Lewis and Roy Orbison, and it's also where Elvis Presley recorded his first ever song, a demo called 'My Happiness'. Elvis later went on to record 23 other songs at Sun Studio. In more recent times U2, John Mellencamp, Chris Isaak and Ringo Starr have recorded at Sun Studio. I stood at the front door contemplating how all these famous musicians, people who had been so instrumental in the formation of modern music, had at one time stepped through this very same door. This was yet another special moment of the world run.

I finished that day just over the border in the state of Mississippi. I had only spent two days in Tennessee but would be back again soon.

I was now in the Really Deep South. I had not realised until reaching the state of Mississippi that there are 'dry' areas within the US. Prohibition was tried in the 1930s and repealed, having been a monumental failure. However, Mississippi had enacted a law of prohibition many years earlier, in 1907, and this law is still essentially in existence in the state now, more than a century later.

I found the situation bizarre but it is actually illegal to buy a beer or bottle of wine or anything with spirits in much of the state of Mississippi, although there is plenty of bootlegging going on and the police clearly turn a blind eye to it. We had a few bottles of red stored in the car, so I was still able to have my couple of glasses each night. Besides, I was only going to be running in Mississippi for a few days.

— 🏃 —

Other than the oppressive heat and humidity of the Deep South in summer, the countryside was beautiful from a runner's point of view. Lush forests, gently rolling hills and rustic townships were the order of the day. And the rivers were a bonus, the slow lazy flow creating a soothing effect as I ran along the banks.

There were also plenty of commemorative plaques to signify important events from the American Civil War. I always found these worthy of a brief stop, acknowledging the ground on which so many battles had taken place and so many people had died. It would have been the perfect running experience if the weather had just been a bit cooler.

I soon reached the state of Alabama, finishing the day in the small city of Muscle Shoals. Here I learned about another piece of trivia that had puzzled me for years. I was aware of the Lynyrd Skynyrd song 'Sweet Home Alabama', which refers to Muscle Shoals and something called The Swampers but I had no idea what this meant. As far as I was concerned, this was as cryptic a lyric as I'd ever heard.

However, on arrival, it was clear to me that Muscle Shoals was a town—but what, then, were 'The Swampers'?

My investigations revealed that The Swampers is a famous local band whose members have been the session musicians for some of the world's most well-known performers. Bands and singers such as the Rolling Stones, Bob Seger, Rod Stewart, Elton John, Joe Cocker and Boz Scaggs have all used The Swampers to back them in recordings and performances. Again, the world run was providing me with more than just a physical adventure; this time it was an education in music history.

Muscle Shoals soon presented me with another puzzle to solve. The city is separated from the neighbouring city of Florence by the wide Tennessee River, with just one motor vehicle bridge and one railway bridge connecting the two. I intended to cross the road bridge, of course.

That was until I reached the southern approach and saw the sign that forbade pedestrians on the bridge. I quickly consulted the maps, only to find my nearest alternative was nearly a day's run further downriver. As far as I was concerned, that wasn't an option; I was determined to cross this bridge, even if it was technically illegal.

There was a set of traffic lights just before the bridge and I waited for those to turn red, then I ran as fast as my tired legs permitted. There was absolutely no room whatsoever outside of the car lanes, so I took up a lane until the lights turned green some 40 seconds later and the cars started racing towards me from behind. But I was only halfway across the bridge.

I had little time to think as the cars bore down on me. So I did the only logical thing—I climbed onto the bridge rail and out of the fast-approaching stream of traffic.

And that's where I stayed while the traffic rushed past, balanced on the bridge rail with my legs dangling on the road side, just inches from the passing cars, while my bottom and torso hung out over the water far below. I am convinced that one or more drivers called the police to inform them of the crazy guy hanging from the bridge.

As soon as the lights changed again to red and the last car passed, I hopped off the rail, back into my lane and sprinted toward the other side. I only made it to the end of the bridge with metres to spare before the next wave of traffic descended upon me. For several minutes after that, my eyes were peeled for quick and easy hiding spots, certain that a police car would come cruising by on the lookout for me. I managed to reach my turn-off before any did. It was another ordeal I didn't want to repeat and one I do not recommend to other runners.

More idyllic terrain followed that day as I crossed back into Tennessee on the Andrew Jackson Highway, finishing at the town of Lawrenceburg. This was the land of Davy Crockett and there were plenty of signs to indicate the fact.

It was also the Deep South, the land of the Confederates, and it was clear that many of the residents of these southern states were still living in the days of the Civil War. For more than a week I'd noticed the preponderance of Confederate flags outnumbering United States flags. Hoisted up household flagpoles, displayed in the back windows of cars and even draped around shoulders, these very tangible demonstrations of Southern defiance far outweighed displays of the national flag in the region.

And tobacco production was clearly still a profitable industry in the south. I had been passing strange crops for some time, confused as to the nature of the flora. It wasn't until I saw the same plants, hung upside-down to dry in sheds, that I realised what they were. Little has changed in this industry over the past couple of centuries.

There were also Amish in the area and I enjoyed waving hello to each horse-drawn buggy that trotted by me. Many of the Amish in these buggies were very friendly, though the occasional individual seemed almost scared by my greetings and would completely ignore me. I was to see many more Amish over the coming months.

The town of Columbia in Tennessee provided Carmel and me with one of the more bizarre human interactions of the whole run. Running along one of the town's main roads, I encountered a stopped car with two women standing beside it. I could see the car had a flat tyre. The women—white and well into their fifties—seemed confused and had no idea what to do, so I decided to stop and change their tyre for them.

Carmel pulled up soon after and observed the strange event unfold. The car was filled with all manner of junk and the trunk had to be emptied of blankets, clothing, gadgets and other paraphernalia before I could access the spare tyre and the jack.

By this time it was clear the two women were very much under the influence of illicit drugs. They were barely coherent and were content to chain-smoke as I went to work. Carmel was as bemused by the situation as I was. The spare was a completely different size to the other wheels, which created a problem when I tried to release the jack.

I eventually succeeded in getting the wheel changed and instructed the two women to go straight to a garage and have a properly sized wheel fitted, as this one was quickly going to shake itself loose or cause damage to the wheel and the car.

But they pretty much ignored me, jumped into their car and promptly drove off on the wrong side of the road, causing several cars to veer wildly to avoid collisions while angrily honking their horns. (This reinforced our assessment of the women's state of mind.) Then, to my disbelief, just minutes later they again passed me, this time travelling in the opposite direction. Although the car was on the correct side of the road, it was not moving in a straight line. I can only hope that they were apprehended and that nothing untoward happened before then. If anyone had been killed in an accident with these women, I would have felt responsible for the driver being back on the road.

The next day's running brought me to Nashville. Another hotbed of the Civil War, this city is the capital of Tennessee and home to the Titans NFL football team. It was not the nicest of times running into the city, as the roads were highly congested and were clearly designed with no consideration for pedestrians. The main road I was running on had no sidewalk and no shoulder. My only option was to run in the lane with the cars, as there was a two-metre-deep ditch between the roadway and the front fences of the residential properties. It was not pleasant running.

Our evening in Nashville, on the other hand, was most definitely pleasant. After a shower and all my usual documentation and blogging duties, we headed down to the Music Row area. Similar to Beale Street in Memphis, this enclave of musicians and entertainers is a must for visitors to the city. We had dinner, checked out several live music venues and just revelled in the atmosphere.

Though country music is not a favourite of mine, there were plenty of variations on the theme to keep me enthralled. I quickly came to the conclusion that Nashville should definitely be on the itinerary of every world runner who enjoys live music.

CHAPTER 12

Hillbilly country

A further day of leisurely running saw me cross yet another US state line on 1 September, this time into Kentucky, reaching the 11,000-kilometre milestone a couple of days later. As the state purports to be the home of Jim Beam bourbon, I expected anything but the pockets of 'dryness' we encountered.

The reality is that there are plenty of dry counties in Kentucky, where it's impossible to buy even a beer or wine. This fact led to a very amusing incident one day in the town of Columbia.

While I was concluding my running one afternoon, Carmel was in a local Walmart store buying provisions. She could not find the liquor division to purchase wine, so she enquired at the counter. Carmel was helpfully informed by the girl on the cash register, 'Oh no, this is a dry county, but you can get most of your needs from the bootlegger.'

Carmel's response was, 'But don't the local police frown on bootlegging?'

To which the girl replied, 'Oh no, that's where the cops go for their liquor too.' And with that, the checkout girl drew Carmel a map so she could find the bootlegger's 'shop'.

When I finished running that afternoon, about 8 kilometres north of the town, Carmel drove out and picked me up. The bootlegger's place was on the way back to our motel so we did a little searching. After noting other cars driving behind a shed, only to reappear a few minutes later, we located the clandestine premises.

Driving around the back we saw a small window in the shed wall. A somewhat scruffy young man came to the window and asked what we wanted. He looked just like Cletus the Slack-Jawed Yokel from *The Simpsons*. Carmel, who found the situation amusing, cheerfully informed him that we'd never met a bootlegger before and what a novel experience this was for us. The guy inside the window was not impressed and asked her to keep her voice down.

At this, an older and sterner man, complete with straggly beard, missing teeth and tattoos all over his body, stuck his head through the hole. We took this as a sign that a more serious approach was required. The police may have frequented the place to do their business but that clearly didn't make the boot-leggers any less nervous about their illegal set-up.

The establishment sold no wine but it now seemed rude and possibly dangerous to drive away empty-handed. So we bought a few Budweiser beers and a small bottle of bourbon and headed off. We thought the whole episode was hilarious and we laughed about it that night over beer and bourbon and Coke.

Moseying on in a generally north-easterly direction, the following day saw me run into the town of Campbellsville, Kentucky. And there in the back streets I came upon the largest single building (by land area) I'd ever seen. It covered the equivalent of at least twenty football fields and looked to be about four storeys high. The enormous parking area housed hundreds of semitrailers and was the centre of a constant stream of the vehicles coming and going. It took me some time to run by the structure, during which I discovered more about this gargantuan operation from the signage at the entrance.

This was one of Amazon.com's largest distribution centres. Yes, the place was full of books! Millions, I'm sure. I had ordered several books from Amazon.com in recent years and I couldn't help but wonder if any of them had passed through this processing centre before making it to Australia.

Further up the road Carmel had another entertaining encounter with bootlegging. It's amazing where these illegal liquor stores can pop up, especially when the adjoining county is dry. This one was in the middle of nowhere, just metres inside the boundary of the next county. Here, Carmel met three Scottish women who were visiting an American relative. The Scots had wanted a drink and because they were staying in a dry county, their host drove them across the county line to find a liquor store.

As I ran up, Carmel, the Scottish women and their host were having a good old chat and laughing at the ridiculousness of the situation. I was obliged to join them all for a few photos. The pictures show that it was lovely and sunny at that time but shortly after a late thunderstorm completely soaked me through before my finish in the town of Lebanon that afternoon.

Another of the many interviews on the road by a local newspaper journalist, about 20 kilometres to the east of the town, was followed by some leisurely running through a pocket of Amish land. As I continued on up the road, Carmel paid a very convivial visit to an Amish farm that sold its produce to the public. She learned from the friendly farmer that male Amish shave until they are married, after which they grow a beard for life. She was desperate to take a photograph of the family but was informed this was not allowed. Apparently, for the Amish, cameras are a symbol of modern and decadent times and they prefer to live in a simpler era. That said, we did notice a lot of inconsistencies in what is and isn't allowed from one community to another and even inconsistencies within communities; I guess it's just human nature to be able to justify anything if you want it enough.

From around this time the terrain began to get a little more hilly, the roads more twisting and turning and the farmland was now punctuated by equal amounts of deep green forest. I was approaching the foothills of the Appalachian Mountains.

Kentucky is an unusual state. Besides such ironic contradictions as being the home of bourbon yet partially 'dry', there are several other strange practices. One example is how the country folk have fenced off public roads. From my perspective, this was infuriating. I would be running down a well-mapped road only to stumble upon a fence across it. On one occasion, I was forced to turn back and find an alternative route. But this alternative turned out to be cursed with the same problem. I'd had enough and decided to risk it, making plans for Carmel to drive the long way around and meet me at the next town.

So I climbed under the fence and continued running, only to find the road peter out into farming fields. Consulting Google Maps, I made my way across country in the direction of the nearest alternative road—the one on which I had originally intended to run. After resuming on my road of choice, I then began to encounter serious gates made of solid steel and concrete. And there were several of these compound-like restrictions.

These were no ordinary gates. I realised there was something seriously worth protecting or hiding if the residents had gone to so much trouble to keep the public out. And here I was right in among it. I was sure that, had the owner of the property seen me, I would have been threatened with a gun—and perhaps more than just threatened. I was relieved when I passed the final gate and met Carmel up the road in the agreed location.

On the afternoon of 6 September, I ran into the city of Danville, which a month later would host the 2012 Vice Presidential Election Debate between Joe Biden and Paul Ryan. Being September, I'd been in the US most of the year; a presidential election year.

Living and talking with everyday people in 'Main Street USA' had given me a particularly unique perspective on American culture, especially in regard to politics. US citizens are like people everywhere—there are good and bad, friendly and rude, outgoing and shy, big and small. But we also know there are nuances to each culture.

The US and Australia, for example, have many cultural similarities. But it was the differences I was interested in exploring further during my time in the country.

Like most peoples, the majority of Americans are quite friendly, especially if you approach them in a congenial manner. They love to find out more about you and where you come from and will engage you in hours of conversation if you allow them. This was very much our experience.

But these often lengthy conversations in an election year elicited a variety of opinions, some quite extreme. The experience led me to a certain conclusion about the prism through which US citizens view the topic of politics. From what I could see, their attitude is unique in one specific way—trust.

In Australia, the country I know best, the usual ideological divide exists. But regardless of which side of politics is in government at the time, and whether the policies that side has implemented are popular or not, in my opinion, most Australians trust that their politicians will strive to make decisions that are in the best interests of the people. In the same way we view our football referees, we may often think the decisions of politicians are misguided or wrong but we rarely question their motive to get it right. We might not like them but we assume our politicians have mostly good intentions.

Many Americans, however, appear to believe differently. There seems to be a deep mistrust of politicians in the US, from the local level right up to the federal tier. In the US, if 'your team' is not in DC, there is a high likelihood you reckon the government has an ulterior motive and is trying to destroy the country for its own purposes.

Conspiracy theories abound. Sure, there are plenty of Americans who do trust the government and undoubtedly Australians who don't. But it appears to me there is a decided leaning toward mistrust of politicians in the US when compared to other cultures I've observed, including my own. Perhaps Bertrand Russell had made a similar observation when he opined, 'Democracy is the process by which people choose the man who'll get the blame.'

Another political curiosity I observed in the US is the way every official post at the local level is elected. In Australia, most official positions, such as the head of the police force, fire brigade and school board, are appointed according to merit in the way any other role is—an application and interview process, administered at some higher government tier. In the US, these positions are elected. It sounds fine in theory but, noting the plethora of placards advertising every candidate in every position in every local government jurisdiction, I couldn't help but feel the process in practice must be very unwieldy. Does the best candidate end up in the job? It seemed to me the most well-known individuals or the ones with the ability to most effectively bankroll their campaigns were likely to end up in these various civil positions.

A more obvious cultural peculiarity in the US is the approach to food. It is no secret that the US has the largest obesity problem in the world and this was glaringly obvious during my time running in the country.

It's not that Americans want to be fat but they have collectively acquired some very bad eating habits over the past half century or so (it should be noted that Australia and some other parts of the world are exhibiting a similar trend). Huge servings at restaurants are taken as a right, where an attitude of quantity over quality prevails. But it was breakfast that really stood out to me.

Motel breakfasts in the US (and most motels include breakfast in the price) are simply atrocious. And I am in no way a fussy eater. We got to the stage where we didn't even bother, preferring to prepare our own (I should say, Carmel prepared breakfast while I got ready for the day).

The standard fare in the motel chains was powdered eggs that tasted like someone had spilt an entire salt shaker into a saucepan of rubber during the cooking process, highly processed cereals like Rice Bubbles or Froot Loops or waffles you made yourself from a white gooey, sugary mixture. But the worst of all was 'biscuits with gravy'—scones with a greasy sausage on top, smothered in lumpy white gravy that was tasteless to my unsuspecting buds.

At one motel I witnessed an American woman of at least 250 kilos, possibly more, place three chairs next to each other so she could sit down. She then came back from the breakfast bar with a huge plate piled high, with food falling off the sides. The base layer was formed with about twenty scone halves; this was then topped with two separate layers of sausages—probably a dozen sausages in all—and finally covered with about a litre of white breakfast gravy. I watched her demolish the lot. I left that morning shaking my head in disbelief.

Dinner customs in the regional US were also a little strange to my mind. One evening Carmel and I turned up to a restaurant in a medium-sized town a few minutes after 7 p.m., only to find the place was closed. But we could see diners inside preparing to leave. Thinking the locked door was a mistake, we knocked a few times. A woman opened the door with an annoyed look on her face, informing us the restaurant had closed at 7 p.m. We asked why. Our temerity in posing such a question elicited a scathing response—'Well, what sort of person would want to have dinner after 7 p.m.?' Clearly in the opinion of this ultra-puritan only deviants and undesirables ate 'that late'. Luckily for us a nearby pizza place delivered till 9 p.m. Unfortunately, their choice of toppings exhibited no sign of anything but highly processed ingredients and lots of cheap and nasty cheese.

There are plenty of people doing their best in the US to change the country's attitude to food. For example, former New York City mayor Michael Bloomberg (who I once met and had a beer with in Sydney in the lead-up to the 2000 Olympic Games) has made particular efforts to enact basic legislation that makes it easier for citizens to choose healthier food. Time will tell if these actions end up making a difference.

As I ran east from Danville, I started to notice the hills becoming more prevalent and the farms more concealed within the forests. I was now running through hillbilly country. This fact was soon brought home to us in a nasty and confronting way.

A few days earlier in Kentucky, Carmel had taken a photo of a duck hunter in a field. He was some distance away and she was unable to discern any detail. When she later reviewed the photo in close-up, the hunter had been aiming the gun directly at her. This was a worry but the danger had passed by the time she realised there had been any danger at all.

However, half a day's running east of Danville a more insidi-ous event unfolded. I was running up a dusty gravel road in a secluded part of the hills while Carmel had gone ahead to look for a shop and was now returning. She could not turn around at the point where she passed me, so she drove on to the first driveway—which I had just passed a minute or so earlier. The driveway led to a ramshackle farmhouse surrounded by trees. There was a public nature strip between the road and the farm's front fence.

Carmel edged the car into the driveway for a three-point turn, without the nose of the car even entering the property. Despite this, a young man ran out of the house and aimed a rifle directly at Carmel's head—from a distance of just 10 metres. He stood there taking aim for a few seconds until he decided she posed no threat and waved her on her way. Carmel backed out and drove up the road to me. She was hysterical and in tears. She truly believed there was a good chance he may have pulled the trigger.

We were later told that this area was the heart of the old moonshine region, where illicit whiskey was produced during Prohibition and beyond. But now the stills in these hillbilly farmhouses concoct crystal meth and the 'chemists' are usually high on the stuff themselves. It's likely this young man's paranoid behaviour resulted from the use of his own product.

There are few situations as dangerous as a paranoid crystal meth addict with a gun. Carmel was very lucky indeed, and she kept close to me after that until we were well and truly out of the hills of Kentucky and the neighbouring states.

The preponderance of guns in the US was another cultural difference that we'd now encountered first-hand—a difference that was a lot more dangerous than the mistrust of politicians.

Life was fairly uneventful over the next week or so as I continued in a generally easterly direction through the hills of Kentucky and West Virginia.

One minor drama involved the fire brigade turning up at our motel room after the fire alarm had been activated. The room included a small kitchen and Carmel had decided to cook a meal that night. There was only a hint of smoke wafting from the saucepan, yet it was enough to set off the alarm. One would think, if the motel offers cooking facilities in the rooms, they'd set the tolerance on the smoke alarms a bit higher.

The running terrain became an increasing procession of forests and hills, although most of the roads ran along the creek and river valleys between the hills. This made it flatter than one might expect. It was early September and the temperatures were starting to drop. This fact, coupled with the shade provided by the myriad of trees, resulted in ideal conditions for covering 50 kilometres or more each day. The roads I chose to run on were quiet and the task at hand was getting easier on a daily basis.

Not long after crossing from Kentucky into West Virginia, I reached the small city of Huntington. This was clearly a university town—along the main street was a 'mini suburb' of sorority houses. One large double-storey house after another was adorned with the customary three Greek letters in various formations—alpha kappa chi, delta lambda pi, beta gamma rho—they went on and on. It was like a scene from the movie *Animal House* and I could only imagine the street parties.

The next afternoon I passed a female 'chain gang', working at tidying the roadside. It was in an isolated forest region, many miles from the nearest town. The bright orange prison-issue overalls were visible from the distance, though it wasn't until I was quite close that I fully comprehended the scenario.

There was a touch of danger involved but it didn't emanate from the prisoners themselves. Two armed guards were also in attendance. They were obviously alarmed at the slow approach of a lone individual on foot, especially given that Carmel had already stopped the car on the road among them. This was highly unusual and I'm sure the guards considered the possibility that we were part of an elaborate jail-break plot. The remote setting would have readily facilitated such an attempt.

I noticed the hand of one guard tense on her pistol as I got within a few metres of her and her vehicle. I smiled as disarmingly as I could, giving a little wave to reinforce my friendliness. Stopping to speak may have been interpreted as an attempt to distract the guards, so I just kept running.

I didn't look back but I could feel the guards' eyes following me down the road. I did manage to slip in a 'Hi' to a couple of the incarcerated women when I was out of earshot of the guards, eliciting an affable nod in response. Our lives couldn't have been more different. I was free to roam around the world. These individuals possessed no freedom to roam at all.

An unexpected feature of running through the Kentucky and West Virginia regions was that I regularly found myself accompanied by dogs. This had occurred previously, and would occur many times henceforth, but never as often as here. It seemed I was a magnet for friendly canines, a veritable Pied Piper of puppies.

The happy mutts would trot alongside me for miles, with no sign of leaving. Often we'd even have to pile a dog into the car and Carmel would drive miles back to where it had originally joined me, which we assumed was close to its home. Otherwise I'd have ended up with a massive entourage of animals in trail, much like the dog version of Forrest Gump's tribe of followers. I appreciated their desire to wander the world with me but watching out for them on busy roads was a stress I didn't need.

We struck another off-road drama in the town of Spencer, West Virginia. I used my credit card to pay for dinner at a restaurant across the road from our motel at the western end of town. A couple of days later I received an email from my bank, informing me that my credit card had been used fraudulently and had, therefore, been mandatorily cancelled.

I spent some time on the phone to Australia organising a new credit card, which was to be delivered to Katie, a friend of Hannah's we knew well, who was living in New York. I was still a month away from New York, so it was lucky for us that Carmel had a separate card on the same account. It was an old lesson learned anew—never let your credit card out of your sight, especially in hillbilly country.

Through the seemingly unending hills of West Virginia, another few days of running carried me to the border with Pennsylvania. As I crossed the state line on 20 September, another historic plaque informed me the state had initially been a land grant from King Charles II of England to William Penn in 1681.

Originally home to several indigenous American tribes, including the Iroquois and Shawnee, Penn was awarded the land as a repayment of a debt from the Commonwealth to Penn's father, thereby dispossessing the 'Indians'. William Penn was reputedly embarrassed when King Charles ordered the colony be called Pennsylvania.

For me, the state of Pennsylvania represented the beginning of running in the colonial part of the US. It was also the twentieth US state I'd run through since starting in California back in February. In the intervening period I had covered more than 10,000 kilometres on foot in the US alone.

CHAPTER 13

Pennsylvania and New York

As I passed the Pennsylvania state line, I began to comprehend what I'd accomplished so far. That night I traced out my track across the US in marker pen. I had run more than 10,000 kilometres in one country, crossing almost the entire continent of North America. And, in just eight and a half months, I'd notched up nearly 12,000 kilometres in total.

There are times when we briefly view reality through what seems like a different lens. This was one of those moments of epiphany. I had always considered myself a sprinter who liked running longer distances. I was now going to have to recategorise myself.

In recent times, despite my protestations, many had referred to me as an ultra-distance runner or endurance athlete. I could now no longer repudiate these labels. I was far from the best, to be sure, but the days of denying I was an ultra-runner were over. There aren't too many alternative definitions for someone who runs across a continent—or four.

Some parts of our lives we plan, others are the consequence of circumstances. For me, graduating from the fast lane to the slow lane was never planned. Rather, it was a case of the latter—a confluence of some unlikely events.

After the euphoria of my initial experience on the football field at the age of ten, I soon settled into several seasons in the sport. This was complemented perfectly by athletics—more specifically, sprinting events. But, by the age of fourteen, I had 'retired', giving away both sports. I'm not sure why—I just did. The next few years I pretty much played no sport at all.

I remained uninterested until I was sixteen when all of a sudden I returned to sport and, without any training whatsoever, I ran a 400-metre race in 51.2 seconds in the state age finals. I wondered what I might have been capable of if I had invested in even a modicum of training in the months before that race—probably 47 or 48 seconds, which means I would have won. The following year I ran the 100 metres at the school athletics carnival in 10.9 seconds; once again, without any training. Now I really started to consider what might be possible.

Speed is a vital attribute for any footballer. And it didn't go unnoticed. The coach of the Warilla Gorillas junior squad

(18 years and under) approached me mid-season in 1978 to join the team. This time I agreed.

A handful of games later and I found myself promoted and playing my inaugural First Grade match at the age of seventeen. It was only a one-off game, filling in for an injured senior, but it was one of the highlights of my life to that point.

By the following season, at the age of eighteen and while still at school, I was an established First Grader. Various newspaper articles of the time focused heavily on my ability to run, including stories from Sydney's leading Sunday newspaper, *The Sun Herald*. The sports pages of that publication and others, especially during August and September of 1981, were effusive on the topic.

Statements to the effect that 'his acceleration is amazing', 'giving Denniss room to move is suicidal', and 'he can step around an opponent with extraordinary ease' left me somewhat embarrassed, particularly as I considered it was my team mates who created the opportunities upon which I merely capitalised. Playing in a great team affords one that luxury.

Newspaper stories, however, tend to take on a life of their own and the articles didn't go unnoticed elsewhere.

As the leading try-scorer in the competition during the 1980 and 1981 seasons, I was regularly fielding questions from the press about graduating to a Sydney club in what is now known as the National Rugby League, or NRL. By 1982 the scene was set—it was time to step it up a notch. I was determined to have a big year on the football field and see where it might take me. But the year didn't unfold as I had imagined. It did, however, begin well.

In April I was selected in the Country team to play City. In those days, this was basically the state selection trial for the

State of Origin, the annual series between New South Wales and Queensland that had been recently established. The City side usually won the match but it was a great chance for boys from the country to showcase their abilities.

I'd heard in confidence that the state selectors were looking to include at least one Country player in the side—and their eyes were supposedly on me. I suspect the selectors considered the wing position the least risky option. So if I had a half-decent game, I stood a very good chance of making the NSW State of Origin side. A token selection, perhaps—but I wouldn't have complained.

Then disaster struck. At a training session in the week preceding the City versus Country game, I tore my hamstring badly. I was replaced for the match by a guy called Phillip Duke. Phillip played very well, was selected in the NSW team and played State of Origin that year.

I was naturally disappointed at my misfortune but I was still positive about my prospects as a professional football player. Then events took another strange turn.

On returning to my club, I found myself demoted to the reserve grade. I was told my replacement had fared well during my weeks with the Country team and that it would be unfair to drop him. Such a policy was unheard of at the club. It puzzled many people, including me.

I didn't play another first-grade game that year. And I wasn't the only one. Another senior representative player from the team that season found himself in the same predicament.

At the club presentation night at the end of year, an official confided that the club had overcommitted on its player contracts for the season. By ensuring certain players didn't play the minimum number of games needed to fulfil their contractual commitments, the club wasn't legally obliged to pay these players.

I received a minimal payment for the season, an unfortunate casualty of bad management decisions. As a university student, football was my only source of income. The money was sorely missed.

Rather than be bitter, I decided to turn the situation to my advantage—I would move to Sydney and trial for a contract with the South Sydney Rabbitohs the following season. After a month of training with the other hopefuls through the heat of January, my chance finally arrived in a trial match against the Balmain club on a humid Sunday morning in February 1983.

However, there were so many trialling aspirants, two separate squads were required for our team, each player having just one half of the game to impress. I got to play in the first half.

By the end of this opening stanza, I was ecstatic. I had scored four tries in just half a game. How could I not be offered a contract?

Unfortunately, my second major disappointment with rugby league management was about to surface. I received a call the following day from the CEO of the Rabbitohs—a call I was eagerly awaiting, so sure was I that I'd be offered a contract for the upcoming season. But it wasn't the conversation I was anticipating.

That year a new policy had been invoked by the Australian Rugby League, restricting each club to signing just two imports (players who weren't local juniors). South Sydney had already committed to their two imports months before.

Completely unaware of this constraint, I and all the other non-local hopefuls had trained and played for nothing. No matter how well any of us had performed in that trial match, we were never going to be offered a contract. I'd finally had enough of football management.

That morning—14 February 1983—I put down the phone and decided I would run my first marathon. I changed into a T-shirt, shorts and a pair of running shoes and headed out the door for my first official training run. I have logged my daily mileage ever since.

That was the day I left the fast lane behind and began my gravitation toward long distances. I probably would never have made that decision had I enjoyed a better experience with football hierarchies. Running around the world may never have eventuated. Was it serendipity? I guess it depends on your outlook.

Pennsylvania's landscape was much the same as West Virginia's. A journey runner could do a lot worse than choose western Pennsylvania as a region in which to do their running. One of the most entertaining evenings of the whole run was had in this state, in the town of Ligonier which, sadly, was not far from where United Airlines Flight 93 crashed into the otherwise idyllic green countryside on 11 September 2001.

It was a Saturday and I had run a couple of hours that morning with a local guy who was out for his weekend long run. He had told me how Ligonier was a very nice town with lovely restaurants and bars, so Carmel and I thought we'd try to have a more regular style of Saturday night—dinner, a few drinks, maybe catch some live music. After all, I'd just passed the 12,000-kilometre mark earlier that day and was in the mood for a celebration. And Ligonier obliged perfectly.

While eating dinner at a cute restaurant bar, we noticed a two-man acoustic act setting up. We decided to stay on and listen for a while. Without telling me, Carmel had mentioned to the two musicians how I used to play in venues just like this and in the same style; singing with an acoustic guitar. The next thing I knew, I was being summoned up to the stage. I hadn't even held a guitar in my hands for some months and hadn't played in front of a crowd for well over a year.

However, it all came back and I didn't embarrass myself too much. I played a Cat Stevens song and a Bob Dylan, then was joined by one of the other guys for a rendition of 'The Boxer'.

The evening was a lot of fun, particularly as our night life had been virtually non-existent since Nashville a month earlier. And the crowd seemed to appreciate the novelty of listening to someone who, while running around the world, had stopped in at their town and put on an impromptu performance.

For me it was a welcome respite from heading straight back to the motel room after dinner. Such occasions are a great way to refresh oneself mentally during any long journey run, especially a run around the world.

Two days later I reached the town of Punxsutawney. Of all the local customs I observed during my run around the world, Punxsutawney has one of the strangest. Every 2 February since

1886, the town officials dress in tuxedos and top hats and force a groundhog named Phil—ostensibly the same animal every year, despite the fact this makes Phil more than a hundred years old—to rise from his slumber.

If Punxsutawney Phil sees his shadow and heads back to his burrow, the winter is supposed to continue for another six weeks. If Phil stays above ground, the winter is supposedly over. Phil is cared for by a self-appointed group of locals known as the Inner Circle and it is also claimed that the cuddly celebrity animal speaks 'Groundhogese' with the President of the Inner Circle—supposedly the only person who can understand this unusual language.

The locals in Punxsutawney take the whole tradition very seriously, probably because it's been bringing a huge amount of tourist dollars to the town every year since the movie *Groundhog Day* made Phil and the town famous. Never mind that Phil's prognostications about the weather have only had a 39 per cent success rate over the years.

I suggested to a local journalist during an interview in Punxsutawney that perhaps the town officials are interpreting Phil's predictions the wrong way around. If not seeing his shadow and staying above ground was interpreted as Phil's way of saying the winter would continue instead of ease, then his success rate over the years would have been 61 per cent and a lot more accurate.

This suggestion was met with a less than enthusiastic response. It was pointed out that my suggestion would imply the President of the Inner Circle has been untruthful about his ability to speak Groundhogese, casting a pall of doubt over the whole tradition. I was told not to push this theory in town, as

I might be running out of Punxsutawney a lot quicker and sorer than I had run in.

The weather continued to cool as I ran toward New York State. The forests and hills did not abate either, until I made it to the city of Erie on the shores of the enormous lake that bears the same name. This was the third of the famous 'inland seas' of the region I had run by—the Great Lakes, the largest group of freshwater lakes on Earth—and I can confirm that such is their size that the lakes really do look like oceans.

I ran along the edge of Lake Erie over the next few days, crossing the state line from Pennsylvania to upstate New York. Cloudy weather in the interior gave way to sunny skies along the lake. The scenery, and running, was spectacular.

We ate one evening in an interesting bar just over the state line; a drinking establishment that had been a centre for liquor smuggling during the Prohibition. Whiskey from Canada, on the opposite shore of Lake Erie, was transported during the night and sold out of the bar. Until, that was, the bar's proprietor failed to return one evening during a storm, presumed drowned, along with his illicit cargo.

Lake Erie eventually narrowed as I ran north-east, until I could see the opposite shore near the end of the lake. By this stage I'd reached the large city of Buffalo. I finished running that day at one of the most famous geographical icons in the US—Niagara Falls.

There was plenty of water in the river and the falls were 'working' well. I'd finished a little earlier than usual so Carmel and I took the Maid of the Mist tour to the base of the waterfall itself. We ended the boat tour quite wet, despite the raincoats that everyone receives. Niagara Falls was well worth the visit, though I'd rate the Grand Canyon as much more worthy of a tourist's attention.

The following week entailed much running through rustic lazy countryside. Initially my course took me along the shores of Lake Ontario, the fourth of the five Great Lakes I'd come in contact with, then along a fantastic cycle path next to the Erie Canal.

The Erie Canal is a waterway constructed in the early 1800s linking the Hudson River with Lake Erie. It opened up a direct trade link between New York City and Chicago, greatly enhancing economic activity at the time. These days the Erie Canal is not as important as a means of transport but it's certainly a nice quiet body of water to run beside.

I was also back in Amish territory. I lost count of the horse and buggies that passed me. Some of these had the archetypal bearded husband on the reins and his wife in the carriage, on other occasions there were several youths in charge of the contraption. I'd wave to each and every one of them, sometimes receiving a friendly response, other times a blank stare.

Running for pleasure was not a pastime practised by anyone in the era of which the Amish yearned to remain. I guess my presence was interpreted as far too modern by some of them.

It was early October and I was heading towards New Jersey. This required me to pass from upstate New York back into

Pennsylvania for a few days, through towns with unusual names such as Horseheads and Himrod.

We survived a potentially nasty delay early one afternoon at the state line between New York and Pennsylvania. Carmel had parked the car and was working on her computer while she waited for me to arrive for lunch. But over a period of an hour, with the engine off and the air-conditioner turned on, the inevitable flat battery occurred.

I'd already headed off after lunch before Carmel attempted to turn the engine on but luckily I was only a mile up the road when she called. Even more luckily, I was right out the front of a garage.

I ventured in and explained the situation to the mechanics who'd never heard an Australian accent in the flesh. The head guy was extremely obliging, driving me back to the car and getting it started with jumper leads. Then Carmel and I followed him to the garage in our car to have the old battery replaced and I resumed my run. All up the incident had inconvenienced me by an incredibly short fifteen minutes. An episode like that could have been much worse.

Autumn was well underway and the trees were beginning to turn a myriad of colours. Even the reds, yellows and oranges came in all manner of shades and hues. The ground was often a thick carpet of leaves, a kaleidoscope of dying vegetation returning to the earth.

It was in this region on 14 October, the day I ran into the town of Nazareth—famous among guitar aficionados as the location of the Martin Guitar Factory and just a few miles from Allentown (brought to prominence by the Billy Joel song)—that I reached the halfway mark of my run around the world. Having chosen to run at least the same 26,232 kilometres completed by Jesper Olsen, it was on this day that I passed the 13,116-kilometre mark.

I still had a tremendous distance to go but, as I'd found in any run or race I'd ever attempted previously, passing the halfway point marks a new beginning. From here on in, the mental aspect would get progressively easier. It was a nice milestone to reach.

The next morning, 15 October, I finally passed over the Delaware River and into the State of New Jersey. And the following day I ran into the town of Princeton, a location important to me on two fronts.

One of the world's most prestigious university towns, Princeton was the home of Albert Einstein for the last twenty years of his life. And I ran right past Einstein's house, stopping to reflect on the fact he'd passed back and forth so many times through the very gate I was standing before.

The other reason for running through Princeton was more personal—in town I would find my old friend Craig, of the Tour de Bois.

Craig's first Tour de Bois was in 1999 and it was real baptism of fire. That year, sixteen of us rode from Wangaratta in Victoria to Wagga Wagga in New South Wales. We had caught an overnight train to the start and rode out of Wangaratta at 5 a.m., having managed only about an hour of sleep on the train that night. A difficult day of cycling into the wind exacerbated the fatigue and all the riders were exhausted that evening when we stopped at the small town of Rand.

The next day, though, all were refreshed and the morning was magical; bright sunshine over endless fields of green wheat and flowering golden canola promised a day of outstanding cycling. And it was, but not quite as envisaged.

The irascible Bob Quin (a.k.a. Quinny), feeling guilty that we'd all been too tired the night before to pump much money through the country publican's till, convinced us to each have a beer at 8.30 a.m. before we started cycling to our destination of Lockhart. New to the tour, Craig obliged along with the rest of the crew.

Twelve beers, four bourbon and cokes and a rum and coke later—per person, that is—coupled with a bit of nude cycling around the car park, finally saw us start riding at 12.45 p.m. Luckily we were cycling on a road that was so quiet we didn't encounter any cars at all. And by some miracle there were no crashes within the group.

While we did, and still do, have outrageous amounts of fun on the Tour de Bois—it's why we do it, after all—that year was an exception; we're not usually that reckless. I remember thinking at the time, albeit hazily, that poor Craig would never return for another tour. But he did—and he still comes back every few years when he can fit the tour into his busy schedule.

Craig is now working in Princeton and lives there with his wife and daughter. Carmel and I stayed with the family that evening, our first homestay for months. The food was superb and Craig brought out a couple of nice bottles of wine to celebrate the occasion. Once again, the evening highlighted the finest of reasons for running around the world.

From Princeton it took me two days to run to the big one—New York City. In between we met some locals at a pub while enjoying dinner at the bar (eating at the bar is a great way to strike up a conversation with strangers). One of these locals, Tom, joined me at various places along the road the next day. He was a proud New Jersey resident and wanted to show me the best of his town.

The residents still often refer to their suburbs as towns, although the old towns in this part of the state have effectively now merged into one gigantic conurbation. As part of Tom's tour, I was introduced to a roadside pretzel and snack seller whose accent was straight out of a movie—real 'Nu Joisey'. The friendly street vendor even gave me a free drink and took a few photos of me next to some recognisable landmarks in his neighbourhood, intending to send these to the local press.

For a runner, New York is one of the most difficult cities to reach, especially from the west. There is only one bridge across the Hudson River that is open to pedestrians, the George Washington Bridge, and the approach from the New Jersey side is fraught with difficulty and danger. Busy highways without shoulders through heavy industrial areas, combined with numerous diversions due to road works, made for a day of running that I did not enjoy.

However, late in the afternoon of 18 October 2012, I finally crossed the Hudson River and proceeded down Broadway to our hotel on the Upper West Side. In the process I passed Columbia University, which I'd visited several times during the previous few years in my role as a member of the Global Roundtable on Climate Change. I was back in relatively familiar territory, although this time having traversed the US on foot instead of in the usual aeroplane.

The studios of Channel 5 in Midtown were our destination the next morning. We raced across town during Manhattan peak-hour traffic, luckily finding a parking spot close to the station headquarters. Shortly after, I made an appearance on New York's main morning television program, *Good Day New York*.

From there it was back to the start location for a lap of Manhattan. I ran down Broadway, past David Letterman's studios and Times Square, and then down Seventh Avenue to the Tribeca office of Hannah's friend Katie.

Katie had been living in New York for a year and her boss Mark was keen to do some running with me. Amid squally rain, Mark and I ran down to the very popular cycle and running path along the banks of the Hudson River and turned south.

I used to make regular trips to New York for work and was here in mid-2001 with colleague Cynthia. We had visited Windows on the World, a restaurant and bar just a few hundred metres from where Mark and I were running. But Windows on the World was no longer in existence. Tragically, only months after my visit in 2001, the venue was completely destroyed on September 11.

Majestically perched on the 107th floor of the north tower of the World Trade Center, Windows on the World never stood a chance when the first plane flew into the building several floors below.

As Mark and I ran past, I couldn't help but feel lucky the attack didn't take place on the day I was at the top of that tower. So many others weren't so fortunate and I spent quite a bit of time contemplating what it must have been like for those who were in Windows on the World that day, trapped above as the fire raged on the floors below and the building eventually collapsed.

It was a time of mixed emotions. I felt lucky to be alive and even luckier to have the opportunity to be doing what I was. I also felt sad for those ordinary people—people just like me— who never got to pursue the dreams they may have had. Who knows, one of them may even have dreamt of running around the world.

The weather had turned nasty and Mark and I were duly drenched by the time we'd run by the New York Yacht Club marina, around Battery Point and back up under the Brooklyn Bridge. Mark had to head back to the office then, so I continued alone through China Town, Little Italy, Soho and up to Central Park via Fifth Avenue and Park Avenue.

The tall buildings of Manhattan were so thickly congested around Midtown that my Garmin device could not connect to the satellites, leaving me without proper data for the day. I finished early in the afternoon in Central Park then headed across to Mark's apartment on the Upper West Side, where he had kindly invited us to stay for the night.

That evening we met Mark and Katie in a bar on Broadway before we all had dinner in a Middle Eastern restaurant on the same thoroughfare—a delicious meal full of exotic taste sensations and a most welcome change from the nightly burger theme of months gone by.

Mark ran with me through the northern half of Central Park the following morning, where we passed many runners training for the upcoming New York City Marathon. Carefully choosing a course through the park that avoided intersecting with any part of my previous route, Mark and I threaded our way through the throngs of hopefuls.

Most of these runners were probably completing their last 'long run' prior to attempting one of the world's best-known marathons two weeks later. The original organisers of the New York City Marathon had devised a course aimed at showcasing the metropolis. My running in the city pretty much satisfied this objective too, ultimately consisting of the best part of a lap around the perimeter of Manhattan Island.

Running through Harlem was interesting and I felt very safe. In the 1970s this would have been unheard of but it's easy these days. Crossing the Bridge into the Bronx, I headed east to Long Island Sound and followed the old Boston Post Road. As the name suggests, this was once the postal route between New York and Boston.

For me it was a nice way to exit New York City, running on a non-freeway which, while still quite busy, was far more pleasant than my entry to the city two days earlier. I finished that afternoon by crossing the state line and entering Connecticut, the 23rd US state of my world run.

CHAPTER 14

New England

The best time of the year in New England is autumn. And we were in the region smack-bang in the middle of that very season. The forests were a kaleidoscope of colours and Carmel was having a ball with her photography. And it was no less enjoyable running through this brilliantly hued landscape.

Two days after leaving New York we stayed with a friend of mine in Connecticut. David Downie had been a key administrator in the Global Roundtable on Climate Change and he and I first met at the inaugural event at Columbia University in 2005. David is just five days younger than me so we also have a generational culture in common. I vividly recall a particularly late night in 2008, featuring rounds of beer and pool in a Broadway bar while pumping dollars into the jukebox.

David and his wife and two children live in a huge house not far from Long Island Sound. Once again, it was a real luxury for us to stay with the Downies and so much better than the motel rooms to which we'd become accustomed.

The whole family took us to one of their favourite restaurants for dinner, then drove us around the streets to look at the various Halloween displays that had been assembled in the front yards of homes in the lead-up to the annual holiday. Residents try to outdo each other with the intricacies of their designs, much like the Christmas lights and displays that adorn suburban homes all over the world.

Two days after that I was nearing Hartford, the state capital of Connecticut. I took a half day off for an interview with the big cable sports network ESPN, who were making a documentary about my run. A fellow Aussie, Jason Bennett, is an ESPN executive living in Connecticut and I sat down with him for a few hours while the cameras rolled. He and his crew then shouted us lunch at a local Japanese restaurant before further filming of me on the road during the afternoon.

It was a very eventful day. On arrival at our motel in the town of Cromwell late that afternoon I met one of the original venture-capital investors in my wave energy company. Charlie was a local Hartford resident, a guy I'd been dealing with since 2001, and he'd made the short trip from his office to catch up with me that afternoon. Charlie had even been on holiday in South Dakota since I'd passed through that state and was very familiar with various places I'd run through, like the town of Wall in South Dakota with its numerous billboards.

And also waiting to greet us were Roger (a.k.a. Chook) and Don, our good friends and the owners of the support vehicle that Carmel had been driving for the past eight months. They had flown over from New Zealand and were intending to travel with us to the end of the North American leg in Boston before driving the car back to its home in Colorado.

We hadn't seen either Chook or Don since Hamilton in New Zealand back in early February. Needless to say, there was something of a celebration that evening, though somewhat restrained in expectation of the following day of running. Chook was a man on a mission, determined to run with me as much as he could.

So the next morning Chook and I set off toward the village of Essex. This is an amazing pre-Revolutionary War town, with many buildings dating back to the 1600s. It was also a ship-building centre and was the construction site of one of the major battleships used by the Americans in the War of Independence.

One of the iconic buildings of Essex is the Griswold Inn, which has been operating since 1776. From 2000 to 2008, I had spent a lot of time in the New England region on the trail of venture-capital funding for the company and I often made Essex my base. And when in Essex I always stayed at The Gris, as the locals call it. We even hosted a board meeting at the inn, one of the unusual locations at which I'd previously met up with Walter from Phoenix.

The Griswold Inn's authentic rooms come with the typical low ceilings of the day and truncated doorways that I had to be careful not to bump with my head. It's a truly charming location, complemented perfectly by the Black Seal bar just up the road.

Chook took it easy this first day, peeling off after 10 kilo-metres to meet up with the support vehicle. I continued through classic New England forest on a fairly quiet road, eventually reaching the Griswold Inn late in the afternoon.

There I caught up with Betsy, who was my company's first US employee in 2002. I hadn't seen Betsy for a few years and she, Carmel, Chook, Don and I revelled in a delicious seafood dinner in the hotel's restaurant. I was now well and truly in the land of the seafood chowder and I didn't waste the opportunity to savour the version the Gris had on offer.

Then it was off to the Black Seal. The 'Seal' has a surprising link to Australia—it sports a plaque on the wall from BHP in Whyalla, South Australia. This remote outpost is where iron ore was once shipped and steel made. No-one in the Black Seal now knows how this curio from Whyalla came to be in the bar. In fact, most locals had no idea what BHP was, let alone where Whyalla was located.

The Seal also holds a special memory for me. Just like in Ligonier, I was once asked on stage to play a set of songs. On that occasion Betsy and my colleague Cynthia had arranged it. The patrons especially liked my rendition of 'The Times They Are A'Changing'.

But that was in a past era. Now I was running around the world and this occasion was more sedate, though we did have a good chat with various local friends of Betsy's over a few beers and wines. As always, though, Essex lived up to its reputation in my memory as a great place to hang out.

Chook and I ran eastward from Essex the next morning, with Betsy guiding us toward the correct on-ramp for the bridge over the immensely wide Connecticut River. Chook managed 16 kilometres with me that morning before he was picked up by Don.

I continued on and, late that day, met the now three-strong support crew—Carmel, Chook and Don—in the lovely historic seaside port of Mystic. Just as I had run through Blythe in California, the setting of one of the Hardy Boys mysteries, I was now running through Mystic, the setting of the *Mystery of the Whale Tattoo*.

As I recollected from the book, Mystic was, and still is, the world capital of scrimshaw. Scrimshaw is the art of engraving images on to ivory and bone from sea mammals such as whales (I did learn things from Hardy Boys books). I didn't have time to visit the scrimshaw museum but I did appreciate the well-preserved townscape.

I was now only days away from finishing the North American leg. This created a bit of a party atmosphere, especially with Chook and Don along for the ride. In the evening, as I was attending to my daily documentation and blog writing, I would be happily informed it was 'wine o'clock'. This became a regular occurrence for the remainder of their time with us. I wasn't complaining. As far as I was concerned, running (what turned out to be) 12,000 kilometres across the US was cause for more than just a single night of celebration.

But it almost all came unstuck. Just a mile or so into the following day's run, with Carmel there taking photographs, I tripped on Chook's heel as I attempted to cross to the other side of the road. Feeling the impact, he turned suddenly as I was falling. This unfortunately resulted in Chook's elbow hitting me squarely in the nose.

The next thing I remember I was 'coming to' on the road surface, with Chook apologising profusely. Blood was flowing freely, especially from my nose but also from cuts and abrasions. It took a few minutes for me to recover and regain my composure. Luckily there was no serious damage done. Chook, a Kiwi, is an old rugby champion and I joked that, when Chook hits you, you stay hit. That's certainly how my nose felt for the next few days.

Despite this unfortunate incident, Chook backed up with a 25-kilometre run across the state line into Rhode Island, baling out around lunchtime. He and Don drove on to Newport, where we were staying that night, with Carmel sticking with me till I'd finished running near the town of Narragansett.

This was also very familiar territory for me, as a former wave energy project was to be situated at Point Judith, just down the road in Long Island Sound. In fact, I'd even stayed in Narragansett once before.

Newport, however, was always the preferred place to stop over when visiting the area. The site of the America's Cup yachting regatta for more than a century, the town is well known to Australians as the place where we, courtesy of the *Australia II* syndicate, finally won the auld mug in 1983. My favourite hotel in town was the Jailhouse Inn and that was our choice on this occasion.

Newport itself is an archetypal seaport, dating back centuries. Just about everything in town has a nautical feel to it. I had previously discovered some of its highlights on work visits to the area. The Black Pearl restaurant on Bowen's Wharf and the numerous bars along America's Cup Avenue were old favourites, especially the blues bar in One Pelham East. Chook, Don and Carmel had never been to Newport, so I decided to show them around.

But that wasn't the sum of us. An old friend and work associate, Gregor, was in Providence at the same time for a conference and he arranged to come down to Newport for the night. Gregor lives and works in Launceston in Tasmania, heading up the test tank facility at the Australian Maritime College (AMC). He's a world authority on boat and ship wakes and their effect on coastal erosion, among other things. My wave energy company had used the services of the AMC on numerous occasions to test our wave energy technology and so I had got to know Gregor well.

Gregor met us at the Jailhouse Inn and we all set off for a few beers followed by a sumptuous New England seafood dinner—replete with chowder, of course. Afterwards, Gregor and I even kicked on for a few more at One Pelham East. It was a worthy return for me to Newport and one I was pleased to share with Gregor. Our personal link was based on things nautical and you can't get much more nautical than Newport.

The next day, before the running began, I took the crew on a short tour by car of the mansions of Newport. On previous visits to the town I had always taken the opportunity to run through the mansion district and along the cliff top behind it. This time I wanted the others to see the same sights.

The whole neighbourhood is very impressive but the place I really wanted to show them was The Breakers, the old Vanderbilt mansion perched over the headland to the south-east of the town. The Breakers is magnificent—a classically designed structure made from stone in an Italianate style. The building and grounds are now under public trust but it is easy to imagine the opulent parties that must have occurred there a century prior, when it was a private residential retreat. Despite being one of the grandest mansions one can imagine, however, it was considered by the Vanderbilt family as only their 'summer cottage'. My support crew were suitably impressed.

An hour later Chook and I were running along the edge of Narragansett Sound. Chook stayed with me for 16 kilometres that morning before he and Don had to depart temporarily to visit one of their business colleagues further north; they would catch up with us the following day just south of the border with Massachusetts. I finished the day in the western suburbs of Providence, where Carmel and I had a quiet night over a pizza dinner.

But it wasn't to stay quiet for long. The weather was taking a nasty turn and it was about to get a whole lot worse. For several days the news broadcasts had warned of a hurricane developing—a perfect storm. And now Hurricane Sandy was heading our way.

History now records Hurricane Sandy as one of the worst to ever hit the US coast and possibly the largest ever hurricane in terms of its diameter. I ran the following morning to Hopkinton, the starting place of the Boston Marathon. The rain had been coming down steadily and the wind was increasing.

I was joined that morning for 13 kilometres by a local runner who had run his first 30-mile race the previous Saturday. He had found me via the tracker on my website. We were both freezing cold and wet by the time we reached Hopkinton. My morning running companion was then picked up by his wife. I was met by Carmel, Chook and Don.

We stood around for a few minutes, which was a bit of a mistake. I soon became hypothermic and couldn't stop shaking. I took shelter in a corner pharmacy but couldn't warm up. I finally decided I needed to change into warmer and drier clothes, though I knew they weren't going to stay dry for long.

Changing outfits in the car was awkward but Chook and I finally managed to set off together that afternoon, running head-on into the hurricane-force winds of Sandy. We stopped briefly to take photos at the start line of the Boston Marathon then battled the elements along the marathon course, always mindful of frequently falling branches. The wind was strong enough to bring down whole trees and we saw many that had been blown over. Luckily, though, we were never underneath one when it fell.

Admittedly, the hurricane was not as intense in Massachusetts as it was near New York City and along the New Jersey coastline. Chook and I even had a bit of fun at times, leaning at precarious angles just to stay on our feet. Still, we were seriously buffeted by the hurricane and were soaked through by the time we made it to our motel.

The next few hours were spent drying out our gear. But we'd otherwise escaped unscathed and I was able to say I ran for seven hours through the fury of Hurricane Sandy. I doubt anyone else on the eastern seaboard of the US ran so far that day.

It was 29 October. The main reason I chose to run during the hurricane was the imperative to get to Boston in time for our flight to South America on the 30th. However, that evening I received a discouraging email. Due to issues related to Hurricane Sandy, our flight had been cancelled and Carmel and I were rescheduled to fly two days later on 1 November.

After the initial disappointment, I quickly accepted this turn of events—there were hundreds of thousands of people who were affected by the storm in a much more serious way than I was. People lost their homes and possessions and some even lost their lives. A two-day delay in my schedule was trivial in comparison and in fact I felt quite lucky to have been minimally affected.

So, instead, the four of us had a few wines and ordered in some pizzas, waxing philosophical as we listened to the rain continue to pour down outside.

We were staying that night in Framingham, a well-known early checkpoint on the Boston Marathon course and the location of a famous medical study through which Yale University evolutionary biologist Stephen Stearns and his associates were able to demonstrate that humans are still evolving through natural selection, even in our modern society. I felt like my body had actually evolved during the ten months I'd been running around the world.

The weather the next morning was much better. The remnants of the hurricane were still in evidence and the damage it had caused was obvious but the conditions for running were relatively fine.

Chook and I headed off again on the marathon course, reaching the famous Heartbreak Hill around noon. We stopped for a drink at a running shop on the hill, where the proprietor kindly gave me a T-shirt from the store. Chook ran with me the whole day and by the time we passed the finish line of the Boston Marathon at Copley Square and finally reached the Park Plaza Hotel he had set a new record for his longest day ever of running—37 kilometres.

That evening the wine flowed freely as Chook and Don were leaving the next day. We indulged in even more great New England seafood, including the mandatory bowl of chowder at a McCormick and Schmick's restaurant, a chain famous for its ocean fare. Carmel and Don were worn out from their lack of running and retired after dinner.

Chook and I, though, had other business to attend to—sharing a parting bottle of pinot noir to celebrate his great effort on the road. He'd run well over 100 kilometres with me through the New England region, experiencing the best it had to offer and at the best time of the year. And for me, that part of the world run had been made more special for sharing it with a mate.

It was also the end of another era that night, with Carmel handing back the keys of the support vehicle after emptying it of all our gear. It had been a great car for such a journey and our appreciation of Chook and Don's gesture was no less great.

We bid farewell to the guys early the next morning and they headed off for the long circuitous drive to Colorado. I then prepared for my final day of running in the US.

I ran north out of Boston, through Salem, the site of the infamous witch hunts of the 1600s, and on to the little seaport town of Manchester. I dipped my toe in the Atlantic Ocean, as I had done in the Pacific Ocean in San Francisco, symbolising the end of my odyssey on foot across the North American continent. I then consumed a large cup of seafood chowder from a convenience store while waiting for a train back to Boston.

Carmel and I enjoyed a final celebratory dinner that evening in the same McCormick and Schmick's restaurant, along with a nice bottle of wine—our last of so many we'd consumed in the US.

The next day we flew out of Boston Airport, en route overnight to Santiago in Chile. I had run just over 12,000 kilometres in the US over a period of eight and a half months. I'd run through snow in temperatures as low as minus 10 degrees Celsius and in extremes of 60 degrees Celsius. I'd run at altitudes as high as 3000 metres above sea level and as low as 60 metres below.

Crossing North America on foot had been a mind-opening experience, tough at times but thoroughly enjoyable all the same. It was the longest leg of my world run and one I could finally tick off as complete.

Now it was time to traverse the breadth of South America. And this also meant crossing the second highest mountain range in the world—the magnificent Andes.

CHAPTER 15

South America

The first time I ever travelled internationally—a trip to Europe in 1986—I experienced an amazing feeling of exoticness. The sensation of novelty was around every turn, emanating from every nook and cranny. The sights, sounds and smells were all new and it felt like there was magic in the air. The landscape was not what I was accustomed to, nor was the architecture or culture. Everything looked and felt so different, creating a heightened sense of adventure. However, as I travelled more and more, this feeling of excitement gradually became less intense.

But this same sensation of exotica all came flooding back as we descended into Santiago, lined on one side by the South Pacific Ocean and on the other by the peaks of the Andes. Passengers crowded against the windows on the left side of the plane to catch glimpses of the snow-capped summits, especially that of the 7000-metre high Aconcagua, the highest mountain in the world outside of the Himalayas.

The thrill of disembarking under a dry cloudless sky, surrounded by majestic peaks and with the thought that I'd soon be running up among those very same peaks, was palpable. This leg was always going to be one of my favourites of the world run.

After buying Chilean SIM cards for our phones, we picked up a hire car at the airport and drove to Valparaiso on the Pacific Coast. I'd heard from Cynthia that this was a city worth visiting and it definitely lived up to its reputation. The old part of the city, perched up above the harbour, was a maze of streets with buildings covered in fantastic murals. Thousands of examples of street art were on display, creating an amazing riot of colour.

Carmel and her camera were in their element. The hotels and restaurants were abuzz with the vibe of adventurous tourists. We took it all in as we enjoyed our first dinner in South America, gazing out over a bay that gradually turned darker shades of blue as the night descended upon the city.

In the morning, 3 November, I set off along the pathway that lines the harbour. I couldn't find an easy way down to the shore to dip my toes in the ocean, so I hung out over the water on a viewing platform. That was certainly close enough to the Pacific to satisfy the required world run criteria of beginning each continent—in this case my crossing of South America—within one kilometre of the ocean.

The change in my running environment was obvious almost immediately. As I passed a fish market, I came within a metre of two policemen wrestling a handcuffed man to the ground. I didn't stop to ask questions. A few minutes later I passed a hotel on the headland with hundreds of young girls screaming and yelling in front of it. As it transpired, the Korean pop singer and dance sensation Psy was staying at the hotel and the throng of young fans were hoping to catch a glimpse.

I turned inland and my running soon became climbing. The roads in Valparaiso were generally good, though there were exceptions. The traffic was held up for miles at one stage due to major road works, making me grateful I was on foot and immune to the delay.

I'd arranged with Carmel to meet me later in the day in the town of Quillota, to the north-east of Valparaiso. I had no trouble surviving in the warm conditions via regular visits to the roadside vendors selling drinks and snacks, so Carmel's continued presence as support crew during the day was not required.

Meanwhile, though, Carmel struggled in Quillota to find accommodation for that night but we eventually ended up in a room in a woman's home. She spoke no English and my Spanish was too rusty to be of any real use. All the same, we managed to communicate enough to get by. It was a bed and I had a delightful night of sleep.

The pitfalls of a strange land came to the fore the next morning, a day in which I passed the 14,000-kilometre milestone. I had set out early and Carmel was to meet me a couple of hours later after visiting the supermarket for supplies. At one point, while running along a fairly main road, I looked at Google Maps to find it had me placed in the middle of nowhere—no roads, towns or any other form of civilisation anywhere near me on the map. But I could see I was in the middle of a built-up area. I decided to continue along the same road and ended up reaching an area that Google Maps finally recognised.

Carmel had a similar experience that same day when she called me for an address she could put into her Garmin; the same routine we had been following for the past year. I duly checked out the name of the thoroughfare on which I was running and provided her with the street name. No match! And without GPS recognition, finding each other was going to be extremely difficult. After much description of how I'd reached my present position and a lot of driving around, Carmel finally found me. We decided to stay much closer to each other from then on.

I was now running in valleys that cut through a small mountain range that preluded the Andes. Farmers and villagers were nonplussed to see a runner in their midst. Stares were often followed by smiles but sometimes by frowns too.

It was warm and dry, bordering on desert conditions, and typical of most of the west coast of North and South America. The town of Los Andes was something of an oasis, though. We stayed at a new hotel that offered great value, both in terms of accommodation and meals. The steaks were as good as you'd get anywhere.

Los Andes was an important psychological milestone for me, as it is situated right at the base of the Andes themselves. It was now time to enjoy some real climbing. In this part of Chile there is only one option by road into Argentina and it begins in Los Andes. Known as Ruta 60 in Chile and Ruta National 7 in Argentina—I just called it Highway 7—this is the main and only road that crosses South America from ocean to ocean in this part of the continent. And so it was that I headed up this highway, along with the numerous cars, trucks and buses.

Up and up I ran, a decent shoulder making for pleasant running, in perfect weather conditions, with Carmel driving ahead to logical stopping points to await me. Despite the constant gradient and ever-increasing altitude, I was feeling terrific. Ten months of running 50 kilometres per day had apparently made me quite fit.

By the end of the day I'd reached an elevation of more than 3000 metres, including negotiating my way up the most amazing set of hairpin bends one could possibly imagine. The view was breathtaking and the road so steep in places that the vehicles laboured past at speeds not much faster than my own running pace. Passengers in the buses were astounded to see a runner battling the same twists and turns as their coach.

By late afternoon I'd made it to Portillo, Chile's number-one ski resort. The hospitality of the staff was first class, especially the lovely Elena, who made us feel like we were old friends.

The day that followed will always live strongly in my memory, the reasons for which have already been detailed in the first chapter of this book. Running to the top of the Cristo Redentor Pass, only to find it blocked by ice and snow, was bad enough. Nearly falling to my death made it so much more traumatic.

As dangerous and life-threatening as it was, I am still very fond of the Cristo Redentor Pass and would like to visit it again. The views were truly panoramic, the air so fresh and crisp and the experience of being at the top of the Andes is one of life's great moments. Falling off a cliff of ice and possibly never being found is one recollection that conjures nightmarish visions when I reflect on the occasion but overall the memories are positive.

A good night of sleep back at the resort in Portillo was enough to revive my enthusiasm after the mishap and we headed through the tunnel once more into Argentina, about 5 kilometres over the border, to the spot I'd stopped at the previous day. Here began the remainder of my descent of the Andes.

The Argentinian side is not as steep as the Chilean ascent but that simply makes the descent a lot longer in terms of distance. I had run about 20 kilometres when I passed a small ski resort town, Puente del Inca. Carmel was nearby with drinks, so I didn't bother to stop in the town.

About 15 kilometres further on, I came to a military road-block. Again, the language barrier created difficulties but we finally realised the soldiers were sending us back to Puente del Inca. Apparently, the town was where the Argentinian immigration office was located and both Carmel and I had failed to be processed.

I was annoyed but we had no option. I jumped in the car and we drove back, finding the immigration facilities tucked away off the road. I hadn't even thought to look in that direction when I ran through the town. Half an hour later saw us both processed and we returned to the checkpoint. A thorough search of the car satisfied the soldiers we were 'clean' and I was eventually allowed to continue on foot.

Ten minutes later I passed two English cyclists who were ascending from the Argentinian side. They stopped and we had a chat. I felt happy that I was knowledgeable enough to inform the pair they had no chance of getting past the snow-covered non-existent road at the top of the Cristo Redentor Pass. They had intended to try exactly that and I'm sure I saved them a lot of time and probably a whole lot of grief too. They would either need to get a lift through the tunnel with a truck or take the risk and ride through. I would not recommend riding through the

Cristo Redentor Tunnel to anyone. However, despite it being technically illegal, I feel it is quite do-able on foot, along the narrow and buckled subterranean sidewalk.

I finished the day nearly 40 kilometres from the town of Uspallata, which we commuted to that night. Uspallata is an 'adventure town', with lots of small businesses catering to thrill-seekers who come there for mountain climbing, white-water rafting, mountain biking, bungee jumping and hang gliding. I loved the vibe of the place and enjoyed running through the town the next day before commuting back again. Two nights in Uspallata was fine by me.

I reached the bottom of the Andes a couple of days later, exiting the mighty range with a distinct suddenness. Unlike many mountain ranges, the Andes finish abruptly on both the Argentinian and Chilean sides and I was suddenly running on a flat plain. My legs were quite sore from more than three days of downhill running and the flat ground seemed to exacerbate the soreness.

Early that afternoon I reached the city of Mendoza, a place I'd been looking forward to with gusto since I began planning for this run. Mendoza is the 'capital' of the Argentinian wine region and it didn't disappoint.

After a struggle to find accommodation, we ended up in a lovely hotel just around the corner from a restaurant strip. Fantastic steaks and red wine at unbelievably low prices made our time there one of the highlights of South America. And, not realising it at the time, we were to spend five nights in the Hotel Princess Gold.

Taking a car from one country to another in South America is a nightmare. Selling a car in a different country to where it was bought is illegal, as is dropping off a rental car. I had investigated the options in intimate detail before starting the run and chose the only real possibility open to us—hire the car in Chile, have Carmel drive it to Mendoza while I ran, leave our gear in a hotel, drive back to Santiago, drop off the hire car, catch a plane from Santiago to Mendoza, pick up a new Argentinian hire car, load it up with the gear that we'd left at the hotel and only then begin running again while Carmel drove the new car. Got that? It was a convoluted solution but it worked well— except for two small spanners in the works.

We'd arranged to return the Chilean car to the airport in Santiago and fly back to Mendoza on 13 November but I'd arrived in Mendoza a day early, on the 11th. So the next day I ran a little way out of the city toward the east and was picked up by Carmel, after which we drove to the airport.

There we bought new Argentinian SIM cards for our phones and arranged the hire of the new car for the following afternoon. Then it was back to the Mendoza hotel for another evening of delicious food washed down by the sumptuous local red.

We were up early the next morning and on the road for the 400-odd kilometres back to Santiago. It always amused and amazed me to drive back over a part of the course I'd recently run. For some reason it seems so much further in a car than by foot.

After negotiating both sides of the enigma that is South American immigration, we dropped in briefly to say hello to Elena at the Hotel Portillo then began the descent. The first drama arose when we reached a set of tollbooths. We had no Chilean cash.

Luckily, we had just enough Argentinian pesos and the kindly booth operator agreed to personally exchange this money into the Chilean denomination. Still, the process took some time to sort out. Quite stressed by the experience, we continued the journey.

Unfortunately, that wasn't the end of the toll road. Another set of booths really brought about a potentially nasty situation. Now we had no money at all, credit cards were not accepted and we had a line of traffic building up behind us. Tempers were starting to flare, with horns honking and shouts emanating from the rear.

After holding up the traffic for nearly ten minutes, the operator finally made an executive decision and waved us through without paying. He had no choice, really, as it was clear we had no acceptable way of settling the debt and he was copping as much abuse as we were. Such are the pitfalls of travelling.

But that wasn't the end of our dramas for the day. In fact, it was about to get worse. Once we'd returned the car at Santiago, we attempted to check in for the flight. There seemed to be some anomaly in our documentation.

The woman at the desk spoke English well and informed us we had not paid the reciprocity fee online—the only way it could be paid. This is a fee related to the fact that the Australian government, in its infinite wisdom, had chosen to charge Argentinians to visit Australia. So Argentina reciprocated and was now charging Australians the same amount. To confuse matters further, the fee only applied to entrance into the country by aeroplane—running or driving into Argentina attracted no reciprocity fee. We were unaware of the impost, an oversight that left us unable to board the flight.

Discussions followed, with suggestions put forward by the airline staff of taking an overnight bus until the manager got involved and asked us down to his office. If we were quick enough and paid the fee online, we might still make the flight.

Numerous staff, including one local who had lived in New Zealand for a while, spent nearly an hour helping us. They logged on to the internet and tried to arrange for us to pay the fee but the internet just happened to go down at that moment.

Time was quickly running out—it's strange how time seems to pass much faster when a deadline is looming. Another Australian, a young backpacker from Brisbane, with the same problem was led into the office too. His fee was paid online on the first attempt.

There was hope! The internet was back up and we quickly settled our dues and were rushed up to check in. Luckily we had arrived at the airport very early that day. Despite all the time we thought we had up our sleeves, in the end we only made the flight by about fifteen minutes.

I was exhausted and fell asleep on the short flight back over the Andes, despite the magnificent view from my window seat. We picked up our new car at the airport and headed to the same hotel in Mendoza for a third night. This time we celebrated overcoming our day of dramatic hurdles. The wine tasted especially sweet that evening.

However, things weren't all good. Carmel was not happy with the new car in the morning. That, and the need to do some further 'housekeeping', resulted in a snap decision to spend another day in Mendoza. The staff members at the hire-car office in town were very helpful but they had no alternative cars. We had to keep the one we'd been given.

Carmel coped amazingly well with driving around the world. In situations where many men and women would fall to pieces, Carmel managed to navigate her way through intense traffic, reverse out of narrow dead-end streets and co-exist with freeway traffic that was, at times, travelling at twice her speed, all the while learning the road rules and driving culture of each country.

Perhaps the most stressful situation Carmel found herself enduring throughout the entire world run was driving alone along a 14-lane motorway in Chicago, with traffic whizzing by her on both sides. There were plenty of other nerve-wracking occasions—how could there not be when driving tens of thousands of kilometres through strange lands—but for the most part, Carmel handled the driving like a true professional.

Her problem in Argentina, however, was with the car itself—more specifically, with the air-conditioning and the locking system. We were about to cross South America with summer almost upon us and a good air-conditioner was important, particularly as Carmel would need to spend a lot of time sitting in the stationary car waiting for me to arrive on foot. This is one of the pitfalls for a support crew on the Argentinian Pampas.

Thankfully, the cooling system in this car was simply of a different style and with a little instruction the problem was solved. The locking system was of the old style—push the button down and hold the handle as you close the door. Fine—except that it was too easy to lock the keys in the car. This was potentially a problem of the highest order, of which we'd have to be constantly vigilant to avoid a disaster.

Once the staff had explained a few things about the nuances of the air-conditioning, soothing Carmel's concerns, we felt the car issue had essentially been solved (though there was nothing much anyone could do in the event of her locking the keys in the car). We then headed off to buy groceries, check out the tourist office for hints on subsequent accommodation and to enquire about our new SIMS, which we didn't quite understand how to operate properly.

A productive day ended with a fourth night in our Mendoza hotel and another pleasant evening on the restaurant strip.

The next morning I finally set off to the east from Mendoza and on to the plains the Argentinians call the Pampas. These ultra-flat grassland plains cover 750,000 square kilometres and are the lifeblood of the country. I would be running through them on Highway 7 for the next thousand or so kilometres.

As I ran along a dusty potholed road that paralleled the highway, I startled a few locals who'd never seen the likes of me. Carmel was again having some difficulties coming to terms with the differences between the physical reality of the roads and what her Garmin navigation system was indicating. GPS systems are only as good as the data that has been input. This almost caused her to lose me at one point, which she was much more wary of in a country in which she didn't speak the language.

But our main problem was that by the time I'd finished running for the day, we had not encountered a single accommodation option. We were tired and opted for the easy solution; drive back to Mendoza for another night in the same hotel.

Although it was now a 70-kilometre commute each way, at least we knew we would have a comfortable night and a delicious meal. And so we were to spend a fifth night in the Hotel Princess Gold—and I wasn't complaining one little bit.

The quiet parallel road petered out a day later and I was forced to run on the highway. This was a lot easier than I'd expected, with a wide shoulder allowing me to stay well away from the traffic.

I'd imagined very little in the way of rain on the Pampas of Argentina. I was wrong. Although most days are, indeed, bathed in brilliant sunshine under azure skies, there are times when those same skies open up.

And when it storms on the Pampas, it *really* storms. One afternoon I watched with trepidation as huge cumulus clouds steadily built for a couple of hours before unleashing their fury on me—and upon every vehicle on that highway.

The hailstones were the size of marbles, and they caused intense pain as they struck my head and shoulders. Luckily I was just 400 metres from an overpass when it started. I took shelter underneath, along with many buses and cars whose drivers were trying to stave off hail damage to their vehicles.

And then the hail really started. Stones the size of golf balls were smashing into the ground at terrifyingly high terminal velocities. I could do nothing other than wait it out. It was far too dangerous for any traffic to move, with visibility no more than a metre or so. The lucky drivers were those who could fit under that overpass with me. The rest had to sit in their cars and suffer whatever damage the heavens inflicted upon their vehicles. Somewhat similar to my experience when running into Phoenix, Arizona, the whole four-lane divided highway looked like a very wet and dangerous version of the freeway gridlock in REM's video of 'Everybody Hurts'. Except that no one was getting out to walk around or to sit on the roofs of cars.

At times, finding accommodation was to prove problematic for Carmel on the Pampas but she always found something when it mattered. Even the small villages seemed to have somewhere we could stay.

We were impressed by the way certain Argentinian towns had set up wireless internet facilities—every resident had access for free. And we were just as impressed with our SIM cards that gave us unlimited pre-paid access to the internet for the equivalent of just twenty cents per day. Try getting that in Australia!

Argentina is broken up into states and I'd already crossed the states of Mendoza and San Luis when I came to a checkpoint on the state border with Córdoba. Here the highway stopped abruptly and was replaced with a two-lane road with little or no shoulders. I had enjoyed running for more than 200 kilometres on that highway, a period that included some novel experiences.

For example, I was surprised at one stage when I ran past two 'working girls' standing on the shoulder of the highway in the middle of nowhere. The nearest town was miles away. Apparently their clients came out and picked them up from this remote 'red light strip'.

Carmel had stopped about half a kilometre further up the road and was waiting for me to reach her. She was shocked yet amused when a car stopped and an old man knocked on the window, asking '*Cuando?*' (How much?) Her horrified reaction quickly alerted him to his mistake and he made a hasty and embarrassed retreat before I reached the car. Carmel and I had a good laugh about it, though.

But now the divided highway was gone and I was forced to run in long grass by the side of the road. This was hard enough but was made even tougher when, after just a few kilometres of running on the grassy verge, I felt an agonising pain sear through my foot. A small wooden skewer had pierced my shoe and was stuck firmly in my foot. It was so deeply embedded that the skewer was pinning the shoe to my foot and I was unable to take off the shoe.

I struggled for a moment then realised my only choice was to pull out the wooden skewer from the outside of the shoe. This actually took quite some force. I could not grip the skewer properly and my fingers slipped off the spike the first few times I tried.

Grasping the skewer as firmly as I could and with a colossal effort, I finally managed to pull the skewer out of both my foot and shoe in one violent action. I almost fainted with the relief. Now, though, I needed to remove the shoe and survey the damage.

There was a puncture wound but it wasn't bleeding too much. My concern was whether I could continue running. I tentatively put the shoe back on and tried a few steps. To my great delight it hardly hurt at all when I ran, so I decided to just keep on running. And, to my even greater amazement, I never suffered any infection or other ill-effects whatsoever from that wound—I felt like I'd dodged another bullet that day.

We stayed in a town with a strange name that night, an eclectic mix of Spanish and Scottish—Vicuña Mackenna. I had stopped about 50 kilometres, or a full day of running, to the west of the town. Civilisation was pretty sparse in this part of the Pampas and it had become clear to us that commuting would be a regular occurrence. Except for the long drive to and from Vicuña Mackenna, shuttling back and forth suited me fine.

Commuting from my finish point to our accommodation had its upside, as it usually meant I could conclude the following day of running in town and we could stay two nights in the same motel room. This was always appealing since it resulted in not having to pack and unpack again that day.

At dinner in the motel restaurant during our first night in Vicuña Mackenna was a table of two men and seven children of a range of ages. Carmel struck up a conversation with one of the men. Mauro and his brother-in-law were taking their combined brood out west for the weekend from Buenos Aires while their wives were on a girls' weekend away. They had already driven some 600 kilometres that day and had another big drive in the morning. We didn't speak for long, this seeming to be another of those innumerable pleasant one-off encounters, like so many we'd had on the world run. But as it turned out, we were going to see Mauro and his family again and again.

The week that followed ran together like a series of Groundhog Days. Long sections of straight road through ultra-flat Pampas countryside made for a reasonably homogenous vista. The highway was still just a two-lane ribbon of tarmac and drivers would often pass by at speeds approaching 200 kilometres per hour. Even when there was no on-coming traffic, I couldn't run on the other side of the road due to cars overtaking from behind. It was simply too dangerous to run anywhere but on the shoulder, where the grass was usually quite long.

And this was dangerous, too—there were rattlesnakes in that grass! I wasn't even aware rattlesnakes reside in South America but Google soon put me straight. And besides, I know they were there because one morning I saw three snakes within an hour!

Each had come to the side of the road to sun itself and I had to be careful not to tread on them. They would retreat from me, usually across the road. But one decided to slither to the centre of the road and stop there.

I tried to scare the snake on to the other side of the highway but it refused to budge, instead just rearing up, trying to encourage me to flight instead. I could see a truck coming in the distance so I tried harder to get it to move to the opposing shoulder. Still it wouldn't budge and the inevitable happened— a squashed snake. Most people would say 'good riddance' but I felt bad. It was my presence that caused its death.

Huge fat lizards a metre long also abounded in the grass but I only saw these in road-kill form. How many of these lizards and snakes I must have nearly stepped on during my 600 kilometres in this roadside grass is anyone's guess.

I consider not being bitten as another bullet I dodged. I was dodging bullets like a superhero might—but I wasn't a superhero and sooner or later one of those bullets would strike its target.

The Argentinian Pampas is one of the world's legendary frontiers. Stretching over a large portion of the country, the Pampas—a local indigenous word meaning 'plain'—is the land of the gauchos, the South American equivalent of the cowboy; men whose work it is to muster the millions of cattle on these vast plains.

In some ways the Pampas is similar to the prairies of North America or the steppes of Siberia; lots of farms and grasslands and little in the way of forests. However, there is a difference. The Pampas is almost exclusively flat. The prairies, which I'd run across just six months earlier, have large regions of rolling hills. There are no such undulations on the Pampas. The horizon is often a long way off in the distance.

Running the west-to-east extent of the Pampas was, I felt, one of the more romanticised components of my run around the world. It might be stretching the point but I felt a little like an explorer when I was out there on the road. Sure, there were plenty of cars zooming by me at high speed but I rarely saw anyone else moving at my pace. Away from the highway the Pampas was a very tranquil place.

Argentina has a reputation for some of the best beef in the world. And I fully concur with this view. In fact, I don't think I've had better anywhere. The country towns on the Pampas had a surprising number of restaurants and cafes and we'd regularly spend balmy evenings sitting on the sidewalks, devouring mouth-watering steaks and sipping fine reds from the region. However, this was not a tourist area and other than us all the diners were locals.

I reckon a tourist to Argentina could do a lot worse than to spend some time slowly making their way across the Pampas.

To me, this was a quintessential period—something unique to an adventure like running around the world.

Three days after we'd met Mauro and his crew in Vicuña Mackenna, their whole contingent, all in one large people-mover, passed me on the Pampas on their way back to Buenos Aires. Carmel had stopped further up the road and Mauro stopped there too, all of them chatting excitedly while waiting for me to catch up. It was a brief but delightful re-encounter, especially when Mauro insisted we stay with him and his family when I reached Buenos Aires. Carmel and I, thrilled to make some Argentinian friends, readily agreed.

A further week of running went by, all of it in similar conditions. Another milestone was ticked off when I passed the 15,000-kilometre mark of the journey, just past the town of Rufino. The running was easy except for the imperative to do so on the grass. It was late November and the weather was almost ideal, though sometimes a little hot—and there was not a hill to be seen.

Because Highway 7 is the main thoroughfare across the South American continent, truck traffic was as prevalent as that of cars. But no matter where in the world I was running, I always found truck drivers to be considerate. Maybe it's because they saw me as a similar soul, living life on the highways. Whatever the reason, I never experienced any unsavoury incidents with trucks.

Cars, however, were another thing. Some cars would try to intimidate me. This is scary initially. But after thousands of miles spent running on the roads of the world, one becomes highly aware of what constitutes true danger. After a while I found myself supremely confident, playing chicken with drivers.

And it was always they who 'blinked first'. Of course, I made sure I was in a position to get myself to safety if needed so I was never in any actual danger. But it was interesting to turn the tables on drivers whose actions clearly demonstrated they objected to me being part of the landscape of the highway.

My hearing played a critical role in my safety throughout the world run. The recognition of danger from behind was tantamount and this sense became finely honed as the run progressed. It was an entirely subconscious skill that I found I'd developed but survival is like that. Ears are secondary only to eyes when it comes to staying alive as a runner on the highways of the world.

And it wasn't just me who faced danger on the road. Carmel had one frightening incident when she was attempting a U-turn and the car stalled on a long straight section of the highway. She couldn't get it restarted and watched as another vehicle bore down on her at a scary speed. Amazingly, she managed to get the car going just in the nick of time, quickly accelerating it out of the way.

Another time she got out of the car to take some photos and, as we had dreaded since picking up the vehicle in Mendoza, she locked the keys inside. We were both very aware of how easy this was to do. Carmel had been constantly heedful about not leaving the keys in the car but no-one can be eternally vigilant. She had managed successfully for two weeks but the inevitable finally happened.

When I arrived at the car, I found a helpful truck driver had already come to the rescue. He was still working on it but assured us the wire coat-hanger he kept in his truck would do the job. Sure enough, a few minutes later the button popped and the car was open. This Good Samaritan really saved the day; our only alternative would have been to break the window.

Accidents on the highway were commonplace and when they happened they were ugly. I came upon one that had just been cleared. The police were still in attendance mopping up the debris. They told me that two trucks had collided head-on, killing both drivers. I was so relieved that I wasn't at that spot a few hours earlier. And then the two policemen, who had questioned why I was running in such a remote area, asked to have their photo taken with me.

The Argentinians are gradually replacing this road with a dual carriageway but it will take decades yet. It was one of the most dangerous roads I encountered in my whole time running around the world. This is despite the fact it is the main highway between Santiago and Buenos Aires, connecting the Pacific and Atlantic oceans.

— ⅄ —

Other than falling over ice cliffs and dodging speeding cars on shoulder-less transcontinental highways, a run around the world involves little that is dangerous. One exception is tripping.

It is unlikely anyone can run around the world without taking a few spills. I'd experienced my first as I was running into Santa Barbara on my birthday, losing a little skin on my hands and elbow. And 'hitting the deck' was reasonably frequent after that.

An innocuous fall near Homer Simpson's nuclear power plant just out of Springfield, Illinois, left me with a bad graze. Whereas a very hard fall in Sheryl Crow's hometown in Missouri resulted in no cuts or bruises at all. Tripping on Chook's feet in Mystic, Connecticut, left me dazed and confused but that was due to Chook's elbow impacting with my nose and not the fall itself.

I had accepted I was going to trip and fall from time to time. It's never nice but a bit of lost skin was not a major concern.

A few days before I reached Buenos Aires, however, I suffered my worst fall of the entire world run. I had just passed some road works which had halted the traffic for an extended period. I, on the other hand, was allowed to pass on the shoulder. It suited me fine, as I got to run on a deserted road for more than ten minutes. All I had to do was periodically glance back to make sure the traffic was still stopped.

But as I once again looked around to check if the traffic flow had recommenced, I tripped on a corrugation in the road and hit the tarmac hard. Because my torso was turned at the time I stumbled, I landed on only my right hand. Although it all happened in just a fraction of a second, I was acutely aware of the sensation of the skin on my palm being peeled off. Before I even got to examine the damage, I knew it was as bad as it gets.

A large coin-sized piece of my palm was missing, and the initial whitish flesh underneath was rapidly filling with blood. I had nothing with which to dress the wound, and had to wait for Carmel to come by about ten minutes later. We spent some time with the first-aid kit, sterilising the area of skin loss prior to dressing it with a bandage. It took weeks for the laceration to heal, with lots of dressings being applied in the meantime.

Perhaps the severity of that fall made me more cautious, for I never fell again on the world run, except for one minor stumble on the Nullarbor.

It's not just parting with skin that is of concern when tripping on the road or sidewalk. Some of my falls caused less outwardly obvious injuries, such as bruised shoulders, hips and elbows. At other times I rolled my ankle when treading awkwardly on objects hidden in the grass, limping along for a while afterward. And it was only for these—the mild trauma injuries—for which I sought medication.

In essence, during the world run I only ever took painkillers or anti-inflammatories to ameliorate the temporary soreness that stemmed from these types of trauma injuries. It is my policy never to mask an overuse injury with anti-inflammatories. Doing so only allows the problem to be exacerbated until finally even the drugs have no effect.

Such a policy served me well. Although I did endure a few instances of niggling pain triggered by the overuse of tendons, such as my ankle problem in the north of the US, solving each by discovering and addressing the root cause proved a much more effective solution.

My philosophy was simple: if it was a sudden painful injury—a sprained ankle or sore shoulder—that was likely to last just a few days, painkillers were fine in the interim, allowing me a more comfortable and enjoyable day of running.

However, if it was an overuse injury with the propensity to be chronic, such as tendonitis, finding the underlying reason and fixing it was my only sustainable option. I believe this was a critical component of my successful run around the planet.

I finally reached the outskirts of Buenos Aires on 4 December 2012. The city centre is home to many famous landmarks and beautiful architecture but the outer suburbs comprise the occasional slum. Integral to my run was the philosophy of seeing the real world, 'warts and all'. This included running through slums and other places that tourists never visit.

I ran through one such slum that afternoon. The streets were gravel—though this is the case in many Buenos Aires suburbs, including the affluent ones—and every shanty house had a dog.

Dogs had been kind to me throughout the run to this point. There'd been countless occasions where they'd bared their teeth and barked ferociously but I know dogs and it was always just bluff. I found that for me the easiest solution was to reciprocate like a vicious animal and they backed off. However, on this occasion a whole pack formed.

In essence, most dogs are cowards, only having the confidence to attack when they are part of a pack. Even though a large group was now assembling, these dogs were all show, growling and barking but not biting—except for one. I saw this particular dog come out of its yard, alerted by the cacophony of the pack. It didn't make a noise.

I turned my head to the front briefly and it pounced, nipping me on the back of the calf. I turned on it angrily and it retreated immediately. The dog seemed to realise it had gone too far; that it had really pissed me off. The entire pack then ran away, either fearing retribution or content that they'd done their job.

The blood was flowing quite freely from several puncture wounds. Carmel was nearby and had seen what had happened. With the help of the first-aid kit we patched up my calf, firstly swabbing it with disinfectant in an attempt to kill any potentially dangerous bacteria imparted from the dog's saliva. I called it a day shortly after. Finally, a bullet had struck.

It was then important to get to a shower, as constant bathing is one of the first tasks required in order to guard a fresh animal bite against rabies. Once a person contracts rabies, it is 100 per cent fatal. I hadn't even thought about having a series of rabies shots before commencing the run. (I've never actually managed to get around to having vaccination injections of any sort prior to any of my travels over the years. Whether it's just good luck or the result of a good immune system I can't be sure, but I've never suffered an illness in any of the more than fifty countries I have visited. I am not offering an opinion on this issue, nor suggesting others follow my example—just stating the facts of my particular situation.)

Rabies is such a rare disease and, besides, the immunisation process is extremely expensive and usually only administered in the ensuing few days after a rabies-infected bite is suffered. I wasn't sure what the incident of rabies was in Argentina but I expected it was high (as it turns out, rabies is rare in Argentina).

We searched high and low for a motel but there were no vacancies. We even stumbled into two motels that charged by the hour. We quickly discovered these were for people who needed to 'get a room'—quite common in Buenos Aires and something of a novelty that is unique to Argentina. We decided against such an abode and kept looking.

Two hours later we eventually booked into a nice little B&B and I spent the next hour washing the dog bite as thoroughly as I could. Rabies takes days or even weeks to manifest itself, at which time it's too late. Research indicating rabies was not prevalent in this country set my mind at ease somewhat but as there is little the medical fraternity can do to determine if infection exists prior to the presentation of symptoms, I still had a nervous wait ahead of me before I could be sure. Needless to say, I avoided rabies. This bullet may have hit me but it wasn't to prove fatal—just a flesh wound, literally.

The next day entailed some very tedious suburbia as I made my way to the Atlantic Ocean. Slums with piles of garbage strewn along the sides of the road gradually made way to more salubrious suburbs near the coast. Carmel lost me a couple of times, which is very stressful in a city of sixteen million. But phone contact always came to the rescue.

After four weeks of running across South America, I finally reached water again that afternoon, 5 December. At the mouth of the River Platte, which is Atlantic Ocean water, I dipped my toe in once again to symbolise the end of my continental crossing.

Traversing South America had involved almost 1500 kilometres of running. As with all transcontinental journeys, it required a sea level to sea level transect, but in this case I had reached an elevation of almost 4000 metres in the interim.

I paused for a brief moment of reflection—and then we were off. Guided by the Garmin navigation system, we made our way to Mauro's place in the north of the city. There we met Mauro's lovely wife Laura and, once again, his four children.

Both Mauro and Laura spoke perfect English. He had spent many years working in the US and she was an English teacher in Buenos Aires. They introduced us to various Argentinian culinary specialities that evening as we discussed all manner of topics, including Laura's favourite footballer Lionel Messi. It was a real treat to finish my run across South America in this fashion and we were deeply grateful to Mauro and Laura for their wonderful hospitality. They were some of the best friends we made throughout the whole world run.

In the morning Carmel and I drove across the city to the airport, a major accomplishment in itself, where we returned the car and headed to an airport hotel. There we organised our luggage, throwing out any non-essentials and packing for our flight. Early the following morning we flew back to Sydney for a break over Christmas and the New Year, prior to commencing my European leg.

I had so far covered 15,414 kilometres of my world run and had less than 11,000 kilometres to go. Other than the sore ankle during the middle of the US leg, I had not endured any run-threatening injuries and was feeling confident about the year ahead.

It wasn't to be quite as simple as that, though.

CHAPTER 16

Western Europe

A week after returning to Australia a strange thing happened. I began to develop a sharp pain in my left heel. This was confusing and counter-intuitive. How could I get through more than 15,000 kilometres relatively unscathed, yet get injured doing almost nothing?

Christmas and New Year's Eve came and went, the pain slowly getting more intense—and more worrying. It was painful when I was doing almost no running, so what would it be like when I was again running 50 kilometres each day? I spent most of our time at home feeling quite depressed, expecting I'd soon be forced to either quit the world run or, at a minimum, to take a long break.

Early in the New Year, Carmel and I flew to Europe, where I was to start running across my third continent. As we disembarked the long-haul leg in Frankfurt, the friendly Qantas flight attendants presented me with two bottles of French Champagne and two bottles of top-notch shiraz, 'courtesy' of the business-class cabin. The gifts were much appreciated and they were to come in handy later in the run.

We picked up our new support vehicle in Madrid—the latest model SUV generously provided by Citroen at cost, an arrangement Libby had facilitated the year before—and then drove to Lisbon where my European run would start. We enjoyed a lovely dinner with long-time friends from the wave energy industry who I'd first met in the same city in 1999.

That night, however, I slept restlessly. I was deeply concerned about my injured heel. How was it going to hold up?

We drove the short distance west from Lisbon to Cabo da Roca the next morning, the most westerly point in all of mainland Europe (only some parts of Ireland are further to the west). A few photographs later, perched on the edge of the high cliffs above the raging Atlantic Ocean below, and I was on my way. It was 24 January.

It didn't take me long to realise the heel was surviving far better than expected. At the suggestion of my cousin Karen, a champion marathon runner in her day, I had inserted some heel lifts in my shoes. These seemed to help. By the end of the day, just a short 36 kilometres to the surfing town of Ericeira (I didn't want to overdo it on the first day back), I was feeling very little pain.

A couple of days later and I declared the injury non-existent—the heel was healed, so to speak. I am still at a loss to explain how I could do so much running without any major issues, get injured while resting, then cure the injury by doing massive amounts of running again. There is some physiological reason, as yet unexplained—something for the podiatrists and sports scientists to ponder.

I was now running through the ancient countryside of Portugal, with innumerable buildings of stone dotting the muted green fields and meadows, punctuated by leafless trees that stood like sentinels of the season waiting to be clothed again by the warmer weather.

The winter season kept the farmers inside during the day and, for the most part, the townspeople inside at night. As restrained as life appeared to be in the middle of winter, there were still some memorable towns I traversed during the Portuguese leg—such as Torres Novas, where we stayed in a hotel with a view across the ancient town square to a medieval castle just 50 metres away.

Portugal had suffered more than most countries at the hands of the Global Financial Crisis and the state of the economy showed in the prices of food and lodging. We were getting amazing value. Equivalent hotels in Australia would have cost five or even ten times what we were being charged. It was great for the budget but I couldn't help feeling a little guilty that we were taking advantage of the economic plight of the country.

It took me a week to run north from Lisbon then across Portugal to the Spanish border on 30 January. Carmel and I had crossed this same border in 1986, with its armed guards and passport checks. Now there was nothing but the decaying remnants of those checkpoint buildings.

Just over the border that night, we stayed in our first Spanish hotel of the run, witnessing first-hand the fanaticism of the Spanish soccer fans during a televised match involving Real Madrid, the local team of the region.

I have always loved the culture of Spain, with its history, its bar hopping, tapas and late-night eating, and was pleased to now be running across the country, experiencing all these delights, albeit attenuated by the fact it was winter. Even the Spanish tone down their social life a little when their days become cold.

Historic Roman cities like Cáceres were a pleasure to run through and, on the day I reached 16,000 kilometres, in a village called Oropesa, we spent a marvellous night in a castle in which Somerset Maugham had once been a guest. We think we may even have slept in his room—but I'm sure they've changed the bed since then. It was truly surreal to sleep in a modern bed, safely ensconced within walls of ancient stone. A balcony with a view to die for and Maugham's former presence perfectly rounded out the dreamlike nature of our stay.

Less than a week of running in Spain brought me to one of my favourites—Toledo. This ancient walled city, home of El Greco the painter in the 1500s, is a truly special place. As well as a tourist mecca, it is now a university town and my arrival coincided with students returning to classes.

An equivalent of an 'orientation week' was in full progress. Parades were endemic, as was all manner of adornment in strange costumes—the dress policy seemed to be one of 'anything goes', with students trying to outdo each other with their creativity and originality. Not to mention great food and wine. Carmel and I strolled through the thousand-year-old streets and alleys at night, happily taking it all in. Toledo was another landmark destination that definitely lived up to expectations.

The afternoon of 9 February concluded with me running up a long and winding road to a mountain village called El Barraco. We were greeted by the congenial proprietor of a small hotel who during the conversation informed us this was the hometown of 2008 Tour de France winner, Carlos Sastre. It was easy to see how Carlos had become such a good climber.

Although the village was small, it contained several restaurants—yet every one of them was booked out. It was six weeks before Easter and it seemed like every local was out for dinner that Saturday night in El Barraco, aiming to gorge themselves on a last big meal before the beginning of Lent and a period of fasting.

Luckily the staff in one bar took pity on us, bringing all the remaining tapas from their kitchen, from which Carmel and I could pick and choose. Fortunately for us, the restaurant-goers, knowing they had a huge meal in front of them, had eaten sparingly of the tapas that evening. All the more for us! The bars emptied quickly as the restaurants opened and we were left almost alone to enjoy our tapas dinner.

After a steady climb to the top of a pass north of town the next morning, I began a long descent into the town of Ávila. Having seen this walled city in 1986, I found it almost unrecognisable on this occasion. The wall, once prominent, is now almost invisible behind the innumerable modern buildings and light industry encircling the ancient part of town. Ávila had lost some of its gloss in my eyes.

Above: Tom, a tiny speck below, running up the most incredible series of hairpins as he ascends the Andes from the Chilean side.

Below: Tom (the white dot on the road in the bottom right), again dwarfed by the Andes as he reaches 3000 metres altitude.

Above: Running the dirt road to the Cristo Redentor Pass, this time at about 3400 metres elevation.

Below: Cans of lentils were one of Tom's favourite lunchtime treats in Argentina.

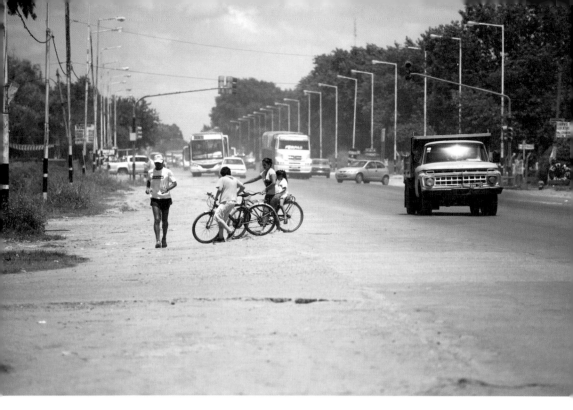

Above: Running in the suburbs of Buenos Aires.

Right: The blood flowed freely when a dog bit Tom on the leg just outside Buenos Aires. But he was more worried about rabies.

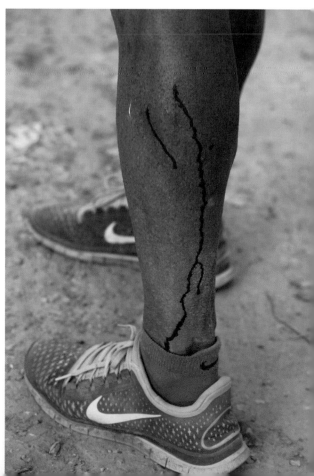

Above: Passing through a village in western Spain.

Below: Celebrating his birthday on the road in south-western France.

Above: Snow running in the foothills of the Pyrenees.

Below: Passing a chateau near Nolay in the Burgundy region of France.

Above: Icicles in his eyebrows, something Tom had rarely experienced in his running career.

Below: More running through snow in Germany. Tom was forced to follow the bike paths, but these had not been cleared, resulting in cold and wet feet all day long.

Above: Running through the main street of the ancient Czech town of Telć.

Below: The Hud (left), Tom, and Dave enjoy a beer in the ancient city of Bratislava, capital of Slovakia.

Above: Crossing the Danube in Budapest with Dave and The Hud.

Below: Simon Bouda and cameraman, Greg, visited Tom on the road in Serbia to film a segment for *The Today Show*.

Above: Tom and Barry crossing the border from Bulgaria into Turkey.
The differences were immediately obvious.

Below: Tom (bottom right of picture) battling the traffic of Istanbul.

Above: Finishing the European leg at the Bosphorus in Istanbul.

Below: Competing for the sidewalk with motorcycles in Batu Pahat, Malaysia.

Above: More battles with traffic in Pontian, Malaysia. Here Tom was just minutes away from finishing the Asian leg of his world run.

Below: Running with Grace between Perth and Kalgoorlie, Western Australia.

Above: Approaching Norseman, WA.

Below: The mind-bogglingly long and straight roads of the western Nullarbor.

Above: Around the campfire at night with Michael (centre) and Jeff (right).

Below: Taking a brief detour off the main highway with Chook, this time on the way to Fowler's Bay on the Great Australian Bight.

Above: Bidding farewell after a month together on the road—Michael, Tom, Carmel and Jeff.

Below: Enjoying a pie for lunch in South Australia.

Above: It was canola season as Tom approached Glenrowan in Victoria.

Below: More brilliant yellow canola as Tom passes a lone sheep.

Above: Mobbed by the press as he finishes at the Sydney Opera House.

Below: Victorious on the steps of the Sydney Opera House.

Finishing in the small village of Villacastin to the east, I awoke the next morning to snow. It was a cold day of running and the first on which I wore my new long running pants (Carmel was sick of seeing me running in shorts in sub-zero temperatures and had purchased some cold-weather attire for me during the Christmas break). No more running in shorts in the snow!

More history was to follow during the afternoon when I ran through the Roman city of Segovia, passing right underneath its amazing aqueduct. Two thousand years old and still going strong!

The snow melted quickly and four days later I had reached Burgos. The old city, comprised of a labyrinth of sandstone, includes one of the most ornate cathedrals in the world. We had stayed in Burgos in 2009 when on a cycling holiday with Libby and we decided to book in to the same hotel on this occasion. It was Friday night and despite the winter chill and darkness it seemed everyone was out on the town. We spent an evening over tapas and tempranillo watching the crowds while the local children, rugged up against the cold, played happily in the town square.

Another four days brought me to Pamplona late on the afternoon of 19 February. It wasn't all easy going, as on one occasion, near the city of Logrono, I found myself in a muddy vineyard between rows of grapes, courtesy of a shortcut indicated by Google Maps. I could do nothing more than traipse through the puddles and mud until I finally reached a dirt track which eventually became a road. But these tribulations along the way were worth the trouble, having now reached the foothills of the Pyrenees.

— ⫰ —

Pamplona, famous for the Running of the Bulls in June, is clearly attuned to tourists. After a walk around the streets fronting the bull ring, we enjoyed more tapas and Rioja wine before an evening meal of local fish. Tapas are different in Spain to what passes as tapas in other parts of the world. Provided free with each drink, these tasty morsels cover the full gamut of food styles, from seafood to offal to vegetarian fare. It was good to be able to choose, as I'm not a big offal fan. Although it's not the tradition with the Spanish, who tend to eat sparingly of the tapas before a proper dinner, we often found the tapas to be worthy of the evening meal in itself.

The next two days were spent running over the Pyrenees. Two long climbs, one on each day, were followed by equally long descents. I was above the snow line and there were plenty of scatterings of white still visible. The Pyrenees are often considered treeless versions of the Alps but this part of the range was heavily wooded in pines and other conifers. The second ascent was on a dirt trail that entailed one of the steepest sections I'd ever run.

I was now in Basque territory and Euskara became prominent on the road signs and billboards. This local language, thought to be the final vestige of the pre Indo-European languages that were prevalent in Western Europe in millennia past, is a descendant of the dialects spoken by the Stone Age inhabitants of that area and era.

The countless high mountains and deep secluded valleys of the Basque country afforded the inhabitants the ability to resist conquer over the aeons, resulting in the preservation of their prehistoric and unique language. Most road signs are now shown in Spanish and Euskara (French and Euskara in the French Pyrenees).

I reached the Atlantic again on the afternoon of 21 February 2013, this time on the Bay of Biscay in San Sebastián. I was met by a local runner—who had a half-marathon best of 61 minutes, which was far better than me; in fact, his time was world class—and he directed me to the promenade where several others from the local running club accompanied me to the finish in the main part of town.

It had been very rare so far to be greeted this way but word had got around and the press were on hand, along with many photographers. I was even provided with a free massage at the ultra-modern gym below the promenade.

We also received a generous discount at one of the most ideally located hotels we've ever stayed in—situated right on the bay above the promenade, with views from our balcony of the wonderful San Sebastián waterfront and old fort. This turreted stone edifice is perched on one of the headlands at the mouth of the bay, providing the harbour with the natural defence that the Spanish Armada found so useful in centuries past.

After my massage—the only massage I enjoyed during the entire world run—it was off to a local running and sports store, Apalategui. This was the store that sponsored the running club that greeted me earlier and the proprietor Felix presented me with a free pair of running shoes. I was very grateful, as these were the first free shoes I'd received during the whole run—every other pair of shoes I wore throughout were bought by me. (These shoes were an attractive light blue colour and I ended up wearing them for some 2500 kilometres, down the Malay Peninsula and from Perth to Ceduna.)

Carmel and I, along with Felix and several other people from the club, then departed for *pintxos* (the Basque word for tapas) before heading to dinner at their favourite restaurant in the old quarter of the city. An entire side of beef was brought out, cooked in Basque-style herbs and spices then sliced into bite-sized chunks. The running club crowd partook heartily, washing down the local fare with equally local red wine. It was a fantastic evening in one of the great cities of the world.

I crossed the border into France on 22 February. Carmel met me in the town of Saint-Jean-de-Luz, where we acquired new French SIM cards. This turned out to be a bad experience. Despite assurances to the contrary, the data on these SIMs never worked the whole time we were in France, therefore preventing the operation of my tracker or of Google Maps in that country.

The following afternoon, after nearly 54 kilometres of running, I arrived in Salies-de-Béarn. Recently the venue for the start of a stage of the Tour de France, Salies-de-Béarn is a medieval town we'd visited with several friends twice previously, in 2009 and 2011. It was also where Carmel celebrated her birthday in 2009. And, coincidentally, on this occasion in Salies-de-Béarn, I would be waking up to my birthday.

After rising to an array of presents from Carmel, a generous breakfast saw me departing through the old town, replete with its thatched roofs and medieval-style wooden houses. The weather was turning cold again and after a long day of nearly 58 kilometres in which I passed the 17,000-kilometre milestone, I reached the city of Pau. This is a large town that features on an almost annual basis in the Tour de France.

I had cycled through Pau in 2009 with a few of my Tour de Bois mates, on our way to Salies-de-Béarn. On that occasion we'd stopped for a lunch of pizzas. This time it was dinner at a restaurant to celebrate my birthday. One year previous I had been running in Santa Barbara in California. Pau was a completely different proposition but that's why one runs around the world—the diversity of experience and culture.

It was snowing heavily in the morning in Pau. The tree branches seemed to have been designed purposely as receptacles for snowflakes—a true winter wonderland. When the snow continued to get heavier, I decided to cut the day a little short, stopping in the city of Tarbes, another regular on the Tour de France. The following days were free of snow fall but the ground was still covered deeply in drifts, making for a unique running adventure.

The snow slowly melted as I made my way through the lower French Pyrenees region, with the white-capped peaks often in sight to my right. Running was usually an easy affair, so long as the wind wasn't blowing. When it was, I found myself requiring my rain jacket to act as a wind break. The extra weight of the jacket left me a little more tired than usual at night. But the most annoying thing was the rustling sound the hood made as it rubbed on the back of the jacket. I was always pleased to shed this piece of clothing when it wasn't too cold.

We met a succession of friendly French farmers during this period, often staying in their B&Bs. One special occasion was at a farmhouse in the small village of Saint-Élix-le-Château. The owners spoke no English but we all got on well regardless, sharing an authentic regional meal of duck and native winter vegetables, washed down with the indigenous red wine. As for the language barrier, we struggled but ultimately succeeded in communicating with each other. A phone call to the couple's English-speaking daughter-in-law helped no end.

For some time I'd been concerned about my ability to concentrate. I'd first noticed the problem in the early part of the US, where I'd often attempt to focus on some issue for the day while I ran, only to realise I'd wandered off into other thoughts just moments later. I had put it down to fatigue. After all, everyone knows it's difficult to concentrate when tired.

But I suspected that months of 'giving my brain a rest' had resulted in a deterioration of sorts. I wanted to perform some brain exercises to prevent further deterioration so I came up with a problem to focus my mind upon while I ran these quiet country roads of southern France. I was familiar with solving mathematical problems with a pen and paper. But this time I decided I'd solve a set of equations completely in my mind as I ran.

The challenge was simple—calculate a formula for the area of a triangle, given only the length of the three sides. Now this may seem easy. After all, everyone knows the area of a triangle is 'half base times height'. Those with a deeper background in the subject may be familiar with formulae that use, for example, two sides and an angle. But the problem I was striving to nail involved no knowledge of the perpendicular height of the triangle, nor any information about the angles. I only had the length of the three sides with which to work.

Despite having a PhD in Mathematics, I had never seen nor heard of such a formula for the area of a triangle. But I was sure it must exist and couldn't be too hard, at least not with a pen and paper. Remembering every line of every equation throughout was, however, a different matter.

It took me a whole day to come up with an answer but I did manage it. I spent the next day double-checking my calculations, though the elegance and symmetry of the formula had already assured me I had got it right.

I'm not sure the exercise resulted in any long-lasting improvement in my ability to concentrate during the world run but solving this task without pen and paper provided comfort that my mind had not completely gone to mush. I had not anticipated such an issue but long-term fatigue during a run of this magnitude most certainly has a potentially debilitating effect on one's mind, and even on eyesight.

Slightly blurred vision was another problem I encountered on a regular basis. It manifested itself in a way that is no different to the blurred vision one might suffer from days without sleep. But the only respite from this condition was rest, my vision improving each time I took an extended break between the continents.

I was now running on infrequently travelled back roads and the snow and cold meant there were even fewer people about than normal. It was a pretty region in which to run, with pristine babbling brooks and rolling green hills in the foreground, complemented by snow-capped peaks in the distance, and I often completed a day in near solitude. I skirted south of Toulouse, through smaller cities like Revel, past the ancient abbey of Sorèze and via Castres.

More than a week later, and after a long climb over a mountain range in the lower Aveyron region, I ran into Saint-Affrique on 3 March. We had visited here in 2011 with friends, staying at a wonderful old B&B. The couple who owned it both spoke English fluently and we got on like old friends. They were delighted to welcome us back and we relished another of those classic evenings of fine regional French fare and local red wine. It was turning into a trip down memory lane.

The owners of the B&B grow much of their own produce and the difference was obvious in the food they served, with seasonal vegetables and herbs dominating. Dinner and breakfast were exquisite and their inclusion of such unusual ingredients as stinging nettle in the cooking was a real culinary revelation. And I'd never tasted so many varieties of tomatoes, each notice-ably unique in its own right.

This part of France is very hilly. Another day of climbing, with the world's highest bridge visible in the distance at Millau, was followed by a massive descent into a small valley. The local pork and offal sausages didn't seem to agree with me that evening and I spent most of the night on the toilet. That morning I left in a weakened state, starting with an 8-kilometre ascent.

Once I reached the top of the climb, the weather struck. The horizontal wind blew the stinging rain straight into my face. I had to cover up, such was the force with which the raindrops were striking my flesh. This included sunglasses for my eyes, despite the gloomy day. I would have otherwise suffered serious eye damage from the bullet-like rain.

Many massive hills later and my day concluded in the town of Ganges. The 48 kilometres of running had left me tired but it had also built confidence. If I could survive a day like that, after losing most of my stomach contents the night before, then I could survive almost anything.

My insistence on running in extremely inclement weather and during other adverse conditions had often drawn comment. Carmel and Libby were incredulous when I'd dug the support vehicle out of a deep snowdrift in Prescott, Arizona. Carmel and others, policemen included, were equally stunned to see me running on days so hot they'd attracted extreme health warnings from the authorities about even venturing outside. But this willingness, I felt, was an important attribute for someone running around the world.

I have always tended to set a running goal and stick to it. It's not even a conscious thing. Once I've loosely decided to run a certain distance, I find it's mentally easier to fulfil that aim than to abandon it.

This served me well during the world run. Dumping my plans for the day each time I encountered adverse weather would have added months to the adventure. Those months would have been well used if we'd been able to make the best of the days off. But by the very nature of the break, we'd have been stuck in a motel room watching the rain and snow or escaping the debilitating heat. That would have been psychological torture.

No, at a mental level it was definitely easier to get out on the road and brave the unsavoury conditions.

This attitude is, however, a double-edged sword. As useful as it is to the cause of circumnavigating the Earth on foot in minimal time, at some point one has to bow to common sense. Only once did I take an unplanned day off, to avoid running in 55 degrees Celsius heat with a chronically sore ankle after the all-night party at Sissy and Bob's in Chicago. In my mind, that would have constituted overstepping the mark. Getting the balance right is difficult but important. In hindsight, I feel I did get it just about perfect.

Two days later I reached another B&B from our 2011 cycling trip, in the town of Mauressargues. Once again we were hosted imperially, this time in a renovated house from the Middle Ages. The structure is so authentic it even has reality TV shows requesting permission to film on the premises.

The owners run a most impressive establishment and we partook of more regional fare and wine. Local organic beef and vegetables and a dessert consisting of a parfait of sweet thistles made for a memorable culinary experience. Our hosts were surprised when I brought out one of the bottles of shiraz from Australia, courtesy of the generous Qantas attendants on our flight to Europe. It was certainly a different style to their usual wine but they loved the drop and it was much appreciated.

A couple more days of running, including a crossing of the Rhone River, saw me saunter in to Malaucène at the base of Mont Ventoux. This mountain, known as the Giant of Provence, is nearly 2000 metres high. It is legendary in the Tour de France and among cyclists the world over.

There are three different roads to the top of Mont Ventoux. One of the great challenges for a cyclist is to climb to the top of the peak from all three directions in the same day. I had accomplished this feat in 2011—more than 4400 metres of ascent in a seven-hour session. It was good to be back in familiar territory just eighteen months later. I wanted to run to the top of the mountain on this occasion but unfortunately the roads are closed in winter.

The next week of running was eventful at times. On occasions running in snow, through former Roman territory littered with fragments of 2000-year-old Doric columns, past France's second largest city of Lyon, I was often kept company by the endless procession of TGV trains travelling at their superfast speed of 300 kilometres per hour. I never tired of seeing these amazing bullet-like pieces of engineering. This was complemented by more pleasant experiences, including a brief visit to the dairy farm of more acquaintances near the city of Mâcon and a stay in historic Cluny, once home to the largest cathedral in the world before it was eclipsed by Notre Dame in the 1100s.

The end of the week saw me finally arrive at an old favourite of ours—the town of Nolay. Carmel and I had stayed in this lower Burgundian hamlet on a couple of previous trips, fascinated by its village square and covered market structure dating back to the 1300s. On those visits we'd always been with friends and this time was no different.

On this occasion we were joined by Judith and Steve, good friends who'd been to Geneva on business from their home in London. Judith and Steve used to live just a few kilometres from us in Sydney and we'd caught up with them on past occasions in a variety of places, including Perth, Melbourne and London. Now it was great to see them again in completely different surroundings.

We partook of dinner that night in a cosy little restaurant on the corner of the archetypal French village square—in fact, if a cartoon version of the township was created it might look just like the village from the *Beauty and the Beast* animated movie.

The evening was one to remember. Amid a room full of local diners, we ploughed through three bottles of the restaurant's finest red as we caught up on old times. Ours was definitely the loudest table in the eatery and the one having the most fun.

Steve dropped me back to my starting point in the morning, 16 March, for a day that included reaching the 18,000-kilometre milestone. After barely fifteen hours together, we were bidding each other adieu. Catching up with old friends like Judith and Steve in unfamiliar territory was a true delight, adding to the colourful sense of diversity I was experiencing during my run around the world.

The weather was not improving as I ran through the heart of French culinary territory, including Beaune and Nuits-Saint-Georges, skirting just to the south of Dijon. I was rarely seeing the sun—the occasional snow was becoming more common—and the temperatures were steadily decreasing.

Running to the east, through Dole and Besançon and the southern suburbs of Montbéliard, had brought me close to the border with Switzerland. In fact, I briefly ran into Switzerland one afternoon before ending the day back in France. I was now in Lorraine, home of the quiche. And that evening we met some fellow diners in a restaurant who were from Luxembourg. They were friends of the famous cycling brothers Frank and Andy Schleck. The people you meet!

I attained a rare feat the next day, certainly for my world run—I ran in three countries in one day. I began the morning in France, reached Switzerland at Basel where I crossed the Rhine River before ending the day in Germany. And I only had to run 40 kilometres to achieve this. The total of my running in Switzerland amounted to just 8 kilometres, the lowest of any of the countries I passed through on the world run. It was 22 March and I was making excellent progress across Europe.

Much of the next week I was running through the lower reaches of the Black Forest. I sought out the quietest roads and though they were hilly at times, it was a beautiful place to run. Traditional villages of the Baden-Württemberg region were numerous and we loved seeing many of the wait staff in the restaurants and bars wearing their local costumes.

Another positive about running in Germany is the proliferation of cycle paths. I had run on a few in France, particularly around Cluny and east of Dijon, but the paths were in much greater abundance in Germany. This was a very good thing as there was little or no shoulder on the actual roads.

And it was even more important because the weather was deteriorating further. The snow was almost a daily occurrence and I was sometimes running knee-deep in powder. When I couldn't find a cycle path, it got scary.

One morning I was running on a road in the snow when a pleasant policewoman stopped me. She explained that I was spooking the motorists, especially when they rounded each of the many bends and suddenly saw me heading at them. She asked me why I wasn't running on the nearby cycle path. I hadn't even seen it as the path was covered by snow. I gladly made the change, although then had to guess where the path was at times. It was virtually invisible underneath the snow.

Every morning my shoes would become waterlogged from the snow and then I'd spend the remainder of the day running with wet and freezing feet. Although it didn't snow every single day while I was running through Germany, it was always grey and overcast—I didn't see the sun once during the whole two weeks I was traversing the country.

Running in snow presents its share of difficulties. Besides cold and wet feet, visibility becomes an issue. Light is very muted in overcast conditions, yet it's so blindingly bright in the sunshine that sunglasses are a must. If the snow is falling at the time, it can be hard to see more than a few metres. This makes running dangerous.

The most perilous aspect, however, was when paths were obliterated by the snow. It could be difficult to know where to run, and who knew what lay beneath! I was constantly in fear of breaking an ankle or tripping on some obstacle hidden just below the pristine snowy crust.

But the snow wasn't a complete negative. The soles of my shoes would develop a thick build-up of compacted snow and ice and this was virtually frictionless when in contact with the snow on the ground. I found that if I slid my feet rather than lifting them off the ground, I could travel significantly faster. I was effectively cross-country skiing in running shoes.

This was a particularly fast mode of travel on the downhill sections. I had to be careful, though, as when the road became too steep my pace would increase to an unmanageable level and

I'd become unstable, many times almost falling or crashing. But it was generally a lot of fun, providing a diversion from the drudgery of running all day through snow and getting me to the end of a day sooner than would otherwise have been the case.

The first big town I came upon in Germany was Ulm. I knew this was where Albert Einstein was born and I was keen to find the exact location. After booking into the hotel, Carmel and I headed across the road to grab a simple dinner. There was a takeaway kebab place close by and we both ordered a falafel roll with extra hummus and tabouleh.

While I was waiting for the falafel, I was thinking about my strategy for discovering the location of Einstein's birthplace. And then I saw a plaque right there on the ground. The kebab place was just metres from the house in which the great physicist had begun his life. The house was destroyed during World War II but the spot was now commemorated by the plaque. The run around the world had now afforded me a visit to the location of both Einstein's birth and his death.

I dropped in to the local Oxfam shop in Ulm the next morning. I was raising funds for Oxfam as part of my run and it was my policy to drop in to say hello if there was an office in town and if it was convenient to do so. We had an impromptu photo session with the staff in the shop and I was on my way east again. That day, 28 March, I reached Bavaria.

A few more days of running through idyllic Bavarian country-side brought me to Dachau, just north of Munich. Dachau was the first concentration camp set up by the Nazis in the 1930s. It is now a tourist destination with a difference and a harsh but important history lesson for any visitor.

The camp illustrates, in graphic ways, the horrors of that time and place. It is clear the German people never want to see the likes of such an institution again.

To my mind, the most hard-hitting display is in a corner of a room once used as a crematorium. On the wall is a photograph of that same corner of the room during the war. Now the building is otherwise empty. Then it was piled high with dead bodies, predominantly Jewish, awaiting burning.

Next to that picture of the bodies pending cremation is another photograph of a bonfire from the mid-1930s depicting a Nazi book-burning ceremony. And between the two photos is a sign highlighting one of the most prophetic quotes ever uttered.

The German poet Heinrich Heine had opined, more than a hundred years prior to the rise of the Nazis, 'When they start burning books, they'll soon be burning people.' Unfortunately, those two photographs were all too graphic a testament to Heine's prediction.

The snow was even heavier the next morning as I headed in a north-easterly direction. The week ahead was cold and wet and I spent most of my non-running time indoors.

During the following week I crossed a wide river several times, sometimes spending many miles running along its banks. It was called the Donau, which I hadn't heard of before. I wondered how I couldn't be aware of such a large waterway with huge barges plying its length. Stupid me—I later discovered that Donau is the German name for Danube. I had been running beside the great river for some time without even realising it.

On the subject of the German language: it is the source of the word 'doppelganger', meaning an identical double. It was entirely appropriate, therefore, that in Germany we met the most authentic doppelganger I've ever encountered. Running a small guesthouse in the little village of Ramspau, situated just north of the city of Regensburg, was the spitting image of then Australian Governor-General, Quentin Bryce.

Carmel and I were discussing the uncanny resemblance over dinner as the lovely old German woman was serving us. We decided we'd tell her. I Googled Quentin Bryce and brought up a couple of images of her on my phone. We showed our host.

She reeled back in amazement, holding her hands to her cheeks, mouth agape and eyes agog. The woman then held her hand on her heart, as if she was going to have a cardiac attack. Tears welled in her eyes as she exclaimed, 'Das bin ich.' ('That's me.') So identical was she to Quentin Bryce, I believe she could have easily passed for her in any situation that did not require speaking. This was a doppelganger in the extreme.

On 4 April 2013, after two weeks running through charming German towns and villages and living on schnitzel each evening (I adore schnitzel), I crossed the old Iron Curtain border into the Czech Republic. The change was immediately obvious.

CHAPTER 17

Eastern Europe

Once a part of Czechoslovakia, the Czech Republic separated from Slovakia after the fall of the Iron Curtain in 1989. As the European Union expanded, the border controls were relaxed and now no one stops those who cross from Germany into the Czech Republic.

The towns just inside the country obviously market themselves to the seedier side of the German population, with strip clubs and the like being advertised on numerous billboards. These establishments disappear rapidly as one goes further into the country, existing primarily just inside the border.

The weather conditions were still grey and cold as I passed the 19,000-kilometre mark of my run around the world on 5 April, the day after crossing into the Czech Republic. It was about this time I came to an interesting realisation. When I bought a drink from a fridge in a shop, the liquid was actually warmer than the sub-zero surrounding air. The interior of a refrigerator is usually set at between 2 and 4 degrees Celsius, which was actually a higher temperature than the outside ambient air in which I was running. This created a bizarre sensation: the objects inside the refrigerator felt hot and whatever I drank—Coke, chocolate milk or orange juice—was warm. It was even weirder to think that these fridges were actually acting as heaters. I guess it proves temperature is just a relative phenomenon.

Just as interesting was the preponderance of the old dreary Soviet-style tenement buildings. These were being converted into modern and colourful versions of their former selves. Despite the winter malaise, the people appeared quite vibrant and were always keen to meet us. And most of the younger ones spoke excellent English. We were finding the Czech Republic much friendlier than we'd expected.

On one occasion in the small town of Kladruby, a series of megaphones attached to power poles kept repeating an announcement in Czech in a dreary monotonous voice. It was a scene straight out of Orwell's *Nineteen Eighty-Four*. However, none of the townsfolk took any notice of the monotonous voice. I wondered if that would also have been the case during the Communist era.

Finding accommodation was not always easy and Carmel had some very stressful times in many of the towns. Acquiring Czech SIM cards was also a painful experience. The reasons are still unclear as to why it took nearly three hours to obtain these phone cards but it probably wasn't helped by the fact a mobile trailer was operating as the local Vodafone store.

After running through the picturesque city of Plzeň, the place where Pilsener beer originated, I reached the town of Žebrák.

Here we had a fantastic meal in a centuries-old stone building. As in Germany, the most abundant dish in Czech restaurants is the schnitzel (although in both countries it tends to be pork rather than veal) and I was keen to compare the national differences. In Žebrák the schnitzels were superb, along with the vegetables, but while the variation wasn't as pronounced as I had expected, it was surprisingly tasty and subtly different. I assume this was the result of the use of local ingredients and a particular regional cooking style.

The following morning it was snowing again but the fall stopped by mid-morning. Though I was unaware of it at the time, the half day I spent running from Žebrák was the last time the skies snowed on me during the remainder of the world run.

That afternoon, 7 April, I arrived in beautiful Prague. A city rich in history and culture, Prague is a jewel in the middle of Eastern Europe. Sitting on the Vltava River, it was bathed in sunshine by the time I rolled into town; the warmest day I could remember since starting in Europe back in January. At just over 50 degrees north of the Equator, Prague was also the most northerly point I reached in the entire world run, roughly equivalent to the 46 degrees south I reached at Dunedin in New Zealand.

We received a great special deal from a hotel in the middle of the old part of the city and headed out to the main square to do the tourist thing. The early evening was spent relaxing in an outside bar below the unique and quirky clock in the Old Town Square, watching all manner of tourists as they checked out the sights.

Unfortunately, I could spare only one night in Prague, heading south-east the next day. It was not a difficult city to negotiate on foot and I found myself back in the countryside by late morning.

The four days it took me to reach the Austrian border were delightful, through quaint towns such as Benešov and past beautifully preserved architecture like that of Telč. This latter settlement, in particular, exhibits one of the most original and well-preserved town squares I've ever had the pleasure of stumbling upon. I'd recommend a visit to Telč to anyone travelling in the southern part of the Czech Republic.

While it never snowed on me again, the temperatures often hovered around zero. There were plenty of places where the evidence of the long winter was still obvious, including many lakes frozen solid. I even ventured out on to one pond where the ice was at least a metre thick. Walking on frozen water is a weird experience; one that's virtually impossible to have in Australia. It's also very dangerous but I checked the strength of the ice before stepping on to it—this pond was so frozen solid it would have supported a car.

After an interesting stop in the city of Znojmo, another quirky architectural delight, I ran across another of the old Iron Curtain borders, on this occasion into Austria. It didn't take me long to cross Austria. In fact, after spending one night north of Vienna and another to its east, I crossed the Danube yet again, this time just before the border with Slovakia. A wonderful cycle path led me across that border and straight into the city of Bratislava, one of the true hidden gems of Europe.

Bratislava is significantly smaller than Prague to its north, Vienna to its west and Budapest to its east, but it's every bit as historic. Its old town quarter is as quaint and picturesque as any of the larger cities of the region but its size makes it much more pleasant and easier to get around.

We indulged ourselves with a couple of drinks in the cobble-stoned main street within the walled section of Bratislava, followed by a great value dinner, once again based around the ubiquitous schnitzel. The morning of 15 April I ran south and out of the city but it wasn't the last time I was to see Bratislava.

About 20 kilometres on I again crossed another ex–Iron Curtain border, this time into Hungary. The buildings at the old checkpoint were completely derelict, destroyed by vandals during the past twenty years. On reaching the large Hungarian town of Mosonmagyaróvár early that afternoon, we acquired new Hungarian SIM cards and I called it a day.

It was now time for a special reunion—with some of our closest friends, back in Vienna.

Carmel and I had been looking forward to the arrival of Jo, Dave, Sue and Greg (The Hud) since they booked their flights late the previous year. And I had scheduled my only day off during the whole European leg in order to welcome them. We'd agreed on a hotel in Vienna. With great anticipation, Carmel and I arrived there late that afternoon.

The others joined us soon after and we celebrated in our room with a bottle of the French Champagne I was given on the Qantas flight in January. Needless to say, a raucous night ensued. The next day all six of us did a walking tour of the famous sights of Vienna, then that afternoon drove the hour or so back to Bratislava. Carmel and I had enjoyed Bratislava so much we wanted our friends to experience the place too.

We all checked into the same hotel from two nights earlier and hit the town. A few ancient stone-lined bars later and we settled on one that served local beer in large glass boots. The three guys decided to try these while the girls stuck to wine. The glass boots held about two litres each, equivalent to around five large beers.

Sitting outside at a table in the cobblestoned street, we were having so much fun we couldn't help but attract the attention of tourists and locals alike as they walked past. Those huge beers in glass boots were a focal point of the merriment. This was especially so when we each reached the lower part of the boot, the angle of the vessel suddenly allowing an influx of air into the toe and causing beer to rush out rapidly, exactly as it does with a yard glass. It was a bit like Russian roulette with beer. Dinner at a nearby restaurant capped off a memorable day.

Dave and The Hud were there to run with me and they didn't waste time. The next morning, 17 April, we drove to my previous stopping point in Mosonmagyaróvár and we got started.

The three of us had been running together for more than thirty years, originally as founding members of the Maroubra Runners Association. We had trained together for the 1983 Australian Marathon, meeting the girls after each Saturday morning long run for an extended breakfast of scrambled eggs and Champagne.

In more recent years Dave and I had embarked on several cycling tours in Europe. Averaging around 130 kilometres per day, we had ridden leisurely on quiet back roads while Carmel and Jo enjoyed their own parallel driving tour, meeting us at the end of the day in a new village. Paris to Rome, Luxembourg to Spain, San Sebastián to Florence—each leg had involved riding through tranquil and historic countryside, punctuated with climbs of the high passes of the Alps, Pyrenees or both. This time Dave was here to run.

And The Hud had run with me on the first day of the world run, from the Sydney Opera House to Bondi Beach, resulting in the running distance that I invented and bears his name—the ultra-tough 167.7-kilometre Hud (sometimes also known as a Hudrathon). Now he was back for more.

The guys took turns, one running with me while the other would drive their hire car, sometimes after putting in a stint on the bicycle they'd hired between them for the journey.

Meanwhile, the girls enjoyed looking around, meeting us occasionally during the day in small Hungarian villages. It was great for me to have company while running and Carmel loved having friends in the car. Each night was an adventure in itself as we explored on foot these towns that rarely see tourists.

Stopovers in Győr and Tatabánya left me just 60 kilometres short of Budapest—a long but manageable day. We had met an expat Scot, Don, the night before at dinner, along with his seventeen-year-old daughter Yolanda, who had just finished eighth in the Czech national cross-country championships. Don joined us again in the morning and ran the first 10 kilometres with Dave and me, directing us on to the back road toward Budapest.

Dave and The Hud again shared the running with me that day, with Dave totalling 39 kilometres. For some time there had been friendly banter building about who among my friends would run the furthest with me in a single day. Chook had held the record for the previous six months with his 37 kilometres into Boston. Now Dave had set a new record on the day I ran into Budapest, pipping Chook by just 2 kilometres. However, that record was to fall many times before the end of the world run.

Carmel, Jo and Sue had found a perfectly situated hotel in Budapest on the banks of the Danube and we made the best of it. We always knew how to have a good time when the six of us got together, as we had many times in Australian destinations such as the Blue Mountains and Noosa, and doing so in more exotic locations like Budapest just intensified this fact.

The next morning saw me head off from Budapest toward the south. The towns were close enough that I didn't need any support that day. Dave and The Hud ran a few kilometres with me in Budapest itself, with Carmel taking photos as we spanned the Danube. Then the guys dropped out for a day off and I hit the suburbs alone.

Although quite a big city, I was into the countryside by late morning, with Dave picking me up that afternoon from the small town of Kakucs. After a unique Hungarian burger experience, complete with pickled cabbage, in the home-grown Kakucs diner, Dave then drove us back to Budapest for another evening with the group.

It was our last night together and we weren't going to waste it. We took a cable car to a castle overlooking the city then had dinner at a restaurant right on the Danube. It was a fitting finale and the goodbyes in the morning were sad—their time with us had been all too short but our friends had regular lives to resume in Sydney. And Carmel and I had a world run to finish, so we drove back to my starting point for the day and I continued running south toward Serbia.

Hungary is a very flat country; certainly the parts I ran through were like green pancakes. Lush farmland bordered the roads on both sides as I made my way through towns that were a mix of the old and the new. The weather had heated up drastically in the previous couple of weeks, with peak temperatures now nudging 30 degrees Celsius.

And the Danube was never too far away. These vast plains have been the site of human civilisation for aeons. Evidence of settlements dating back tens of thousands of years has been uncovered. The fertile and easily traversable ground, coupled with warm summers, made it easy to see why prehistoric humans would choose this region as home. Criss-crossing the country on foot, just as these peoples had done so many centuries earlier, created a sense of living in another age. Well, at least I tried to imagine it so.

On 23 April I reached the border with Serbia. Serbia was not yet a member of the European Union and, as such, a passport was required at the border crossing. Thus far, I'd only once had to pass an immigration checkpoint on foot, high up in the Andes when crossing from Chile into Argentina. Having to run up to the passport control point at a border crossing made me a little nervous. I feared the immigration officials would consider

the situation unusual enough to detain me for questioning. So I approached the booth cautiously with Carmel crawling along beside me in the support vehicle. As it turned out I had nothing to worry about, though the checkpoint official did indicate it was rare to see someone passing by on foot.

Having obtained new SIM cards (once again) in the northern Serbian city of Subotica the next day, I lazily made my way south in lovely sunny weather. Three more days of running on flat roads under equally warm and sunny skies and I crossed over the Danube for the umpteenth and last time during my transit of the city of Novi Sad.

Half an hour later, I reached the 20,000-kilometre mark of my run around the planet. This was a giant milestone in my mind. The end of the run suddenly seemed so much closer.

Serbia was an unexpected surprise. The people were perhaps the friendliest in all of Europe and the incidence of English-speakers was certainly the highest. Hotels in Serbia were good yet cheap, the food was of a high standard and the people only too willing to help if we had any questions.

At one point an old man saw me approaching. He must have known I was not a Serbian by the look of me. He didn't speak English but gestured to me to wait a moment. He re-emerged from his house with a silver key ring emboldened with an ancient insignia and the word SERBIA in Cyrillic script. The old guy simply wanted to present me with a memento of his country to let me know that he was a friend, and this was despite never having seen me before.

I later asked an English-speaker why, as visitors, we were encountering so much goodwill. He explained that Serbia had gained a bad reputation throughout the world as a result of the Balkan Wars—those of the 1990s and also from past struggles—and Serbians wanted to correct this view whenever they interacted with tourists (and interaction with tourists is rare outside of Belgrade).

To me, it was confirmation that there are nice people wherever you go in the world (and, no doubt, some nasty ones too). No nation has a mortgage on friendliness and decent people.

After a very pleasant stay in the town of Indija, where hundreds of locals were out in the town square that evening, I was met the next morning by a crew from Channel 9 Australia. Journalist Simon Bouda and cameraman Greg had been covering the Anzac Day commemorations at Gallipoli, flying to Belgrade that morning from Istanbul. Lots of footage was taken on the road as I approached Belgrade and Simon even ran with me for a short while in the western suburbs of the city.

We all ate together that night in the popular tourist section of the capital before more filming and an interview on the banks of the Danube the following morning. It was intriguing to observe how television segments like this are created and the experience certainly provided a break from my normal routine. The segment appeared on *The Today Show* a few weeks later.

Belgrade is a big city and not an easy place in which to find someone. I often worried that Carmel would lose me in the confusion of cities like this, particularly when I was navigating my way along side streets and back roads. But her skills with the Garmin were second to none and, yet again, she found me with relative ease that day on the eastern outskirts of the metropolis.

The terrain was becoming more undulating as I ran in a generally south-easterly direction from Belgrade. And this began to exacerbate a problem I was developing. For the past month a pain in my foot had been getting worse. It was where the plantar fascia tendon attaches to my right heel. On the flatter regions of Hungary and Serbia it was bearable but running up hills was now resulting in increased pain.

My only previous problem with an injury had been in the middle of the US, almost a year before. I had alleviated that issue with arch supports. And then the rest days I took during our time in Chicago and then back in Australia, in order to renew the terms of the visa waiver, had cured the problem completely.

But this pain had not responded to any treatment or shoe modification and I was starting to become deeply concerned. Although it never stopped me from running my usual daily distance of around 50 kilometres, I was not enjoying being on the road—pain will do that every time.

I had wracked my brain for a solution but everything had failed. Until, that is, I had an inspiration. What if it wasn't the running but something else I was now doing differently? After all, I had survived more than 20,000 kilometres of running so far without a problem and my shoes, pace and running style were unchanged. I must have altered something else in my daily life.

It finally occurred to me that the beds we'd been sleeping in were different. I sleep mainly face down, hanging my feet over the end of the bed (I've tried sleeping on my back but always wake up the other way around). Although this sleeping style is not a deliberate decision, hanging my feet over the end of the bed does allow my feet to rest at the normal angle to my legs while the body attempts to heal overnight any slight tendon damage from that day of running.

Since reaching Germany, the beds had been predominantly a wooden outer section with the mattress inset into the frame. As comfortable as they otherwise were, this bed geometry had been preventing me from hanging my feet over the end. This meant the overnight repair process was occurring with the tendons in an unnatural position—those at the front of the leg were lengthened while those at the back of the leg and foot (the Achilles and plantar fascia) were shortened. Any new micro-fibres regenerated in the plantar fascia overnight were, therefore, too short and were instantly snapped the next day when I started running again. This was causing a gradual build-up of inflammation, leading to the pain I'd been experiencing. At least that was my theory. But was it correct?

I decided to do whatever was necessary to ensure I slept with my feet at right-angles to my legs. This essentially involved re-engineering the bed, with pillows if necessary. After the first night, the pain was significantly reduced. Was I correct in my diagnosis and treatment? The signs were good.

After the second night, I felt no pain at all. Problem solved! I've never had an injury heal so quickly and so simply. I felt on top of the world, now running without pain for the first time in many weeks.

I reached the city of Niš in southern Serbia on 1 May. Carmel and I had previously visited Niš in 1986 when Serbia was part of the old Yugoslavia. On that occasion we were travelling with a few good friends, Vanessa, Peter and Robyn, and we stayed two nights in the camping ground—on one night enjoying an impromptu fancy dress party which I attended as an elephant. We still talk and laugh fondly about that party, decades later. If anyone had suggested then that I'd one day be back in Niš as part of a run around the world ... well, you know how the saying goes.

In fact, the travelling we did with Vanessa and Peter throughout Europe in 1986 set me up well in my mind for tackling the continent again on foot. Having initially met the couple in a camping ground in Praia da Luz in Portugal (more recently, and sadly, the location where three-year-old Madeleine McCann went missing), we ultimately journeyed together throughout the Greek Islands, Turkey, Bulgaria and many of the old Yugoslavian nation states. During our time together I gained a valuable insight into the geography and culture of these Eastern European countries, leading to an even more valuable confidence in regard to crossing the region on foot. I knew where I was going and I knew what to expect.

Now here I was again, 27 years later, at the scene of our infamous fancy dress party. This time there was no evidence that the camping ground ever existed. It was no doubt the victim of progress and development. We did, however, stay in a pleasant hotel on the banks of the river that flowed through town and enjoyed a delicious meal of Balkan steak at a restaurant in the back streets while being entertained by local Serbian musicians and dancers.

Heading east from Niš, I had an unusual encounter. It's now possible to drive on freeways all the way from Istanbul to the Atlantic Ocean, except for pockets in Serbia and Bulgaria—and this stretch was one of those pockets. I was on a very quiet back road that paralleled the construction of a new freeway section, one that will ultimately reduce these gaps even further.

But there appeared to have been some protests and resistance to this construction. When Carmel tried to take a photo of me with the new freeway in the background, an armed guard immediately drove up to us and threatened to confiscate the camera, even though we were in an entirely public place.

The construction company was obviously very sensitive to criticism of the new road in the distance and were not allowing any photographs of it to be taken. We promised not to take any more and the guard reluctantly allowed us to continue up the valley.

At the top of a long climb, there was another surprise awaiting us. A mountain shepherd was tending his goats. He was tiny, perhaps four and a half feet high, and was dressed in the local indigenous attire. He spoke no English but was delighted to have his photograph taken with me. Just a little man with a handful of goats—these were the very people I most enjoyed meeting on my run around the world.

The township of Pirot was my destination that day. This was a community nestled in a serene valley in the lower reaches of the Transylvanian mountains, with a notable difference— a derelict castle right in the middle of town. This magnificent building had clearly once been a vital regional structure. It looked at least a thousand years old and was now in a state of disrepair and overgrown gardens. Still, it was easy to imagine the castle as it may have once been, lorded over by the likes of the Ottomans or Vlad the Impaler. This was a real relic, with no modifications or renovations to pander to tourists—just an original castle allowed to decay naturally with the passing of time. It was exactly the sort of 'off the beaten track' spectacle I loved to stumble upon.

I reached the border with Bulgaria on 4 May. This was another crossing that demanded a passport and other documentation, such as proof of car ownership or hire. Thankfully, I was allowed to pass through on foot with barely a question asked. I ran for another couple of hours until mid-afternoon, finishing my day well inside the borders of the country. There wasn't much time for meandering because, in Bulgaria, Carmel and I had another important appointment to keep.

Close friends Debbie and Barry were meeting us in the capital, Sofia. We drove the 40-odd kilometres to the city, using the car's navigation system to find the apartment they'd rented. After a happy and animated reunion we celebrated with Champagne in the stylishly converted Communist-era tenement. Barry had taught me at high school back in the late 1970s and it was great to have them both with us for this unusual and exotic part of the journey.

Carmel and I had passed through Sofia in 1986 but unfortunately we couldn't stay overnight on that occasion, due to the thirty-hour transit visa we'd acquired. This time we got to experience the centre of the city, with friends, amid the buzz of a Saturday night.

Sofia is a city that does not see the level of tourism of other European capitals. This, to me, is a bonus. Its architecture is a mix of the ancient and new with centuries-old ornate buildings coexisting with the more practically designed (and less attractive) Communist-era tenements and more recent structures.

Like in other former Eastern-bloc nations, the grey buildings of the past are rapidly becoming multi-coloured.

And the eating culture is quickly catching up with international trends too. Whether this is a good or bad thing, it did provide a level of comfort and familiarity when ordering dinner in the restaurant district that Saturday evening.

But there were still hints of authentic Bulgarian food in what we ate, even if we did have to consciously look for it on the menu—essentially little variations on cuisines of neighbouring countries. Every little bit counts when it comes to cultural experiences and seeking out the real thing was worth the effort.

The three-strong support crew accompanied me by car the next morning to my starting location outside the city. I ran just over 42 kilometres into Sofia, almost exactly a marathon, while the others drove off to enjoy some of the sights of far western regional Bulgaria. I didn't need support that day, having taken note while driving the previous afternoon that there were adequate shops and service stations along the road into the city.

The four of us again savoured a night out in Sofia, this time with an eclectic mix of local and international food styles that proved fascinating as well as tasty. I'd describe it most succinctly as a combination of Bulgarian, Greek, Turkish, Lebanese and Italian—and delicious.

The next week or so was a great running adventure. Beautiful weather, although a touch hot at times, was paired with a unique countryside and culture that few international runners have ever had the pleasure of experiencing. And Barry joined me on the road for part of each day.

Barry had never been a runner. He had played lots of touch football, cricket and tennis in his life but pounding the pavement was not something he was accustomed to. Yet he took to it like an old pro, always keeping pace and never struggling or suffering much from soreness in the mornings after.

The scenery was truly idyllic and rustic. Fields of grain, lazily swaying in the gentle breeze on the flatter plains, were juxtaposed with forests of deep green on the hillsides. And in the background snow-capped mountains towered impressively over the tranquil scene.

Large contingents of gypsies plied the back roads on which I was running, dressed in traditional costume and all in wagons being hauled by horses. This was not a demonstration for tourists. These were real people going about their lives in places that tourists never see.

I thought it was great. I would wave and smile at the occupants of each wagon that passed me and was invariably rewarded with a reciprocal response. At times I had to pinch myself!

One morning I found myself forced to run on the freeway for a few kilometres, including in a tunnel through the mountainside. That made me nervous enough but as I emerged from the tunnel I saw a police station on the nature strip between the two directions of the freeway. Panic almost set in as I imagined myself being arrested, until I realised the police building was abandoned. I then took the first available side road off the freeway.

This route was initially pleasant but it didn't last long. The road deteriorated rapidly and I was soon running rough. To refer to this track as a road is a tenuous call. And it got worse—a lot worse.

After a few kilometres I called Carmel and instructed her not to follow me on the same track. It was a mix of deep potholes and boulders as big as soccer balls. But by then the support vehicle was already on this non-road and couldn't turn around. Eventually, with Barry and Deb's help, Carmel managed to do a multi-point turn, although the undercarriage of the car had taken a bit of a beating by the time they re-emerged on the freeway.

It was definitely the right decision, as the road quality declined even further—to the point where I ultimately found myself on no road at all.

Google Maps was incorrectly specifying my position as being on a road. But it was also showing another more important road a few hundred metres ahead. Was this also a phantom thoroughfare? I would never know without exploring the option. Besides, I had nowhere else to go.

So I simply parted the bushes and saplings and ploughed through the long grass. Finally, and with much relief, I did indeed reach the more major road indicated by Google Maps—though this itself was nothing more than a dirt track. It may sound humorous now but incidents like that are quite distressing at the time.

The ancient city of Plovdiv was a worthwhile addition to the itinerary. Founded more than 6000 years ago as a Neolithic settlement, making it one of the world's oldest cities, Plovdiv was once a fortified Thracian stronghold until captured by Philip of Macedon (father of Alexander the Great). It has changed hands many times since. Well-preserved Roman ruins can be found throughout the city, including a great amphitheatre.

We all had a walk around town before dinner that evening, taking in this most historic of cities. As a history teacher, Barry especially enjoyed wandering through the city, regaling us along the way with stories of Basil the Bulgar Slayer, the Byzantine Emperor from 976 to 1025 AD.

Barry's mileage was also increasing on a daily basis, running with me in the afternoon while Carmel and Deb went sightseeing. I would worry that the girls didn't have enough to occupy themselves in the isolated countryside but each evening they'd assure me that, like myself, it was impossible to be bored with the unusual and eclectic sights regional Bulgaria had to offer.

We loved staying in small villages such as Gorski Izvor. Here we sampled authentic central Bulgarian village food. I interpreted this as a mix of several other styles: German-influenced meat, Turkish dips and Hungarian goulash-like vegetable dishes. It was served by the proprietor who doubled as a waiter and then tripled as a comedian.

After the meal our larger-than-life host treated us to some free Bulgarian pure spirit—call it Bulgarian schnapps if you like—which nearly blew our heads off. He firstly handed me my glass and said, 'Good for running.' After a quick nod to Debbie, he then passed a glass to Barry with the comment, 'And good for sex, too.' I'm not sure how true that is, but I know that many laughs were had that evening. If nothing else, it was definitely good for our outlook on Bulgarian life.

Another unique stay—in a Gaudi-like designed hotel in the town of Harmanli, constructed to resemble a fairy grotto—was followed by a run to the Turkish border. Barry and I jogged along a section of freeway that was under construction just prior to the border. There is no better place to run than a brand new freeway on super-smooth pavement with not a car to be seen.

The border itself took some time to negotiate. We had to show documentation at five different checkpoints. Once through, the scenery changed immediately. Within 100 metres we ran by a large and ornate mosque on our right, with the sound of the faithful being called to prayer emanating from the minarets.

We continued a few miles down the highway to a roadside hotel. The place obviously catered solely to the passing trans-port trade, most of which were truckies. It couldn't be called quaint but we weren't complaining. The food in the cafeteria downstairs was delicious—tasty marinated vegetables and Turkish dips—and we could even buy Efes, the local Turkish beer, in the small adjoining supermarket.

The morning of 12 May I ran through the city of Edirne. This was a real delight. The local Turkish people were busily going about their daily lives—as was I, though it was a rather unusual daily life I was living. Edirne is an ancient city (as are so many in this part of the world) and the mosques were huge and spectacular.

Later that morning, as I ran along an excellent back road that paralleled the freeway a few kilometres to the north, I was passed by four young French cyclists. A little later I caught up to them at a service station. The usual photo opportunity ensued, along with a vigorous session of patting the friendly dogs that were residents of the station.

These cyclists were simply riding. They had no fixed itinerary or timeframe—they just rode wherever their fancy took them. It was a refreshing attitude to travelling and to life in general.

The five of us had a nice chat before I started running again, leaving these young adventurers to their lunch of cheese and crackers. I was to see them again in the days to come.

An hour later I reached a junction in the road that, as an Australian, bore some significance. The road to the right headed south to Gallipoli. I had looked at ways to incorporate Gallipoli, known as Gelibolu in Turkey, into my run. Unfortunately, I just couldn't make it work.

However, Carmel and I had visited Gallipoli with friends Vanessa and Peter in 1986, gaining an invaluable insight into the importance of the locale in the Australian psyche. A pilgrimage to the iconic site is commonplace now. In 1986 it was quite rare. Standing on the beach, looking up at those hills on which so many had died, had been a much more meaningful experience than simply learning about the historic event in a classroom half a world away.

Barry joined me again during the afternoon and we relished some more running on well-surfaced but near-deserted roads. The culture was certainly more exotic than most places I'd run through and Debbie and Barry were loving the experience as much as Carmel and I were.

We had our difficulties with accommodation in some of the smaller establishments but this ultimately added to the feeling of novelty. Passing through towns and cities such as Babaeski, Lüleburgaz and Çorlu provided a unique insight into modern Turkish life. Dinners were especially appealing. New taste sensations were high on the agenda for all of us, as were our conversations with the inhabitants of these regional Turkish cities.

On 15 May, Barry ran the final 15 kilometres with me to Kumburgaz. It did not escape me that, on the same day the year before, we'd celebrated Libby's birthday in the pan-handle region of Nebraska. It would be difficult to find two more different locations, geographically and culturally, on the face of the Earth.

Kumburgaz is effectively a western suburb of Istanbul, situated between the great city and the smaller establishment of Silivri. Our abode that night was one of the most special places we were to stay in during the whole world run.

Built right on the edge of the Sea of Marmara, the hotel and our top-floor rooms overlooked the water, which glistened like a jewel in the late afternoon sun. Nearby, the wailers in the minarets of various mosques were calling the people to their prayers. Standing on the balcony and taking it all in I couldn't help but compare the scene to a movie—the sights, sounds and smells were intoxicating. What else could we do but submit to the atmosphere.

So Barry and I had a few beers while Debbie and Carmel sipped wine and we watched the sun set slowly over the water as we soaked it all up.

The subsequent morning involved my entry into Istanbul itself. With a population of sixteen million in 2013, the city had more than doubled in size since I was last there in 1986. It was also the equal largest city (with Buenos Aires) that I was to traverse during the entire run around the world, eclipsing even New York.

The roads were ultra-busy and required a lot of concentration. As I ran down a long straight thoroughfare, alongside cars stuck in the ever-present Istanbul traffic jam, I heard my name being called. It was the French cyclists passing me again. They were obviously very relaxed about their riding, as they'd taken as long as I had to get from Edirne to Istanbul.

Barry joined me for the last 14 kilometres of this, the final stage of my run across Europe. We loped along much quieter streets, with the sea sparkling on our right. The two of us stopped to eat some cooked fish at a roadside stall before passing between the beachside mansions and the airport, directly under the flight path of the planes coming in to land.

Then the four French cyclists passed us yet again. They were certainly in no hurry, leisurely enjoying their journey with many regular and long roadside stops.

By mid-afternoon on 16 May 2013, I had completed the transit of my third continent—from the most westerly point in Europe to the most easterly. I climbed down a concrete wall and dipped my toes in the waters of the Bosporus Sea, marking the end of the stage.

I had run 5594 kilometres in Europe over 113 days with just one rest day, averaging 50 kilometres per day. And Barry, despite no previous background in running and no training, had run 100 kilometres with me during the previous twelve days.

The momentous day ended at the nearby hotel that the girls had booked, celebrating with the last bottles of the French Champagne and shiraz from the Qantas crew, who we toasted for their generosity.

The four of us did the normal tourist thing the next day: visiting the Blue Mosque, the Grand Bazaar and several other well-known sites in the city. A final night of celebrations was enjoyed before we said our goodbyes; Carmel and I then driving off to the west while Debbie and Barry stayed on in Turkey for more touring.

Unfortunately, our Citroen support vehicle had to be returned to Munich, some 2100 kilometres away. It took us just over two days to complete the drive, much of it identical or very close to the same route I had run. As was always the case, I was amazed at how far it seemed in a car. It definitely didn't feel that far on foot.

After a night in a Bavarian hotel near the airport, we dropped the car back the next morning and checked in for our flight to Malaysia. I had now completed three of the four continents essential to satisfying the requirements of a world run.

And I had now covered a total of 21,008 kilometres—with just over 5000 kilometres to go.

CHAPTER 18

The Malay Peninsula

Asia was not one of the four continents I had chosen to traverse from ocean to ocean. Those four were North America, South America, Europe and Australia. But I wanted to do some running in Asia regardless and the Malay Peninsula seemed as good a place as any in which to fulfil this aim.

We flew into Kuala Lumpur, the Malaysian capital, enjoying the pleasures of a window seat that afforded us views of the lush vegetation and palm plantations on approach. At the airport we purchased new SIM cards and picked up the keys to the hire car we'd booked online, then walked outside. The oppressive humidity hit us immediately like a punch in the face. Running here was going to be interesting—and a struggle.

My sponsor, Asia Pacific Digital, has a strong presence in Malaysia and a special evening was arranged for me to meet the staff and some of the clients of the company. Recently stepping into the role of CEO of Asia Pacific Digital, my good mate and member of the Tour de Bois, Roger Sharp, flew in from his new base in Singapore especially for the occasion. I hadn't seen him on the run since the first few days in New Zealand nearly seventeen months earlier, on that occasion staying with him and Christine at their place in Queenstown.

The event was held in a hotel function room high above the city, lights shimmering in every direction. I gave a speech and overview of the world run so far then eased back and enjoyed the company and camaraderie of the audience. The party kicked on till the wee hours; luckily I hadn't planned on running the next day, which was spent doing some shopping for necessities and generally relaxing and recovering from the intercontinental flight.

By 24 May I was ready to start my short Asia stage, a few hundred kilometres from the outskirts of Kuala Lumpur to the outskirts of Singapore.

The first day of running in Malaysia was the hardest I've ever had on the road. After a long stint in the European winter, I was simply not accustomed to the heat and humidity of an equatorial environment. I began running on the coast, a little to the south-west of the KL city centre. I felt fine early on but as the day wore on, my ability to cope wore out.

Carmel went ahead to find accommodation so I resorted to regularly buying drinks from roadside vendors—drinks that came in plastic bags, tied at the top with a straw protruding.

Food from these same vendors was limited to balls of dough that hid delicious curry-based inner fillings.

And I often shared the road with water buffaloes that refused to budge—it was me who had to move aside or deviate around these huge beasts as they casually chewed on the grass at the side of the thoroughfare.

By the end of the day, however, I was completely shattered. I had not once suffered chafing between my legs so far during the world run but the constant sweat induced by the humidity that day had caused the worst case of chafing I'd ever experienced in my life. Blood plasma, a clear fluid tinged with yellow, oozed from the chafed area, which was swollen and bright red. And my energy levels were absolutely depleted by the humidity as well.

I was an exhausted wreck by the end of my 50 kilometres, which felt much longer than that. I could not envisage how it would be possible to run the next day. I had a shower but when the water touched the chafed skin the stinging was excruciating, as intense as a wasp bite. I was almost crying in the shower, screaming each time a fresh batch of water came in contact with the area.

I tossed and turned during the night, which added to the feeling of exhaustion in the morning. A torrential equatorial downpour delayed my start by half an hour, which added annoyance to the pain and fatigue. I finally got going and to my surprise I gradually felt better the further I ran. Needless to say, Vaseline featured heavily between my thighs.

My route was right along the coast of the Straits of Malacca, starting in the village of Masjid Tanah. Local Malay people live along just about every inch of this coast and they found my presence bewildering. As beautiful a stretch of coastline as it is, there are very few Western tourists visiting the places I was running. And if they did visit, it wasn't on foot.

At one point I got turned back when the road passed through an army base. I ran to the booth at the checkpoint, attempting to explain to the young soldiers on guard that Google Maps indicated this was a public road. I soon realised this was a fruitless exercise and quickly abandoned the strategy when I sensed one of the soldiers become annoyed at my persistence and tilt his assault rifle in my direction. I had to take the long way around, adding about 10 kilometres to my day.

Late that morning, as I was winding my way along a road through the jungle, I heard a loud rustling in the bushes. Suddenly, an enormous komodo dragon burst from the undergrowth, almost colliding with me. I think it was just as afraid of me as I was of it. The lizard was more than 3 metres long from head to tail and its front legs and shoulders were the size of my arms and shoulders. In its mouth was a furry animal—I think it was a baby monkey.

Luckily for me there was a large culvert under the road at just that spot and the gigantic reptile raced into the pipe and was gone. I stopped for a moment to calm down and gather my wits. I doubt I was in any real danger but the surprise alone was the stuff of heart attacks.

As I made my way through the jungle, I watched numerous tribes of monkeys going about their activities in the trees above. I even saw a monkey that had been hit by a car, perhaps the most unusual road kill I'd observed during the whole world run, though probably not uncommon in this part of the world.

As I was running through a typical Malaysian town later that morning, with its cornucopia of roadside stalls thronging with people, I was surprised to hear someone mimicking the distinctive voice and laugh of comedian Rodney Rude. What Rodney Rude fans were there in regional Malaysia?

It turned out to be Roger. He and Christine had hired a car and driven from Kuala Lumpur to meet us. I knew they were hoping to meet us on the road but I had no idea when and where. Roger got changed into his running gear. He was going to do a few kilometres with me.

At that point Carmel arrived and related a unique experience she'd just had. Stopping at what she thought were food markets, she'd walked into a tented marquee area. It was actually a wedding and the reception was in full swing. However, instead of being asked to leave, Carmel was invited to meet the bride and groom and their parents, to have official photos taken with them and to sit down for lunch on the bridal table. She mingled for a while but declined the meal. She was even given a parting gift! Carmel was completely nonplussed that such hospitality could be shown to a total stranger. I guess the wedding party felt she added a unique touch that would be remembered forever by the bride and groom, such was the novelty of her presence—the only Caucasian guest at the wedding.

Roger ran with me through the heat and humidity for about 7 kilometres and then Christine took over while Roger drove their hire car, Carmel leading the way in the support vehicle.

Christine and I did another 5 kilometres into the heart of the city of Melaka (Malacca). The history of European settlement in this city goes back several centuries and there are even archaeological digs unearthing old churches from the 1600s.

Roger had booked himself and Christine into a hotel so we thought we'd register at the same place. But there was only one room left—the penthouse where, we were told, kings and presidents have stayed. On a budget, I politely declined and started walking away.

But the next thing I knew I was being led to this penthouse by the hotel staff—Roger had discretely arranged for us to stay there that night. Carmel and I had bunked in some pretty nice digs since beginning the world run but this huge room was the most extravagant by far, including a view over the entire city and out over the Straits of Malacca. We struggled to thank Roger and Christine enough.

That evening the four of us walked to the old part of town, eating dinner less than a metre from the edge of the river. When I awoke the next morning, however, Roger and Christine were gone. Their only option was an early flight to Singapore and they had to drive to Kuala Lumpur first to catch the plane. No matter, as we would be seeing them again soon in Singapore.

Each day got progressively easier as my body acclimatised to the humidity. The omnipresent roadside drink vendors kept me hydrated and I was enjoying the curry dough balls, particularly the rendang variety. It was all so cheap too, allowing me to survive through the day on the equivalent of a couple of dollars.

The days were spent running along roads that were lined with tall palms and through quaint villages of simple wooden huts with locals relaxing on verandas, punctuated in the evenings by stays in some of the bigger towns like Muar and Batu Pahat. We had a wonderful experience while wandering around the night market at Batu Pahat where we met a local guy of Chinese descent—as the only Westerners there (a somewhat bizarre term, I know, given Australia is actually to the east of Malaysia), we were a curiosity and, besides, he wanted to practise his English.

Talking with these locals prompted me to finally solve a mystery I'd been puzzling over for months. Naturally, nearly everyone I met asked about what I was doing and I'd then describe my run around the world. In the ensuing conversation, though, the listener would subsequently make a comment about my 'walk'. This misunderstanding had me baffled—I'd explained the concept of running around the world simply and clearly enough, I thought—but it finally clicked in southern Malaysia when the confusion again came to the fore while talking with our newly found friend in the Batu Pahat night market.

I had also often used the term 'circumnavigating the Earth on foot' in the many conversations on the topic. It had finally become obvious to me that 'on foot' conjures up the image of walking in most people's minds. For some reason, the majority do not equate running with covering ground 'on foot'.

Yes, walking and running are both forms of covering ground on foot and either one, or a combination of both, is perfectly allowable within the 'rules' for circumnavigating the Earth on foot—which requires nothing more than traversing the Earth using one's own two feet. However, I'm a runner, not a walker, and the difference was crucial to me and so from then on I went to some trouble to always specify that I was running around the world.

On a technical note, before commencing my run I had envisaged I would do about 95 per cent running and 5 per cent walking. As it transpired, my actual run–walk ratio was more in the order of 98 per cent versus 2 per cent respectively, meaning I walked just a few hundred of the more than 26,000 kilometres of the journey.

By the end of the month, on 29 May, I had reached the city of Pontian on the far south-western coast of the Malay Peninsula. That was where I'd decided to finish the Asian leg of my run. I had originally wanted to run across the causeway to Singapore, but recent changes to the laws now precluded anyone crossing the causeway on foot—running or walking. Pontian is on the same latitude as Singapore and not far away, so it was only a minor adjustment to my plans.

Once again, I dipped my toes in the waters of the Straits of Malacca to mark the end of the stage and Carmel and I celebrated that balmy evening with more sumptuous Malaysian food—prawns, whitebait, octopus, calamari, fish and anything else they could pull out of the ocean, and some Tiger beers—seated right by those same Straits of Malacca.

We drove the short distance to Johor the following morning, on the other side of the causeway from Singapore, dropped off the hire car then took a taxi across to Singapore and to Roger and Christine's apartment. I had a pre-arranged interview and photo shoot with *The Straits Times* newspaper in the botanical gardens and that evening we attended another Asia Pacific Digital function, this time with the company's Singaporean staff and clientele. Again I gave a talk about my run and then we enjoyed another stellar evening. It was nice knowing I didn't have to run the next day because the party didn't finish until 3 a.m.

I just lazed around the next morning while Roger went to work and Carmel and Christine hit the shops. I did, however, muster enough energy to take the Sharps' Labrador for a walk up the street and back.

Early that evening Carmel and I caught a cab to the airport for our flight to Sydney. This was the last international flight of the entire world run—there had been 21 flights to that point—so I decided to splash out and use the last of my frequent flyer points to upgrade us to business class. It was a fitting way to end the international stage of my run around the world.

There was now only one more country for me to run across—Australia.

CHAPTER 19

Australia begins

Carmel and I arrived in Sydney on 1 June 2013, which happened to also be the birthday of our daughter Grace. So there was much to celebrate that evening, followed by catching up with family and friends over the next few days, before we were off to Perth to start the final leg of my odyssey. Grace came along to travel with us from Perth to Kalgoorlie.

I was well aware during the planning stage of the run that the biggest timing consideration was the seasons and so I had ensured that my presence in various locations coincided with the less intense climatic conditions—where possible. As such, I had avoided the deserts of California and Arizona in summer as well as winter in the New England region and the Andes. As previously described, though, despite the meticulous planning, I barely succeeded in the Andes. I also failed to avoid parts of northern

Europe during winter and was caught out by the summer in the mid-west of the US, though I couldn't have predicted it was going to be the hottest summer ever recorded in those parts.

The other major seasonal extreme I knew I had to avoid was the Nullarbor Plain during the Australian summer. In the warmer months—December to March—conditions on the Nullarbor can be as bad as the deserts of Arizona. This was why I arrived in Perth at the start of winter.

Although a bit cold by Australian standards, winter on the Nullarbor is infinitely preferable to summer, where daytime temperatures often average 50 degrees Celsius. And there was an added bonus for me: running across Australia in winter would mean that I would finish my run around the world in Sydney in early spring—one of my favourite times of the year in the city and perfectly comfortable for running.

In Perth, we were picked up at the airport by a long-time friend, Robyn, who we'd first met while standing in a queue at the Bulgarian Embassy in Istanbul in 1986 with Vanessa and Peter. And she had been one of the participants in the impromptu fancy dress party we enjoyed in the city of Niš in Serbia, which I'd run through just a month before. We toasted our arrival with some French Champagne at Robyn's place in City Beach. I was about to embark upon my final leg of the world run—the home straight—so I was in a celebratory mood. The Champagne went down very nicely.

Then it was over to the Mossman Park home of more good friends, Shane and Denise, who had kindly invited us to stay the night. This was particularly handy as their place was near my starting point the next morning. Shane and Denise prepared a delicious meal, befitting of a 'last supper'—which is how it felt for me, the night before embarking on the final 5000 kilometres of the run, right across Australia.

Shane and I had collaborated in the early days of the wave energy company, including an unusual field trip together that took us to exotic places such as the southern tip of India and the Azores Islands in the middle of the northern Atlantic Ocean—almost as unusual as some of the places I'd recently run through. Shane had also been a decent middle-distance runner when he was younger and he and I both have similar 800-metre personal bests of around two minutes. These days, Shane farms and exports abalone—one of his products is canned abalone and, thanks to his gift of a few cans, Carmel and I were to enjoy this delicacy in a most unusual location later.

Also at dinner that evening were old friends Kim and Brynn, who lived in Sydney in the mid-1990s, along with two of their children. I had trained and run with Brynn during his first marathon in Sydney in 1994. And the last time we'd set eyes on the two kids, they were both under ten years of age. Now they were approaching their thirties—not really kids anymore.

Earlier that afternoon, Barry's sister Julie, who lives in Perth and had followed the run with particular interest during the time Barry was running with me across Bulgaria and Turkey, had dropped her car around—a red Hyundai Getz. We were to use it as our support vehicle until we were joined a few weeks later by more friends with a caravan for the journey across the Nullarbor. Without all these friends and their contributions, we would have really struggled with the cost and logistics of support vehicles throughout Australia, and indeed the world.

Everyone from dinner met again the next morning, 10 June, at Cottesloe Beach for breakfast. I once again dipped my toes in the Indian Ocean then those assembled formed a gauntlet on the sand for me to depart through.

And then I was off. The two youngsters, both keen runners, accompanied me through the riverside Perth suburbs and into the city. The weather was spectacular and the city sparkled in the sunlight with the river glittering in the foreground. And Barry's sister met us alongside the river for a brief hello, too. A local Perth Channel 9 crew arranged to meet me on the riverbank in the city and did some filming, with the segment appearing the following day on the evening news.

I finished my first day of running in Australia, a gentle 40 kilometres, in the Swan Valley at the home of some more old friends, situated in the farming belt on the eastern edge of the city. It had been more than a decade since we'd seen them and it was tremendous to catch up over another superb dinner. If nothing else, running around the world facilitates many happy reunions.

The following day involved a long climb into the hills east of Perth. It was good to be back in Australia for the surety of food styles. One thing you can be certain of at any Australian bakery, takeaway or service station is a good old meat pie. And I certainly had a craving for this Australian culinary icon.

Pies may not be to everyone's liking but they were high on my list after a year and a half in which there was not a meat pie to be seen. The first few days out of Perth saw me sampling pies in just about every bakery I ran by, much to Carmel and Grace's surprise. They were sticking to healthier fare.

Two days later we were joined in the evening at a pub in the town of Northam by Shane and another old mate Kim. They'd driven from Perth to spend the night with us. I'm glad my metabolism was running on overload, processing the six pints of beer like it was water. For reasons probably related to enhanced metabolism, most runners seem to have a propensity for drinking beer like it's soft drink. Not all are so proficient, however, on the red wine.

Sitting in a pub with family and friends over a few ales made the run feel so much more like home. Whether it's the Tour de Bois or a run around the world, there are few things more enjoyable than an evening in a country pub with your mates. As remote as the roads may have been, I certainly wasn't lonely.

Each day Grace would run for about 5 or 6 kilometres, which was pretty good for someone who hasn't done a lot of running. Her preference was to finish the day with me, with the sun low on the horizon at our backs.

At times police convoys would force the traffic to sit on the side of the road while gigantic mining vehicles passed by, taking up both lanes and then some. As a runner, though, I wasn't compelled to stop. I simply moved further on to the always ample shoulder and even in among the trees if the load was wide enough.

The winter mornings in rural Western Australia were very cool and I often had to help Carmel scrape thick frost from the windscreen before she could drive. On one occasion poor Grace spent the entire night with woefully inadequate bed covers, hardly sleeping due to her shivering. I was always heavily rugged up for the first hour of each morning's run but once the sun was well into the sky I would strip down to just a T-shirt.

My general preference was to run on the road, which was often devoid of traffic for long periods at a time. And when it wasn't, I would run on the redder-than-red dirt by the side of the road. This was the Great Eastern Highway, the main road from Perth to Kalgoorlie and the final (the most western) segment of the 4200-kilometre route across Australia from Sydney to Perth. At 600 kilometres, it was a long and relatively remote section of road but exciting to run on nonetheless.

Sometimes there was a parallel dirt road that provided access to the equally long 600-kilometre Coolgardie water pipeline, a hundred-year-old engineering marvel in itself. This side road varied from just a few metres from the highway up to several hundred metres away. I would usually run on these deserted dirt tracks when I could.

The long remote stretches were broken up by visits to places like Meckering, 130 kilometres east of Perth, interesting primarily because it was almost totally destroyed by an earthquake in 1968. I ate lunch in Meckering while reading the signs on the former main street indicating the buildings that once stood on each plot of now vacant land.

As the next week wore on, I passed through typical Western Australian rural towns with their wide, dusty red street shoulders, such as Cunderdin, Kellerberrin, Merredin and Southern Cross. There was little on the road to occupy my mind during the daylight hours. Other than running through a town or two, each day was spent in relative isolation amongst the low scrubby vegetation and tall but often sparsely populated eucalypt trees.

Nights were almost always spent talking with locals over a beer or wine.

A very social evening at the Carrabin roadhouse is a case in point, made even more special by the most delightfully friendly resident cat, creatively named Puss Puss. This social feline would race out to meet every car that stopped for petrol and came in to the motel rooms to visit everyone who stayed. Puss Puss was well fed and not looking for a meal. He was just hyper-interested in anyone and everyone—I declared him the world's friendliest cat.

As I moved east, the towns started to become more and more sparse, supplanted by the legendary roadhouse. Each of these remote establishments catered for petrol, takeaway food and general supplies, and had a motel and the necessary restaurant in which to feed travelling guests.

Yellowdine was the perfect example. With a normal population of four, this megalopolis swelled to six on a Wednesday during the shift changeover. Considering how small and remote these places were, the food was surprisingly good, though I suspect a hatted restaurant was a long way off yet.

The stretch from Southern Cross to Coolgardie is a 180-kilometre expanse of nothingness; just long straight sections of road lined with eucalypts—no towns, no farms, nothing. A distance of 180 kilometres was awkward, as my normal daily effort of around 50 kilometres didn't divide into it nicely. However, three days of 60 kilometres was perfect and so that's how I tackled this stretch.

The downside of the lack of towns was that Carmel and Grace had to drive back and forth a few times from our accommodation but it was better than sleeping in the car. The girls had started to leave food and drink drops for me whenever they needed to head further down the road. This worked very well, allowing me to get through these long days without the regular accompaniment of the car.

On 20 June I ran through the village of Bullabulling, with its population of two. I failed to see a soul. Later that day Grace joined me as I finally ran into Coolgardie just as the setting sun was casting a spectacular glow over this former epicentre of goldmining.

Sadly, most of Coolgardie's century-old two-storey buildings have been torn down, leaving just a few grand old structures to remind modern residents and visitors of its past glory. Still, we enjoyed our two-night stay at the Goldrush Motel, courtesy of the proprietors who gave us a generous two-for-one deal on the accommodation. They also were the carers of several social cats, including Bruce, Kitty and Kitty's cleverly named identical twin Not Kitty, plus four of the most playful kittens one could hope to meet.

I ran a relatively short 38 kilometres into Kalgoorlie the following morning. Founded a few years after Coolgardie, Kalgoorlie is now the much larger town and has become the centre of the goldmining industry in Australia. The town's evolution owes a lot to Herbert Hoover, a US mining engineer who played a part in bringing modern (for those days) mining techniques to the region. Hoover went on to eventually become President of the United States in the turbulent years from 1929 to 1933. Various monuments and plaques in the city bear testament to Hoover's one-time presence.

On the morning of 22 June, the shortest day of the year in the Southern Hemisphere, we dropped Grace at the airport for her flight back to Sydney. It was an emotional parting as we knew we wouldn't see her again until I finished at the Opera House in September. As I ran south of the city that morning I could see Grace's plane fly up into the cloudless blue sky. I stopped and watched as it gradually became a dot, finally disappearing from sight.

Nights spent in Kambalda and Widgiemooltha, where we stayed in the smallest room of the entire world run (just 2.5 metres square and known as a 'dongle'), were soon followed by the passing of the 22,000-kilometre mark. A day later I reached Norseman and the start of the road across the Nullarbor.

There we met a contingent of television workers filming a documentary on caravanning across the Nullarbor. The host was Frankie J. Holden, one-time front-man of 1970's rock band Ol' 55 and now television presenter. We talked and laughed over a few wines, swapping stories from the road. The fact our lives were so different yet similar provided the spark for an interesting evening of conversation.

By this stage I was beginning to wonder about the date I would finish in Sydney. Many people would be relying on knowledge of a precise date in order to plan for the event. I did some mental calculations on the road, with the help of the calculator on my iPhone. I knew the intended distance was 26,232 kilometres, which amounted to the equivalent of 622 marathons.

It didn't take long to realise I would be reaching Sydney after a world run of close to that same number of days. In fact,

I worked out that if I made it home by 13 September, this would be exactly 622 days since I began the world run at the Opera House. I had been averaging nearly 50 kilometres per day since the start but I would need to increase this to about 53 kilometres per day for the remaining 4000 kilometres if I was to finish by 13 September. So I started running further each day.

As I ran out of Norseman I passed a major road sign highlighting the distances to towns and cities down the road. The next real town with a grocery store was Ceduna, more than 1200 kilometres away. There was nothing in between but roadhouses, each with a population of around eight people, and these were sometimes 200 kilometres apart. The next city was Adelaide, which was more than 2000 kilometres via the route I was taking.

The distances seemed daunting. And I was now about to enter a legendary no-man's-land; a stretch of terra firma as vast and empty as the steppes of Siberia—the fabled Nullarbor Plain.

Early one morning on the western end of the Nullarbor, I stopped by the side of the road to answer the call of nature. I suddenly jumped backwards as fast as I could. Via my peripheral vision I thought I'd seen a snake in the grass. As it turned out, the object was simply a curved stick but my instinctive survival mechanism had kicked in with an unconscious 'just in case' reaction.

Running around the world affords a lot of time to reflect on all manner of topics, delving into each in far more detail than is possible during one's normal busy existence. The experience with the snake/stick was something I pondered quite deeply as I whiled away the time on the roads of remote Western Australia in the days thereafter, coming to a greater realisation of how, as people, we think and arrive at our conclusions.

We humans are very adept at imagining we see things that aren't really there, as this 'ability' has served us well during our evolution. It's better for a person's chances of survival to imagine a false threat than to ignore a true one.

My brain had received information based on a partial image—an image that loosely resembled a snake—and had conjured a life-and-death situation out of it. Despite having incorrectly processed the limited information available to me, my instinctive thought processes had nevertheless ordered my body to react instantaneously by 'getting the hell out of there'.

This was a classic 'better safe than sorry' reaction; an impulse that has evolved in humans and other animals as a way to survive in a world in which one false move can lead to demise. Early humanoids that erred in this way 99 times out of a 100, and reacted appropriately the one time it really was a snake, lived to have heirs, while those who erred the other way, failing to recognise the potential danger in time, ended up dying of snake bite and possibly leaving no heirs.

While this survival trait has proved to be a positive evolutionary factor, it is not without its negatives. Seeing patterns and shapes that aren't really there, such as the coils of a snake, has little downside if we get it wrong, but a large beneficial upside if we get it right.

The problem is that humans also have the ability to conjure in their minds a myriad of patterns that don't really exist and then build belief systems around that imagined concept.

Running around the world had given me ample time to think about many topics and one of those pertained to why people believe what they do. Humans believe in all sorts of things that have no basis in evidence or fact. Conspiracy theorists are an example of this trait gone haywire.

So many things people blindly accept as true are simply wrong, based on nothing more than a flawed imagination. As the old saying goes, 'Everyone has the right to an opinion, but that doesn't mean every opinion is right.'

But most false beliefs are harmless—getting it wrong is usually not a big issue. In the majority of cases, such as with my reaction to the perceived snake, believing something that isn't true won't get you into trouble. But sometimes it will.

The snake example is a simple case—to determine whether it was real or imagined, I only had to look again from a safe distance. But not every imagined 'reality' is so easily discerned or corrected. Luckily, a method has been devised to sort through the evidence and sift out the real from the imagined in these more complex cases.

It's called science. Science is not physics or chemistry or biology. These are nothing more than subjects of research that make particularly good use of the scientific method. Science itself is a philosophy whereby one does not accept an ideology per se without facts and evidence to back it up.

Believing something to be true is not good enough. One must gather verifiable evidence and data, check that their belief is consistent with those facts and be willing to change that belief if the evidence is contrary. Although it's not practical to follow this methodology in all aspects of our lives, evidence-based decision-making can still be loosely adhered to by individuals—and should be mandatory when it comes to public policy-making.

Unfortunately, too many of society's leaders—political, religious and others—have no interest in making decisions based on facts. They prefer to stick with an ideological belief they've held for years, sometimes since childhood. The world would be a much more peaceful place if everyone was more questioning of the beliefs they hold, insisting on hard facts and evidence before making any decision that affects themselves and others in a material way.

People often ask me what I used to think about as I ran along remote highways like those of the Nullarbor. The above is a good example. Running around the world allowed me to explore many such issues in my mind.

Carmel continued to organise food and drink drops ahead of me along the vast and lonely highway, before continuing on to arrange accommodation for the night and then returning to shuttle me back and forward if required. I would work out which kilometre markers I preferred and Carmel would hide the goodies in the bush at the side of the road. Both the food and the drinks were in sturdy plastic bags, allowing me to easily carry the rubbish with me until I reached a roadside bin in one of the regular rest bays provided for weary drivers and truckies.

One day, however, I ran up to the pre-arranged location, looking forward to lunch, a drink and the chocolate treat with which I liked to end the meal—but the food and drink wasn't there. In their place were the plastic bags with numerous holes ripped and chewed into them. At first I thought kangaroos were to blame but on closer inspection and analysis it became obvious the perpetrators were crows. Big black birds were eating my supplies.

Carmel would henceforth need to be more creative when she dropped the food. And creative she was, from then on building elaborate stone cairns, hollowed out to make space for the food and drink. Not only was she a pretty face, she also would have made a great stone-age engineer.

After Norseman the road became even lonelier, with a noticeable reduction in traffic. It now consisted of just those driving across Australia from Perth to the eastern states or vice versa. Vehicles were sporadic, passing me about once every minute on average; occasionally it was even as long as five or ten minutes between vehicles.

And most would toot their horns and wave because they knew something unusual was afoot, literally. No one runs on the Eyre Highway in the middle of nowhere without a reason and a cause. Many would have guessed correctly that I was running across Australia. Most, however, would not have guessed I'd already run around the rest of the world by that stage.

Two nights staying at the wonderful setting of Fraser Range Station, where we met a couple of girls cycling across Australia, eventually led to me passing the Balladonia Roadhouse on 29 June. I stopped 40 kilometres down the road, with Carmel shuttling me back to the camping ground. I was looking forward to this day—our great friends Michael, Annie, Jeff and Guenolee were arriving with a caravan owned by Jeff and Guen.

This was the changeover point. From here, Annie and Guen would drive the borrowed car back to Perth while Carmel, Jeff and Michael would accompany me across the Nullarbor with Jeff's car towing his caravan. This was a different support vehicle and accommodation arrangement to anything we'd had so far on the run around the world, and Carmel and I had been looking forward to it.

It was hugs and kisses all around when we all gathered back in the Balladonia camping ground, the six of us celebrating with a 'home-cooked' meal in the van and an equally delightful, and compulsory, few bottles of nice red wine. Our four friends had been travelling in the north-west of the state for several weeks and, as we basked around the fire under the crystal clear night sky, we revelled in hearing of their adventures.

I said my goodbyes and thankyous to Annie and Guen over breakfast as they prepared for their 1200-kilometre drive to Perth. Michael then dropped me back to my starting position at the beginning of the second longest straight stretch of road in the world.

How was my head going to handle 146 kilometres of running without a single bend or kink in the road? Nor any sign of civilisation! There was no turning back now. This was adventure running at its best.

CHAPTER 20

The Nullarbor

A peculiarity of the Eyre Highway—the only paved road across the southern half of Australia—is that it doubles in several places as an aeroplane landing strip. The first of these is just to the east of the Balladonia Roadhouse and I was thrilled to find myself running on a runway, no pun intended, complete with all the usual markings on the tarmac of any airport.

This hybrid road–runway was wide and about a kilometre long; just enough for light planes to land for emergency purposes, usually as part of the Royal Flying Doctor Service. Although I passed many of these landing strips across the Nullarbor, I never once saw a plane land or take off. It's clearly a fairly rare occurrence.

The longest straight stretch of road in Australia—and the second longest in the world—was actually a joy to cover on foot. I thought I'd get bored but the subtle undulations meant it was rare for the panoramic view in front of me to extend more than about 10 kilometres at a time. The top of the gentle rise in the distance provided me with a focus for the next hour or more. Though I would eventually reach the crest to find that a similar vista lay straight out in front of me.

I was passed at one stage by a former Dutchman who was cycling around Australia. He stopped to talk to me, with Jeff joining us soon after on the bike he'd brought along (Carmel and Michael were ahead in the car). We spoke for half an hour, me on foot while the other two slowly pedalled alongside.

My support crew and I spent two nights along this straight expanse, camping in the bush at the side of the road. In the evenings the four of us sat nestled around the campfire with a red wine in hand while gazing at the unrivalled view of the Milky Way. There can be few places on Earth that afford such clear views of the heavens as the Nullarbor.

Eventually reaching the end of the mind-boggling 146-kilometre straight stretch at Caiguna, we each had our first showers in three days. It's not easy going without a shower after a full day of running. The best I could do on those shower-less occasions was to sponge myself down but it wasn't quite the same as the feeling of freshness one derives from a real shower. I was very pleased it was winter. Summer would have been a much smellier affair.

I was running down the road on my own the next day when I spied a convoy of pink vehicles ahead, slowly making their way in my direction. As I neared this most unusual sight for the Nullarbor, the cars and vans came to a stop and I noticed a video camera was aimed my way. Then from behind one of the vehicles emerged a cyclist.

It was AFL star Shane Crawford, who was riding from Melbourne to Perth in aid of breast cancer, hence the pink. He had been taking shelter from the fierce headwind, the same wind that had been making my day much easier than usual. His crew had been informed I was not far up the road and they were ready to go with the cameras. The contingent was large—twelve people and four vehicles—and they all milled around while Shane conducted an impromptu interview with me on the road.

We spoke for about ten minutes before I was on my way again. The fact that I was on my own, running more than 26,000 kilometres around the world, while Shane was cycling 3600 kilometres with a full contingent of professionals in tow, was not lost on the unassuming celebrity. He was almost apologetic as he mentioned this point. The interview appeared nationally the next evening on the *AFL Footy Show*.

That same afternoon I ambled in to the Cocklebiddy Roadhouse, later partaking of a fantastic meal in the restaurant. My lamb shanks with mash and roasted vegetables were as delicious as I'd ever tasted and the others enjoyed their dishes equally. It was amazing that a roadhouse more than 1000 kilometres from the nearest city, and with a population of just eight, could turn out such high-quality food. Not all the roadhouses provided the same standard but they were generally more than adequate and we were rarely disappointed.

Despite the lack of variety in the landscape, I was revelling in each day on the road. The weather was perfect—cool temperatures and clear blue skies—and the evenings we spent around a campfire were among the best of the whole world run.

Most runners will admit they enjoy the sport because it affords them a brief moment of peace in an otherwise hectic day. For me, this was nirvana—I was running in one of the most peaceful of all places on Earth and I got to do it all day, every day.

When a town was too far for me to reach that day, the routine was simple. One of the guys would ride some of the day with me, while Carmel and the other would drive ahead to find a good camping spot near to where I wanted to finish the day. They'd then unhook the caravan and drive back to give us directions to the campsite, which was always off the road and out of sight. Whoever was cycling would then ride ahead while I'd make my way to camp at a much slower pace, picking up the judiciously placed food and drink drops along the way. It was a highly efficient operation on the part of everyone involved. And Jeff would often finish the day running alongside me.

By this time I was putting in long days. One occasion was just short of 68 kilometres, almost setting a new record for my longest day of the whole run. Because I was now so fit and the weather conditions ideal, I could have run much further each day had it been necessary. In fact, I was feeling so comfortable with days of 60 kilometres or more I reckon occasional days in excess of 100 kilometres would have been entirely possible.

However, running so far in a single day would have meant starting and finishing in the dark. It was always my philosophy that running around the world was about more than just the running. Starting at a civilised time of the morning and finishing before dark was an important component of this philosophy.

My daily routine had changed little in the year and a half I'd been on the road. I would wake at a similar time each morning, usually around 7.30 a.m., drink my chocolate Nesquik ahead of breakfast and then don my running gear. I would hit the road by 8.30 a.m. on most occasions, always running at a similar pace and for similar distances—most days between 50 and 60 kilometres.

I would usually run for 10 kilometres between drink and food breaks, with lunch somewhere around 30 or 40 kilometres into the day. Most days would finish between 4 and 5 p.m., upon which I would attend to my documentation and blog posting. After a shower (or sponge bath when camping out on the Nullarbor), I'd then enjoy a few glasses of wine with dinner. I was usually in bed around 10 p.m.

There were variations, of course, but the routine was remarkably consistent. I'm not normally such a creature of habit in my daily life but the task at hand demanded regularity. However, I was never inflexible if a worthy variation to the routine presented itself.

It wasn't such a hard life to bear. And, besides, I could see the end in sight.

At the outset of the world run, my two big concerns were injuries and sickness. I've never been one to be injured too often, though I knew I wasn't immune. Likewise, I have rarely been sick, but it can happen. Both issues took on an even more uncertain hue, given the unknowns of how my body would react to running so far every day for such an extended period. Injury was something I could have some control over. Sickness was more of a lottery, especially considering the unusual places I would be running.

As it transpired, there would appear to be some evidence that running around the world actually enhances one's immune system. By the time I was on the Nullarbor, I virtually felt impervious to illness. Was I just lucky not to have had any health issues on the road? Or was I born lucky, with a strong ability to fend off infection? Maybe there's a little bit of truth in both but I believe there's a lot more to it than that.

I have long been one not to shy away from contact with the real world. Society has, to a large degree, been conned into believing there's a big bad world of germs out there and that we must use all manner of cleaning and disinfectant products, coupled with an avoidance bordering on paranoia, to guard us from these microscopic perils.

I've never subscribed to this theory. Yes, I'm meticulous about washing my hands after using the toilet and I don't eat rotten food or indulge in any similar extreme practices. But I've always been one to drink water from the taps in every country I've visited, including places like Mexico, China, Namibia, Brazil and even India.

Sometimes I might end up with a mild stomach irritation and some low-level diarrhoea but this is just my body's way of getting on top of a foreign invader, gradually building an immune system capable of dealing with most common bacterial and viral infections. It's sort of like a natural immunisation program. I would never be silly enough to wilfully expose myself to deadly diseases such as ebola or cholera, or to drink the water from the Ganges. But I do believe that the less dangerous and more everyday type contaminations are better to be faced on a regular basis.

As I ambled along the highway on the Nullarbor, nearing the end of the odyssey, I found myself briefly contemplating this long-term health policy on my part. I do believe it was another important contributing factor to what got me all the way around the world devoid of any adverse wellbeing issues.

Across the Nullarbor, I was being intermittently passed by trans-Australian cyclists, each riding slowly alongside me for a while as we conversed. The only person I passed on foot was a sixteen-year-old boy from Adelaide, walking around Australia in the opposite direction as he raised funds for childhood cancer. When two people pass each other on the Nullarbor on bikes and/or foot, they never forego an opportunity to have a yarn. And probably half of all the cyclists who passed me were international travellers, fulfilling the once-in-a-lifetime desire of attempting one of the world's most unique and remote road trips.

A Friday night in the Madura Roadhouse was a treat, with the restaurant bar featuring both the NRL and AFL match of the evening. I'd had virtually no exposure to either sport for two seasons. At night these roadhouses attract travellers like moths to a flame. The bar and restaurant at Madura were packed with drinkers, diners and football fans. I was introduced to many people that evening, most of whom I'm sure I'll never see again—but that's the nature of travelling the world. It's a constant procession of hellos and goodbyes. In fact, the reality couldn't be expressed any more succinctly than through the sentiments expressed in a Rodriguez song—hello only ends in goodbye.

Madura, 530 kilometres to the east of Norseman on the Eyre Highway, sits on the ridge between two major plateaus, one almost 100 metres below the other. I even had to descend a small pass into Madura. Once on the lower level, it immediately became obvious that this region had once been part of the sea floor. A little research confirmed this fact.

Billions upon billions of fossilised shells and other sea creatures lay all over the ground, including right alongside the road itself. I stopped regularly to inspect these artefacts from the distant past—remnants from the Pliocene Epoch, a time well before recent Ice Ages. It amazed me to think that each of these myriad fossils was at least a couple of million years old.

Another night camping out led to us meeting a couple of musicians on a tour around Australia. Pete and Elle were in their seventies and happened to have set up camp near to ours. The six of us got on tremendously well and we were to see Pete and Elle many times again as we crossed the continent. They even gifted us a copy of an album they had recorded which became a regular on the car's CD player.

The following day, 7 July, was another special occasion. Our long-time friends Jane and Peter were to meet us on the road. They had driven from Sydney and had picked up supplies for us along the way.

Running on my own, I observed an approaching car and caravan slowing ahead. The driver shouted an obscenity at me. It took me a second or so to realise it was Peter displaying his warped sense of humour. It was a warm reunion, though I did decline his offer of an immediate beer on the road.

Peter and Jane had never met Jeff and Michael but they all immediately hit it off and suddenly I had an entourage of five people, two cars and two caravans. That night we all stayed in the camping ground at Mundrabilla, where Frankie J. Holden had told us he'd given an impromptu performance on his way through a couple of weeks earlier.

The next day I ascended another pass back to the upper plateau again. This time I was at the Eucla Roadhouse, just short of the Western Australian border with South Australia. All day I could see an amazing set of sand dunes ahead of me, looking like a mirage. They were the Eucla Dunes, a relatively recent addition to the landscape.

A rabbit plague in the 1890s denuded much of the area, resulting in sandy hills being exposed. Quasi-living things that they are, these dunes grew and migrated, gradually engulfing the town. The present version of Eucla is several kilometres to the north from the historic earlier settlement. The support crew ventured out to inspect the giant dunes while I ran and talked to a herd of kangaroos eating peacefully by the side of the road.

Peter is a chef and he amazed us with his culinary skills that night. And this was just one of many times he repeated the feat. Whether it was pasta, pizza, crepes, curry, casserole, steak and vegetables or scrambled eggs, Peter would cook up a storm on minimal kitchen equipment, aided by Jane. It was like having our own little restaurant on the Nullarbor and Jeff and Michael were particularly impressed.

— 🏃 —

I crossed the state border the next morning, 9 July, and finally reached the famed cliffs of the Great Australian Bight. My transit of Western Australia had taken me a month and involved nearly 1600 kilometres of running.

During the afternoon a heavily packed-up car slowed and pulled alongside of me. Four young guys gave me a friendly hello and it turned out that one of them was the younger son of Kim and Brynn; his elder siblings had run with me from Cottesloe Beach to Perth. Having embarked on a surfing safari to the eastern states, the boys had expected to catch up with me somewhere on the road. They could hardly have missed me. Such meetings on the Nullarbor were surreal, usually with no other sign of human activity in evidence. We spoke for a while, with the car casually rolling along at my pace in the middle of the road, then they headed off to continue their own adventure, the vehicle slowly disappearing into the distance, the way they always do on the Nullarbor.

The highway runs within 100 metres of the high cliffs that front the Southern Ocean on this part of the Nullarbor and the six of us camped that night less than the length of a cricket pitch away from the precarious vertical drop of 100 metres. The winds were gale force and the caravans rocked and swayed, resulting in a nervous sleep for all. It was too easy to imagine a gust picking up the vans and depositing them over the nearby edge of the precipice, to be smashed on the rocks below. No wonder Jane, who is a little scared of heights, suffered a sleepless night.

I began running early the next morning, having a specific plan in mind—I was going to set a new daily record of 70 kilometres. The crew passed me at the 25-kilometre mark, going ahead to heat a frozen meat pie in the van oven for my late-morning snack. The two cars stayed on while I continued down the road.

Just short of the 35-kilometre mark, as I was running along a particularly straight stretch of road up the slightest incline, I spied a weird sight ahead. Motionless in the middle of the road was a man, with a dog walking around in front of him, his car parked on the side of the road. As I got closer I realised that the gait of the animal was not that of a dog. In fact, it was a large goat.

When I was within earshot I called out, 'Now, that's something you don't see every day on the Nullarbor.'

The man replied, 'Neither are you.'

There had been no traffic for at least five minutes and none came along for another ten while we talked in the centre of the highway. Jimbo was a travelling comedian and his goat was called Gary. Jimbo marketed himself as Australia's crudest comedian and was on his way to a gig at Karratha, in the iron ore region of Western Australia. He took some creative photographs of Gary and me in the middle of the long straight Nullarbor Highway. Gary was initially patient but as he tired of posing for the camera he would alleviate his boredom by butting me in the legs. This was a truly surreal interlude in the middle of nowhere.

I mentioned to Jimbo that my support crew was just up the road, so he and Gary stopped and chatted with the team on their way by, leaving one of his DVDs for us to later sample. It turned out he wasn't joking about the crudeness of his material. I thought it was hilarious, though it wouldn't be to everyone's taste.

It was just on dark when I finished my 70-kilometre day. I was picked up by Jeff and shuttled a few kilometres down the road to our camping spot. Another brilliant meal prepared by Peter really hit the spot and we all sat around the campfire that night toasting my new record with glasses of red from bottles of donated wine.

Kemenys, the well-known wine retailer in Bondi, had kindly couriered us a case of wine on the road. The owner felt I needed to keep my strength and spirits up with a few glasses each night.

And the especially clear sky that night provided an even more spectacular view of the Milky Way than usual.

When Europeans first encountered this vast plain, they were bedazzled by the lack of trees, hence naming it *Null Arbor*—Latin for 'no trees'. The setting is simply beguiling. To run here is to run on another planet.

I would often go for as long as fifteen minutes without a vehicle passing me, during which time I could have been the only person on Earth. I'd stop and merely listen, the only sound being the gentle throb of blood pulsing in my eardrums. The tranquillity was dreamlike—and definitely a high point of running around the world.

Although the broader Nullarbor is loosely considered to stretch from around Norseman to Ceduna, a distance of 1200 kilometres, the true treeless-plain component is nowhere near as extensive. The treeless section through which the road passes was only a half day of running for me, although it's much wider further inland.

That flat and treeless half day, however, was a unique experience, made even more special because I saw dingoes on three separate occasions. Each creature was very shy, sprinting away at top pace as soon as it noticed me. It was also the day, 12 July, I passed the 23,000-kilometre mark of the journey.

Every few days as we crossed the Nullarbor we would encounter Elle and Pete and catch up on their latest adventures. They liked to stop for three or four days in one location, then would pass me on the road before stopping again. Each time they came by they'd pull over and offer me a drink and some food.

And sometimes when Carmel came by, she would drive slowly alongside me during lulls in the traffic with Cat Stevens' 'Miles from Nowhere' blaring on the car's sound system. Listening to that song in an otherwise silent and desolate environment invoked a special sense of relevancy.

On average we'd camp two of every three nights, savouring a shower and restaurant meal on the third. On 13 July we camped just past the Aboriginal settlement of Yalata. For some time I'd been anticipating this day too—for when I arrived in camp, with Jeff running the last section with me, we were met by Chook and Silvia.

I hadn't seen Chook since Boston, nine months earlier, and the last time I'd encountered Silvia on the world run was when I passed through Hamilton in New Zealand a year and a half earlier. They had flown from New Zealand to Adelaide, hired a campervan, and drove nearly 1000 kilometres to meet us.

We celebrated yet again—celebrations were a regular theme on this run and were becoming more common—this time as an expanded group with fine food and drinks around the campfire. And the next morning we sang 'Happy Birthday' to Michael, showering him with the best available gifts that could be bought on the Nullarbor. Needless to say, Nullarbor roadhouses are not renowned for their wide-ranging gift-shop sections.

Chook and Silvia are both runners and they spent the next few days taking turns, one running with me while the other drove their van. Jeff would often join in too, if he wasn't cycling or driving.

I took a detour off the highway to the seaside fishing mecca of Fowlers Bay. This allowed us all to stop for two nights in the same idyllic location. On their 'day off', Michael and Jeff went fishing on a charter boat, catching some of the biggest snapper I've ever seen. We feasted on the fish that night around a communal campfire and I was thrilled to have snapper burgers at lunchtime for several days after that.

After 1200 kilometres without seeing a grocery store, I ran into Ceduna on 17 July, accompanied by Jeff, Chook and Silvia over the final 11 kilometres. The whole support contingent had driven ahead to set up for the night in Ceduna and Michael had then dropped the three runners back to finish the day with me.

It was a little weird seeing a proper town for the first time in nearly a month. And Peter and Jane, who had departed temporarily to visit some other sights for a few days, had returned for this very special and auspicious occasion—it was Carmel's birthday. I quickly showered and got myself ready for the much-anticipated evening.

There were eight of us in the pub that night, savouring the delights of the most expansive menu we'd seen in a while (with limited supplies on the Nullarbor, even Peter's talents couldn't hope to compete with the variety of food on offer in a real town). This was nicely complemented by an equally extensive wine list. It was the biggest celebration we'd had for some time.

Carmel had now experienced birthdays in Chicago and Ceduna in consecutive years. She's probably the only person on Earth who can say that—just as I'm probably the only person on Earth who has celebrated consecutive birthdays in Santa Barbara and Pau.

Chook and I ran the first 11 kilometres together the next day. He didn't want to do too much, for the following morning he was going to have a crack at Dave's record for the longest distance run with me in a single day. All eight of us camped out that night, retiring early to allow Chook the maximum rest. The next morning Jeff shuttled us to the starting point under cool but sunny skies. Chook wasn't sure how far he'd run, but he was adamant about reclaiming his record from Dave and he needed to chalk up 40 kilometres to do so.

By the 20-kilometre mark Chook was starting to tire but a second wind kicked in around 25 kilometres. His resolve was unwavering and this was especially evident when Silvia joined us a little later. The inevitable fatigue set in past 30 kilometres but by mid-afternoon Chook passed the 40-kilometre mark and gave an ecstatic whoop, knowing he was the record-holder once again.

I asked him how much further he intended to run. 'I'm going to do the whole day with you,' was his steely response.

And run the whole day he did, with Silvia there too, encouraging him during those final kilometres. The last 11 kilometres was into a howling headwind but Chook fought through, reaching the end of our running day in the town of Streaky Bay late in the afternoon. He was completely shattered but he couldn't have been happier. Having never run further than the 37 kilometres he covered with me in Boston, Chook now possessed a personal best single-day running distance of 55.57 kilometres.

For my 21st birthday I received a pewter beer mug. Several of my school friends also received similar mugs for their 21st birthdays that year. Annually since, four of us have endeavoured to get together for a day to drink beer from our pewter mugs.

Now, more than thirty years on, we tend to simply meet each year for a pub crawl in an agreed location. In 2012 I was running across North America and South America and the 'Pewter Mug Day', as it's come to be known, did not eventuate. We didn't want to miss another year so plans were hatched for the guys to meet me somewhere on the world run.

Unfortunately, not everyone could be there but Bill and Tony agreed on a date that would see me somewhere in the vicinity of the Nullarbor. As it turned out, my increased daily distance since Perth meant that I had passed Ceduna by the planned date, so Bill and Tony flew to Port Lincoln, hired a car and drove up to Streaky Bay to intersect with me there.

The guys had the pleasure of witnessing the closing stages of Chook's epic 55.57-kilometre run and we all celebrated the achievement that evening over dinner in the pub. There were now nine in the support crew—the greatest number so far. Chook was a weary warrior that night but ecstatic all the same.

The next day I ran a short 30 kilometres out of Streaky Bay. Chook and Silvia departed that morning, passing me one last time on the road where we said our goodbyes—at least for this visit. Bill and Tony drove out around lunchtime to pick me up and transport me back to town. A quick shower and it was on—the 2013 Pewter Mug Day.

The three of us, plus Jeff, started in the van with a few six-packs while watching Jeff's team, Essendon, play in the televised AFL game. Then it was down to the pub to meet Michael, where another game was on TV—this time it was Michael's beloved Collingwood going round. Unfortunately my NRL Rabbitohs weren't a TV game that weekend.

It was a relaxing Saturday afternoon, replete with views across the sunny bay. Bill, Tony and I can't drink as much beer as we used to, so dinner back at the vans with the rest of the crew entailed red wine instead. It wasn't a normal day for me but it was a nice psychological break from the usual routine. An evening barbecue on the beach in such a beautiful spot, with all eight of us in attendance, was the perfect finale to a memorable day.

And I pulled up pretty well the next morning—full of beans, in fact. Bill and Tony had to drive back to Port Lincoln for their return flights so they dropped me at my starting point on their way. Unfortunately, the Pewter Mug Day was a briefer occasion this year than we'd have liked but everyone, especially me, was glad the guys had gone to the trouble to be there.

We were now on the Eyre Peninsula and farming land became prominent. Peter and Jane had again headed off for a few days in the Flinders Ranges but were going to return later. So now we were down to four again.

A wet and windy night in the otherwise beautiful location of Venus Bay, with its mirror-like protected waters and almost untouched beaches, where we again ran into the female cyclists I'd met more than 1000 kilometres earlier at Fraser Range, and it was farewell to the Great Australian Bight as I headed inland across the peninsula.

Most afternoons Jeff was joining me to run the final part of the day. He'd usually do at least 5 kilometres and had even run as far as 21 kilometres with me on one occasion. During these times he started to notice something he considered highly unusual.

Until very recently Jeff had been a senior executive with CSL, an Australian blood products company that is now a major international player in that field. His background as a biological scientist engendered a curiosity in him when it came to human physiological processes. And he believed there was something quite curious about how my body had adapted to running around the world.

The issue, something I'd noticed as well, was how often I urinated while running during the day. I reasoned that carrying excess urine in my bladder for extended periods was not an efficient physiological practice, so my body had 'evolved' to get rid of the waste on a regular basis. But they weren't small pees. Every 4 or 5 kilometres I'd 'have to go' and the volume was similar to what most people would consider a normal amount.

There's nothing too unusual about that—one would immediately assume I was drinking large amounts of water and, consequently, observing it coming out the other end. But this was the odd thing that Jeff had noticed—I wasn't drinking very much at all.

Jeff was adamant that I was taking in much less fluid than I was evacuating during the day. He was keen to do a scientific experiment and carefully measure all fluid inputs and outputs to test his observation. Of course, this was not practical. But both he and I agreed the anecdotal evidence appeared to suggest I was suffering from a liquid deficit during the day. Yet I wasn't feeling dehydrated in the slightest. So how could this be?

Jeff's hypothesis was interesting and somewhat from left field. Humans, as a rule, lose moisture during expiration. That is, every time we breathe out, a little bit of water vapour goes with the breath. (Anyone who's blown on the lenses of sunglasses to clean them knows this.) However, there are plants, and supposedly some members of the animal kingdom, which can do the opposite—they absorb moisture from the atmosphere. Such life-forms have evolved to do this as an adaptation to living in arid environments. If there's not enough to drink, then why not simply breathe in the water? Jeff wondered whether somehow my body had made a similar adaptation as a result of a year and a half on the road, with my lungs processing water vapour in reverse.

Jeff and I both found the hypothesis hard to believe, and we still do, but it was difficult to discount the theory completely. To this day, we still can't explain the mystery of the missing fluid in the 'water in–water out' equation. Perhaps one day a proper study of this potential effect will be initiated and the conundrum will eventually be solved.

Four days after leaving behind the Great Australian Bight to venture across the Eyre Peninsula, we were joined by another old friend from the Tour de Bois—Eric. An energetic man of Latvian origin, Eric had taken on the role of support crew during my final major training campaign, accompanying me for several days as I ran through the countryside of western New South Wales. His contribution to the world run was, therefore, more than trivial.

Eric had flown to Adelaide, hired a car and driven 400 kilometres to find us that evening. However, our phones were out of range and, to add to that, we'd camped about 200 metres off the road. There was no chance Eric was going to find us in the dark.

Luckily, the next morning my phone found just enough signal to pick up a text message Eric had sent. Shivering all night, he had slept in sub-zero temperatures on the ground next to his car on the side of the road, about 10 kilometres down the highway. I managed to get a return text to him and we finally found each other, just before I was ready to start my day.

On the campfire that morning we cooked the abalone we'd been given by Shane in Perth. All of us, Eric included, were amazed at how delicious it was. How many people had previously eaten abalone cooked this way in the secluded reaches of the Eyre Peninsula? Not too many, I'm sure.

Eric was there for more than just a casual visit. The aura about the record for the longest run with me in a single day was building among the Tour de Bois and Eric intended to have a go at it. His previous longest run was 35 kilometres. If he wanted to beat Chook's recent benchmark, he needed to run at least 56 kilometres. As I said to all the guys who fancied themselves at setting a new record, I would run as far that day as it took for them to break the record. If they were up to it, then so was I.

There wasn't much on the road on 26 July for Eric and me to get distracted by, the only town being the awkwardly named Iron Knob. Eric's calves began to pack it in around 15 kilometres and I gave him no chance at that stage. But, as Chook and Dave had shown on previous occasions, the Tour de Bois are made of sterner stuff and Eric kept going.

Like Chook a week earlier, Eric tired badly over the final couple of hours but he finished with a withering burst when I pointed out a sign up ahead that would be our stopping point for the day. When we reached that point, with Michael and Jeff waiting in the car to pick us up, Eric had set a new record with 56.28 kilometres—more than 20 kilometres further than he'd ever run before.

The crew were again joined that evening by Jane and Peter, back from Wilpena Pound in the Flinders Ranges, all of us staying at an eccentric camping and motel site called Nuttbush, which was actually a working sheep station, with shearing sheds and all. Peter whipped up a fantastic spaghetti bolognese as we celebrated Eric's startling achievement. Chook was one of the first to send his congratulations.

Unfortunately, while the rest of us were keen to do justice to the occasion, Eric was so completely exhausted he could do little other than eat his meal and fall into bed. That's what 56.28 kilometres of running does to the uninitiated.

Eric did manage to back up the next day for another 25 kilometres. He surprised me, as I thought he'd be lucky to be walking. But that's the Tour de Bois for you.

That day I reached Port Augusta at the tip of Spencer Gulf, a major transport node on the trans-Australian route. This was also a major nexus in my crossing of Australia, as it was where Jeff, Michael and the caravan were leaving us for their drive back to Melbourne.

Other friends of ours had driven Carmel's car across from Sydney. This was, coincidentally, identical to the support vehicle Chook had lent us in New Zealand—a silver Honda CRV. This was now to become the final support vehicle for the rest of the world run. We were again up to nine in the support crew but only for that one night.

It was time for a final evening on the town with Jeff and Michael. Just for something different, we enjoyed a nice meal and several bottles of red wine at a pub down the road, interspersed with regular short speeches and moments of toasting and congratulations. The morning-after was another for sad goodbyes but we'd be seeing Jeff and Michael again in a few weeks, a fact which tempered the emotions a little.

Eric again ran 25 kilometres with me that day alongside the calm waters of Spencer Gulf. He had run a total of 106 kilometres with me in a little over 48 hours. Eric then drove back to Adelaide in the afternoon for his return flight to Sydney.

Back on my own again, I enjoyed a magnificent climb up and over the lower Flinders Ranges and down into the town of Wilmington on the eastern side of the range. There I lunched on one of the most tasty meat pies of my life, made by a local woman called Old Ev.

Peter and Jane stayed with us that night in the quaint village of Melrose, the mountain biking capital of Australia, nestled at the base of Mount Remarkable, with Peter again doing the cooking. The next morning they also said goodbye to us for the final time on the world run and headed back to Sydney themselves.

It was the end of an era. After a long period with travelling companions, a veritable party on the road, it was now back to just Carmel and me—but not for long.

CHAPTER 21

The valleys of wine

The lower Flinders Ranges are one of the most pleasant places to run on Earth. The roads are good and the traffic quite minimal; the countryside and farmland are idyllic, the mountains spectacular and the townships and villages are rustic and charming.

Wirrabara, 28 kilometres south of Melrose, was one of those quaint towns, with its wide streets and shops fronted by verandas. It was also a bit special because here we were met by Carmel's brother Bernie and his wife Lesley. Like Jane and Peter before them, they'd also driven from Sydney with their caravan to join us on the road.

From Wirrabara, the vehicles then continued south to the town of Laura to arrange accommodation for the evening while I completed my day of running; a lovely late afternoon of golden sunshine and flat roads that included the historic village of Stone Hut.

We were met that evening by more mates from the Tour de Bois. Bob and Sue Quin had flown to Adelaide, along with Rod Coy, a.k.a. Reefton Humblewood (yes, that's the name we know him by) and his partner Sarita. Even though it had only been two days since the last batch of friends left us, it was a great joy to be a crowd of eight again, with animated conversation over dinner—a tasty lasagne, home-cooked by Lesley.

Over the next two days, with a bit of commuting to and from start and finish points, my run straddled the town of Clare, allowing us all to enjoy a double night in this delightful place. The morning of 31 July, I passed the 24,000-kilometre mark to the north of the town, marvelling at the colours of the crops that were just starting to benefit from the upcoming warmth of spring. It was exactly one year since I had passed the 10,000-kilometre mark in Missouri.

Bob and Reefton had dropped me at my starting point that morning and Bernie and Lesley picked me up in the afternoon, allowing Carmel a support-free day. She put it to good use, having her hair done at a Clare salon. She even booked me in for a haircut that evening before dinner.

Haircuts had proved problematic on the world run. I'd had a haircut just before I started in Sydney, then went nearly five months before another, which was only achieved because I was back in Sydney for a few days to meet my US visa requirements. My hair was quite wild by then. After that I usually cut my own hair every couple of months. Actually, I would cut the front and sides and Carmel would cut the back. It was far from professionally done; more of a cobbled job borne of necessity. So it was nice to have a proper haircut in Clare for a change.

Known as one of Australia's premier wine regions, the Clare Valley is just as much a treat in which to run. And the people are just as nice too—at one point Carmel pulled up in a driveway to get a photo of me in the background with a vineyard in the foreground. When a man came out and asked what she was doing, Carmel gave him a full rundown on my endeavour, including how I like to indulge in a little red wine each night. It turned out he'd seen me interviewed by Shane Crawford on the *AFL Footy Show*.

So then this wonderful man, Scooter Smith from Cardinham Estate, donated a dozen bottles of red for my nightly 'sustenance'. This came in very handy. The previous case donated by Kemeny's for the trip across the Nullarbor had been enjoyed long ago and was now a distant memory.

The next day I managed to make it to the upper reaches of Australia's best-known wine region, the Barossa Valley. Widely considered to produce the world's best shiraz, the Barossa is, therefore, one of my favourite wine areas. Reefton and Sarita had left us earlier that afternoon and Bernie and Lesley were to meet us later in Adelaide; it was now just Bob and Sue accompanying us through this must-visit area for wine buffs.

A night in Kapunda was followed by a day running through the Barossa towns of Nuriootpa and Tanunda, culminating with a stay in Lyndoch. Bob and I enjoyed an NRL game on TV in the local pub that Friday night over chicken parmigianas.

For the most part, the weather had been kind to me across Australia. Now, though, it was getting noticeably colder and the skies were threatening. And then it hit, just as I ran down a long incline and into the northern suburbs of Adelaide. In the atrocious weather I ploughed through Gawler and Elizabeth, at times in appalling horizontal rain, and finally entered the city's CBD. It was 3 August and I had spent nearly two months running in the wilderness.

Adelaide is very picturesque, often referred to as the City of Churches due to the large number of these highly ornate buildings dotted around town. The city is also home to arguably the most beautiful international cricket ground in the world, the Adelaide Oval. The weather, however, didn't do Adelaide justice that day. I was glad I'd visited several times before and experienced the city in its usual glory. We stayed in a trendy modern apartment that Saturday night in the centre of the city, savouring a pasta dinner at an Italian restaurant in the company of our four travelling buddies.

Running to the east from Adelaide entails the Adelaide Hills. I had always thought of these as hills, as the name suggests, not mountains. But a 600-metre climb is definitely bordering on mountainous as far as I'm concerned. Bernie and Lesley passed me towing their caravan just as I hit the climb itself and we exchanged a final goodbye. I wasn't to see them again until I passed near to their place in Sydney the day before I was to finish the world run.

Then the climb began. I was horrified when I reached a section where the parallel cycle path finished and a sign indicated that the freeway was off-limits to pedestrians and cyclists. This wasn't in the plan. There was absolutely no alternative. I had to either proceed illegally or make my way through thick mountainous forest on non-existent paths. I chose to proceed illegally.

I stayed as far over to the side of the freeway as possible, climbing the constant gradient against the oncoming traffic. I hoped it would only be a short section after which I could exit on to a side road but it just kept going on and on. Google Maps showed me where I could finally escape from the freeway but would I reach that spot before being arrested?

And then it happened. A Highway Patrol police car pulled over in front of me with its lights flashing when I was only 400 metres from the off-ramp. As the officer walked towards me, I steeled myself for a reprimand but he was friendly and polite. He informed me that several motorists had called in to report a runner on the freeway. Apparently, I was spooking the drivers. 'Many are of a nervous disposition and can't handle any distraction on the road,' he said, almost apologetically, adding that even a person running several metres away on the shoulder of the highway was enough to disturb such drivers. I told the officer why it was important for me to be there, after which he was even more sympathetic. He simply asked me to exit at the next available option and wished me luck with the world run.

So I started off again but then, just 200 metres further on, another Highway Patrol car stopped with its lights flashing. I don't know if it's typical of the South Australian police force but this officer was just as pleasant as the first. Another brief chat, another polite request to take the next exit, and off I ran. A few minutes later, the side road appeared on my right and I was off the freeway and back on legal ground.

But now I was at the top of the climb and this was where the really hilly stuff began. The descent on the other side of the

Adelaide Hills is not the constant gradient of the approach from the west. The hills are rolling—more down than up but there's still plenty of up. The running is challenging, with a rhythm difficult to establish, but it is interesting. The highlight was the oldest German town in Australia, Hahndorf, where the mid-1800s stone buildings are still in stellar condition. Another magnificent pie for lunch set me up for the afternoon.

I finished the day in the village of Kanmantoo, with just one accommodation option. Bob and Sue joined us for an incredible home-cooked Italian meal whipped up at late notice by the proprietor. It was the Quins' last night with us and we treated the evening appropriately.

Bob decided to set his own record the next morning. In true 'Quinny' style, he was going to run, not the furthest but the least distance with me (of those who actually ran any distance with me at all; zero didn't count). He joined me just after my start and jogged an impressive 100 metres, beating Reefton's previous minimalistic record of 400 metres.

And then Bob and Sue departed for Sydney. Now it was again just Carmel and me, and this would be the case for the next few weeks; something we hadn't experienced since Europe. Temporarily, at least, it would no longer be the perpetual party we'd been experiencing of late. But the upside was we could both get a little extra rest each evening.

I now had less than 2000 kilometres to run and for the first time I was developing a sense that my trek around the world was nearing the end. After more than a year and a half, I had less than six weeks remaining on the road. Passing through the town of Murray Bridge and across Australia's longest river, the Murray, I cut a lonely figure as I headed down the highway towards Melbourne.

Nearly three years earlier I had organised the annual Tour de Bois ride along this exact same stretch of road. At that time I'd already planned the world run and knew I'd be running here again at the end of it. For that reason I chose to run much of the Tour de Bois route that year, rather than cycle—it was great training for the real thing. The Tour de Bois support vehicle would pick me up after half a day of running and we'd catch up to the cyclists, at which time I'd jump back on my bike.

I specifically recall a road sign just before the town of Keith. It read 'Melbourne 500 km'. Back in 2010 I remembered thinking how I'd be seeing that very sign again when I was almost finished running around the world. Now, on 8 August, when I finally saw the sign again, just as I'd visualised, I had a strange sense that I'd actually been able to see into the future three years earlier—everything was just as I'd imagined it to be. It was more than déjà vu. Never before had I sensed living the same event across such a span of time. It was also a classic case of the visualisation of a goal and the subsequent achieving of the same.

Over the ensuing week I ran through quintessential country towns, inland from the Limestone Coast—towns such as Tintinara, turning right at Bordertown, through the tiny village of Frances, via Naracoorte, Penola and on to Mount Gambier. In fact, 450 kilometres of the run was identical to the Tour de Bois course of 2010. The highlight was running through the Coonawarra wine region, where the road was lined for miles with vineyards and cellar doors of some of Australia's most well-known winemakers.

Except for the day into Adelaide, I hadn't had much in the way of rain through Australia, or during the whole world run for that matter, having only been drenched on a few occasions. But the region around Mount Gambier is known for its winter squalls and I got soaked the afternoon I ran into the city.

After an interview with the local paper, Carmel and I went out for a nice Thai meal before a relatively early night. Unfortunately, we were about to receive some dreadful news.

The next morning, 13 August, Carmel received a call she had feared. Her mother Dulcie had not been faring well of late and the expectation was she would not live much longer. At the age of 95, this was not entirely unexpected but it's still devastating news when you receive it.

Carmel needed to get back to Sydney so she could then drive to Kiama on the south coast to see her mother. Dulcie had previously told Carmel that under no circumstances was I to stop the world run on her account. Carmel needed to leave but the expectation was that I would continue. This posed a logistical issue. The weather was not hot, the region was not isolated and I could survive all day without support, but how could my gear be transported each day from town to town?

There was only one viable alternative if I was to continue with the run—we needed a replacement. Michael had previously offered to act as support crew in the case of just such a situation and so we called him in Melbourne and he readily agreed. So we packed up all our gear, careful to separate what I needed from what was to stay in Carmel's car, and she began the 400 or so kilometre drive to Melbourne airport. The aim was for Carmel to intersect with Michael along the way. At that point my gear would be transferred to Michael's car.

Thankfully the day was cool and, after crossing the South Australian–Victorian border early in the day, I'd covered 44 kilometres without food or drinks by the time Michael reached me in the mid-afternoon. I was very appreciative of Michael's willingness to be part of the support crew again—this time solo—as it meant I was still on track to finish by the planned date of 13 September; a date around which many people had begun to make preparations.

The days after Michael arrived were cold and sometimes wet too, but Michael did a sterling job. His negotiating skills in the pubs were second to none, often scoring us a drastically discounted or even free room. Casterton, Coleraine and Hamilton were all encountered and enjoyed before I reached Penshurst, where I was a special guest-speaker at the football club's weekly Thursday night dinner.

The previous year in the US I'd experienced many chance encounters of an historic nature. Abraham Lincoln's boyhood home, Billy the Kid's jail and Elvis Presley's recording studio were all examples. In Australia, however, with its shorter period of recorded European history, I was not expecting similar experiences. I was soon to discover otherwise, with the small town of Coleraine surprising me.

Pleasant as it is, this otherwise nondescript country outpost lays claim to an unusual historical fact. Fleeing an upcoming arranged marriage in Poland, a young Helena Rubinstein moved to Coleraine in the 1890s to live with her uncle. Helena soon set up a fledgling cosmetics business, gradually expanding the enterprise into Melbourne. But that didn't satisfy this ambitious young woman. She eventually migrated to New York, creating one of the most successful cosmetics companies in the world. Her battles with Elizabeth Arden are, purportedly, legendary. Though the cosmetics industry means little to me, I still appreciated the historical significance as I ran past the little house where Helena instigated her international empire.

After my speech to the football club in Penshurst, I was joined on the road by a local female dairy farmer Clare, who ran 32 kilometres with me. A running enthusiast, she'd been following my progress for most of the world run, initially having no idea that I planned to go through the area. But having watched the tracker on a daily basis over a few weeks, Clare soon realised that eventually I would be running past her farm.

And it wasn't just Clare who ran with me that day; her young nephew and niece joined us too, with their mother driving behind as back-up. Even Clare's parents were there, acting as an additional safety vehicle to buffer the grandchildren against fast-approaching traffic from the rear.

Most of the family peeled off in the village of Caramut, with just the two of us continuing. I eventually waved goodbye when we reached her farm. After 32 kilometres of running together, we parted company, both richer for the experience. Clare was soon to embark on her own adventure, running and cycling 10,000 kilometres on trails throughout southern Australia.

It was a very windy day and I was constantly buffeted by extreme gusts, sometimes blown off the road and on to the grassy shoulder. I hadn't gone too far when I answered a phone call. It was my cousin Karen. She and her husband Michael were travelling in their car and were just 15 kilometres away. They were on a short holiday and had planned on intersecting with me somewhere in Victoria. Karen had placed third in the state marathon championships when she was nearly forty years of age, so she knew all about long-distance running.

Karen checked my position on the tracker and they drove out to meet us, catching me during a short drinks stop I was having with Michael at the support vehicle. It was a timely reunion as I hadn't seen Karen for almost exactly ten years. She and I then ran the rest of the day into the town of Mortlake, with the two Michaels driving ahead to arrange accommodation.

The next morning, 18 August, I received the call from Carmel I'd been dreading. Her mother had passed away during the night. It had been a peaceful passing. The best thing was that Carmel and her siblings got to spend quality time with their mother for a few days before her death. They had said their goodbyes in person. I was pleased also that Hannah and Grace had been able to see their grandmother in those final days.

I dedicated my run that day to Dulcie.

Karen ran with me that morning before her husband picked her up and they continued on their journey. I ran on through the town of Camperdown and finished the day some distance down the road. Michael arrived for the commute back into Camperdown with some interesting news.

He'd booked us into a motel in which the proprietor had given him a tip for a horse that was running that Saturday afternoon. Michael had decided to put a few dollars on the horse. It was just about to race as he pulled up to me on the road. The horse duly won the race and returned more than $300. Our accommodation, meals and drinks—and then some—were effectively free that night.

The following lunchtime I passed through Colac, hometown of Cliff Young. Cliff had set Australia alight in 1983 when, as an unknown 61-year-old, he lined up at the start of the inaugural Sydney to Melbourne Ultra-Marathon race. The best and most well-known ultra-marathoners in the world were all competing and then there was Cliffy, looking like the relaxed country character he was, at the back of the pack.

But Cliff was not deterred. Despite initially being far back in the race, over the coming days he gradually made his way through the field and into the lead. He remained there for the rest of the race, with enormous crowds lining the streets of Melbourne to cheer him on to the finish line. It was the ultimate sporting underdog story.

I rightfully paid homage to Cliff on my way through Colac. His was a far greater achievement than anything I could ever accomplish on the road.

It was winter in Victoria and the weather reflected that fact. Gale-force westerly winds hammered me on numerous occasions and rain squalls were not uncommon. And it got colder the afternoon of 19 August as I gradually gained in elevation on my way up to Ballarat, having passed the 25,000-kilometre mark earlier that morning. By the time I reached the outskirts of the city, the temperature was just above freezing.

Michael and I were met in Ballarat by Jeff, who had caught the train from Melbourne. He just couldn't stay away! The next morning Jeff ran 16 kilometres with me along dirt trails through the forests. I finished the day in the middle of farming land, with the guys transporting me to our accommodation in Bacchus Marsh, just a day's run west of Melbourne.

Here we were joined by Carmel, who had spent the past few days helping with the funeral arrangements for her mother. Carmel would be flying back to Sydney two days later for the funeral itself. We had, at length, discussed me taking a break from the run to attend the funeral but Carmel and other family members had insisted that this would be against Dulcie's wishes. And so I continued the world run.

I ran to the western suburbs of Melbourne the following morning. Carmel and I then headed to Michael and Annie's place in the city to get ready for a special function. For some time, my sponsor Asia Pacific Digital had been planning an evening with their staff and clients. The most difficult part was the timing, as it had been hard to give a precise date for my arrival in Melbourne so many weeks in advance. But I did provide just such a date and I managed to keep to it.

Carmel and I had invited several friends along as well—people who had been following the run the whole time but whom we hadn't seen until arriving in Melbourne. A great evening was had by all and I was pleased to be able to give a speech without feeling too jaded by the fatigue of a year and a half on the road.

I completed my leg into the city the next morning, accompanied for part of the stage by another of the Tour de Bois guys, Beaver. In the CBD I conducted three different media interviews, including one with Channel 7 News in front of the Melbourne Cricket Ground. Turning north, I left the city, running the last part of the day with a friend of Hannah's. Brad and Hannah had appeared together on a reality TV program earlier in the year and he had been following my run ever since. Brad's parents picked us up late that afternoon for the commute back to Annie and Michael's.

Earlier that day Carmel had flown back to Sydney for the funeral of her mother—one that was well attended by family and friends alike. From all reports, there were many fine sentiments expressed and the occasion did justice to the life of Dulcie Breen. While I wasn't there in person, I was certainly there in spirit as I ran that day, constantly thinking of Dulcie as the funeral was taking place.

Early in the evening of my second night staying at Michael and Annie's, Dave arrived. The last appearance Dave had made on the run was in Budapest. He originally intended running each day with me in Victoria but the plans had changed a little and now he was to be the support crew until Carmel arrived back after her mother's funeral.

Much of the following day's running was identical to my 2009 Melbourne to Sydney run, including our stay in the town of Kilmore. Dave and I are both South Sydney Rabbitohs supporters so we relished watching our team win the game that was on TV that Friday night.

The next day was 24 August, a year since I'd been running in the Deep South of the United States. With less than 1000 kilometres to go, the complexion of the run was now fundamentally different.

A few minutes after I started that morning, I noticed a guy in running gear waiting up the road ahead of me. It turned out to be one of the senior executives from Asia Pacific Digital. He'd driven from Melbourne especially to run with me that Saturday.

We soon passed through the town of Broadford, with Dave leaving the car and joining us on the road. It was a fine morning for running and the extremely quiet back road made the running even more pleasant.

A couple of hours later Carmel arrived in her car, having flown back that morning. She was accompanied by Jeff and Guenolee who were in their own car. They'd picked Carmel up from the airport and driven her to the support vehicle's location in Broadford, where Dave had discreetly hidden the keys behind one of the tyres. Carmel had thoughtfully bought us each a meat pie and these were eagerly consumed on the side of the road.

Dave and I then continued on but soon after he called it quits and hopped in the car with Carmel. I finished a long day in Nagambie, having enjoyed running for much of the afternoon on a deserted parallel side road.

Five of us stayed together in a cabin that evening, partaking of a delicious home-cooked meal whipped up by Guenolee, whose

French background and culinary skills provide her with a decided advantage when it comes to the art of food. And, to top it off, we were entertained by an exciting win in the final seconds of the game by Jeff's Essendon boys over the unpopular Carlton club.

The competition among the Tour de Bois was now getting seriously hot. There wasn't much time left before the record would be decided for good. Who would run the longest distance with me in a single day? This friendly competition proved very important to me during the latter parts of my world run. Focusing too much on oneself can lead to boredom and negative thoughts. Immersing myself in the aspirations of others was a very positive distraction that greatly benefited my outlook as I inched my way toward the finishing line.

In tandem with the competition for the longest single day was the struggle for the furthest total distance run with me. But Chook had seemingly put this out of reach of anyone else. Several guys were already totalling more than 100 kilometres, including Dave, Barry, Eric and Jeff, but Chook had amassed more than double that distance.

But the talking point of the moment was the single-day record and Dave was going to attempt to reclaim what he felt was rightfully his—the record he first set the day he ran into Budapest with me. Eric was the current record-holder with 56.28 kilometres so Dave needed to run at least 57 kilometres to top him.

Jeff ran the first 14 kilometres with us that morning of 25 August before Guen collected him and they headed back to Melbourne. I would see both of them in Sydney in a few weeks.

Dave and I continued; the road was very quiet and we enjoyed a pie for lunch from the impressive bakery in Murchison before sauntering up to Tatura. Dave was beginning to tire by the time he passed his previous record of 39 kilometres but was determined to go all the way. His pace slowed to barely more than a walk but he just kept on going. I was texting Chook and Eric with updates on Dave's progress; Eric, as the current record-holder, was getting nervous.

I agreed I would run the necessary 57 kilometres that day if Dave was up to it—and he was, stopping precisely at that exact distance. It was a mighty effort and one Dave will remember for the rest of his life—it was the furthest he'd ever run by a margin of 15 kilometres.

The three of us ordered in home-delivery pizzas at the hotel that night and soon after dinner an exhausted Dave was asleep before we even realised it; just like Eric and Chook had been after they'd made their own record-breaking runs.

The next morning Carmel drove Dave to the railway station at Benalla for the trip back to Sydney. It was back to just the two of us again for the next few days.

The weather was warming up a little and the canola fields were more yellow than the brightest of canaries. I knew this country well from past Tour de Bois—it was Ned Kelly territory. Shepparton, Dookie, St James, Glenrowan and Beechworth all passed by in a blur and before I knew it I was crossing the state border and entering New South Wales—my home state. I hadn't run in New South Wales since the first day of the world run, twenty months prior.

Carmel's niece and her kids came out to meet us on the road and some of her friends joined me for the final stage through Wodonga and into Albury. I had now returned to home territory, ready for the final leg of the run to Sydney.

CHAPTER 22

The home straight

The final leg promised to open memorably and the reason was simple. The night I reached Albury was also the night The Hud and Sue arrived for another stint on the road with us. Like Dave and Jo, their last appearance on the run had been in Budapest, where the Hud had taken a slightly backseat role relative to Dave in terms of the running.

But this time The Hud was on a mission. He knew there were limited opportunities remaining for anyone to break the single-day record. And he intended to not only break that record, he was going to put it out of reach once and for all.

The Hud and I started out on the morning of 30 August in brilliant sunny weather and he was primed for a big performance. It may sound strange but watching the excitement and trepidation in each of the guys as they psyched themselves up for their respective record attempts was of more interest to me than my own running on those days.

I have always attached more importance to athletic endeavours that entail a degree of uncertainty. With less than 1000 kilometres to go, there was now little doubt I'd attain my goal of running around the world. However, there was nothing certain about these guys attaining their personal goals. And their goals weren't trivial. None of these friends had ever previously contemplated running as far as they did with me. It was an honour to be part of the ambitions of each and every one of them and one of the greatest pleasures of my run around the world.

Traversing the northern suburbs of Albury, The Hud and I and gently rose in elevation to the high point of the day at the 15-kilometre mark. Carmel and Sue stopped by with a drink. The girls were almost as interested in the record attempt as I was, demonstrating perfect support-crew duties that day.

The Hud was itching to go, setting an unsustainable pace in the early stages. I had to regularly reel in his enthusiasm as it was definitely not a pace I was up for. He was fresh but I had more than 25,000 kilometres under my belt. The Hud slowed it down a little and we pushed on. We passed the girls again from time to time; they would stop and walk for a while as we caught up, providing a drink if necessary.

By the 33-kilometre mark we'd reached the town of Gerogery. A quick lemon squash at the pub and we were on our way again. The Hud is an old hand at distances like 33 kilometres so I didn't expect him to be having any troubles at that stage. We were now on the Olympic Highway and The Hud got even stronger, pushing a little ahead of me then waiting as I caught up. The girls delivered us a pie each at the 40-kilometre mark. The Hud was still full of beans.

All this time I had been texting our progress to Chook, Eric and of course Dave, who held the current record of 57 kilometres. They couldn't believe The Hud was on track. Some doubters (not those three, though) had scoffed at the possibility of The Hud running more than 50 kilometres in a day. I knew better. As we ran into the town of Culcairn, The Hud had chalked up more than 52 kilometres. Despite some signs of fatigue, he was closing in on Dave's record.

A final drink followed by a bit of food and we departed on a quieter road towards the village of Morven. By this time Sue and Carmel were also getting excited about The Hud's effort. They kept in close contact as he knocked over one kilometre after another.

Those final kilometres were starting to show on his face but The Hud's resolve was not wavering. We passed the 57-kilometre mark; then we passed 58. We stopped for a brief ceremony of congratulations with the girls. The Hud had the record. But although I asked if he'd like to stop there, he wasn't ready to pack it in yet. He wanted to take it to the next big figure— 60 kilometres.

And so we ran 60 kilometres that day, pulling up stumps as we entered the town limits of Morven. The Hud had never before in his life run beyond the standard 42.2-kilometre marathon distance. But now he had run 18 kilometres further than a marathon—and was the new record-holder for the greatest distance covered on foot with me in a single day of the world run.

We celebrated that evening with the girls in the Culcairn Hotel. The food was surprisingly good, the wine splendid and the night was capped off nicely by another Rabbitohs win on the Friday night TV game (The Hud is also a Souths supporter).

Not to rest on his laurels, though, The Hud backed up by running the entire next day with me, too—the only person to do that. His additional 51 kilometres gave him a two-day total of 111 kilometres. The other guys were astounded.

The Hud had effectively put the record out of reach and no one attempted to beat it after that. Chook, Eric and Dave all sent their congratulations. They knew they'd have struggled to match The Hud that day.

During the second day on the road, The Hud had tired noticeably but he never looked like faltering. He set his goals and went for it in true Tour de Bois fashion, just as the other guys had done before him.

And we had a few moments along the road to distract him from any woes he may have been feeling. Jo's uncle and aunt visited us for a while (that's Jo who travelled with us from Vienna to Budapest), Carmel's niece and her husband and kids dropped by on their way to a rugby grand final in Wagga Wagga and our dear friend Jenny turned up too.

Jenny had been a crucial member of the support crew for five weeks through California and Arizona. This was her first time back with us since then. Her presence elicited a feeling of the early days of the world run, when I was crisscrossing the US countryside with fresh legs and a sense of awe as to the journey that still lay ahead.

In my mind the run around the world had assumed the role of a microcosm of life—the early months akin to childhood, when the whole world is new and each day an adventure. With a wiser head and slower legs, the latter part of the run had taken on the feel of a twilight phase of life. Having Jenny back evoked a sense of meeting up in later life with an old childhood friend, reliving stories from a mystical past era.

The Hud and I reached the village of Mangoplah, finding Carmel, Sue and Jenny having a wine on the steps in front of the pub; celebrating The Hud's achievement, no doubt. The Hud and I had lunch and moseyed on.

We finished the day 14 kilometres down the road and commuted into Wagga Wagga for Saturday night with the girls. It had been a sterling two days of running by The Hud. And I never doubted him.

I'd been looking forward to reaching Wagga Wagga since the beginning of the run. Watson, a friend from the 1970s, lives in the town and he'd been following the run since the beginning. 'Watto' and I go back nearly 40 years. We played in a four-piece band together and, with five others (nine in total), we were involved in a car accident in 1977 that could easily have claimed everyone's lives.

The car, a station wagon with three people squashed in the far back of the vehicle, skidded off the road and over an embankment, landing nose-first in a dam, where it quickly started to sink. Due to the pressure of the water, the doors wouldn't open and the car was soon completely submerged. However, with what seemed like eternal patience and an amazing lack of panic on the part of everyone, the windows were eventually wound open and we made our getaway into the murky water, swimming to the side of the dam. The car rapidly sank into the depths of the dam but not before all nine passengers had managed to scramble to safety.

Watto is a keen runner himself, with several marathons to his credit. He and I hadn't seen much of each other recently, though the car accident group had a 'third of a century' reunion a few years back and I caught up with him then. However, he has been an avid follower of the run and my go-to man whenever I struggled with a simile or risqué euphemism in my blog. Watto always came up with a brilliant figure of speech for the occasion, often from left field. Though sometimes a little too salacious to use in my daily missive, each and every offering from Mr Simile was nevertheless appreciated.

Watto and his wife met us at our accommodation—a popular pub in town—where old stories were exchanged throughout drinks in the bar then dinner. Carmel, Sue, Jenny and The Hud were interested to hear the tales of my days before they knew me, including that of the car crashing into the dam. It was another great evening but over all too soon: a world run waits for no one and the next day I was on my way again.

The morning of Sunday 1 September dawned warm and sunny. After our customary 'pinch and a punch' introduction to a new month, on this occasion with me prevailing over Carmel, we reluctantly bid adieu to our three companions—Sue, The Hud and Jenny. Each was required back in Sydney for work on Monday morning.

Carmel dropped me at my starting location where I was joined for the run into Wagga Wagga by a local farmer (no, he didn't run in gumboots), who had found me via the tracker. The weather continued to be kind, as did the early spring countryside. Fields of green wheat and yellow canola were complemented by the purple of Paterson's curse, creating a patchwork quilt on the landscape. Hannah and Grace both called me for Fathers' Day during the morning.

Running through Junee early the following morning, I rejoined the Olympic Highway. I had suffered on this stretch during my 2009 Melbourne to Sydney run but this time I was revelling in the fact I felt so fit and strong. Mid-afternoon we were again joined by more friends.

Kate, whose father had known Carmel's brother Bernie since childhood, had been in communication for some time about running with me. She and her father and his wife had driven from Sydney, meeting us between Junee and Cootamundra. Kate and I ran the final 17 kilometres of that day together, the opening 14 kilometres into Cootamundra the next day, following up with the final 16 kilometres that afternoon into Harden. Kate had only recently taken up running and her total of 30 kilometres on her second day was the furthest she had ever run in a 24-hour period. She capped that off by running the first 15 kilometres with me on the third day of her visit. Kate and her family had to go back to Sydney in the afternoon of 4 September—but Kate would be back.

Carmel and I stayed that evening in the charming village of Binalong, halfway between Harden and Yass, where I was given a welcome by some locals who had set up a finishing ribbon for me to break through on my arrival at the pub. Word was obviously getting around.

The next couple of days were hilly and the terrain was becoming drier. That said, the countryside was still a joy to be running through, punctuated by lovely transits of historic villages like Bowning and larger towns like Yass.

Having reached the Hume Highway, the main thoroughfare between Sydney and Melbourne and the busiest freeway in Australia, I was elated to find a parallel side road which used to be the old highway. Although ragged in parts, it was still in remarkably good condition overall and there was absolutely no traffic on it. This fortunate situation continued for a couple of days, with the side road extending a considerable distance either side of the village of Gunning.

On 6 September I concluded my day of running just 10 kilometres west of Goulburn. Carmel picked me up and shipped me into town to our motel. I went through the usual data download, documentation and blog writing then had a shower. As I was getting dressed, there was a knock on the door. I opened it to a big surprise.

Standing in the hallway were Debbie and Barry. It had been nearly four months since their last presence on the run, back in Istanbul. It was fantastic to see them. Then, not long after that, another long-time mutual friend of the four of us, Richard, arrived as well.

Richard and I go way back as runners. In fact, it was an impromptu 5-kilometre race we had along the highway while holidaying at Nambucca Heads, just after the Christmas of 1982, which had inspired me to begin running seriously. On that occasion I went out hard and was leading at the halfway turnaround point. However, Richard ground me down on the return leg, passing me to win comfortably in a time of 19 minutes

24 seconds, 11 seconds ahead of me. I had intended to treat the race as a training run ahead of my impending trial with the Rabbitohs but it had a deeper and more profound effect than that.

That unofficial race with Richard was a turning point. I was infatuated with the feeling of racing, both the physical and mental aspects. I didn't mind being beaten, so long as I felt I'd performed to the best of my ability. And I knew I could do better than 19 minutes 35 seconds for 5 kilometres.

The 'best of my ability' was still an unknown and I wanted to find out what my limits were. As it turned out, I was never going to be a great long-distance runner, but I didn't care. I just wanted to be the best that I could be.

Once the decision was made to give up football for running, the future fell into place very naturally. As time passed I gradually reached my limits, or very close to them. Personal bests—of 16 minutes 34 seconds for 5 kilometres, 33 minutes 50 seconds for 10 kilometres, 73 minutes 52 seconds for a half-marathon, and 2 hours 49 minutes and 14 seconds for a marathon—are now well behind me. Racing is not a focus of mine anymore but testing myself with new challenges still is.

We all had dinner that evening with another of the Tour de Bois stalwarts, Poddy, and his wife Ann, residents of Goulburn. Dinner was enhanced by a third consecutive Friday night Rabbitohs game. Sadly, this time the team lost to Richard's evil Roosters.

A short 11-kilometre run into Goulburn in the morning was followed by a jaunt along the freeway with Barry, Richard and my cousin Karen, who had turned up again for a lightning visit. As I reached the town of Marulan, a popular rest stop for Hume

Highway travellers, I was surprised by a roadside visit from an uncle, aunt and cousin I hadn't seen in decades. They lived locally and drove to the side of the freeway to await my passing. Every day seemed to deliver a delightful surprise.

After a quick lunch and a diversion into the primary school to vote in the federal election, I headed off with Barry, finishing the day with a further 8 kilometres. That evening we all had dinner with my newly reacquainted relatives in the pub in Marulan.

During that day, 7 September, I had achieved two major milestones—passing 26,000 kilometres and completing 99 per cent of the journey. The end of my run around the world was nigh.

Running from Marulan to Moss Vale was busy. During the morning Karen joined me again, after which Barry and Richard turned up along the road, followed by Greg Ellis, a journalist from the *Illawarra Mercury* who had followed the world run more closely than any other, writing regular updates on my progress in his newspaper column. He even did some running with us while conducting interviews; not just with me but also with the others. Everyone had a story to tell as far as Greg was concerned.

Carmel had me don a long wig and beard for some Forrest Gump–type photos that appeared the next day in the *Mercury*. Everyone joined in for the photos, including Debbie, who I had never seen run before; she actually has some style.

Another of the Tour de Bois, 'Mother', and his wife, dropped by on the quiet back road for a hello on their way south. Mother had spent several days in the support crew in 2009 when I was running from Melbourne to Sydney. It was the efforts of friends like that, driving many hundreds of kilometres each way to lend a hand, which made that first run from Melbourne to Sydney possible. And, without that run acting as a precursor and 'test run', the run around the world would not have occurred. The contributions of Mother and others cannot be underestimated. On this occasion he wanted to at least be there in person, even if it was just briefly.

For a period that day, way out there in the bush and miles from nowhere, the road had become very congested.

After the departure late in the morning of Barry, Deb and Richard, I was joined again by Kate. Karen was still running with me at the time. The two girls and I jogged down the road to Bundanoon for lunch, after which the girls did some shuttling back and forth to pick up cars while I continued running. Karen stayed all day and we finished in Moss Vale that afternoon. Although we joked about it, both Karen and Kate insisted they weren't competing to see who could be the woman to run the furthest with me.

After so much running on my own during the previous year and a half, I was now virtually never on my own. Though a little part of me yearned at times for the solitude to which I had become so accustomed, I was certainly relishing the recent company. And it was to continue.

The next day I was visited on the road by Gregor, whose last presence on the adventure was in Newport, Rhode Island. He'd driven up from Tasmania en route to Sydney and sought me out via the tracker. It had been almost a year since Gregor and I had enjoyed a few beers in Pelham One East, the blues bar in Newport.

At that stage I was only just past the halfway mark of the world run. I was now seeing Gregor with less than 1 per cent of the run to complete. For some deep internal reason, linking the run through these associations with people I met at different stages was vital to me. It somehow drew the whole run together in my mind and made it feel like a shared experience.

Soon after Gregor's departure I was met by Matt, a friend of Kate's, who ran with me from Robertson to Albion Park. The 700-metre descent of Macquarie Pass was as spectacular as it was hard on Matt's thighs. Kate appeared at the end of the day and transported him back to his car, while Carmel and I commuted to Debbie and Barry's home in Kiama. We enjoyed dinner at the local pub with several friends and family from the town.

It was Tuesday 10 September, the fourth last day of the whole run, and it was hectic—the main reason for this was that I was running through the town where I grew up.

I started the morning with Barry, who accompanied me over the initial 10 kilometres. He had organised a visit to my old school, Lake Illawarra High, where he had worked for 37 years. Many students from the cross-country team, as well as staff from the school, including the deputy principal, ran along with me.

Lots of old school friends and former teachers came out that day to meet me on the road and say hello. I was greeted at the school by more students and staff, including the principal. I was also presented with an official school jersey and a donation from the school to Oxfam. The school visit, in particular, entailed a lot of media attention, including another appearance by Greg from the *Illawarra Mercury*.

Then it was down the road to my mother's place for a visit. A crowd of family members had gathered out the front, many having not seen me since I began the world run some twenty months earlier. From Mum's, I ran with my sister Linda, who had organised a very successful Oxfam fundraising event a month earlier, and my brother Paul, across the Windang Bridge.

A host of other friends and relatives joined me that morning too. There were so many people from my past—it was like being transported back several decades. I thoroughly enjoyed meeting each and every person who came out to see me that day. But perhaps the highlight of the morning was my Fifth Grade teacher meeting me on the shores of Lake Illawarra. It had been more than 40 years since I'd seen her. A run around the world provides all sorts of extraordinary occasions and opportunities but this was one of the most memorable.

The afternoon was hot and dry as I ran north past the Port Kembla Steelworks and on into Wollongong, with more runners who I didn't know but who had been following my progress. In the city of Wollongong, I met Carmel and Hannah for lunch. It was the first time I'd seen Hannah in three months. She then joined me for a few kilometres; the last time she'd run with me was in Missouri, more than a year earlier.

I rounded out the day by running to the northern Wollongong suburb of Thirroul, where D.H. Lawrence had lived for a period of time while writing the novel *Kangaroo*. That afternoon Karen met me again for her fourth stint, along with Tour de Bois stalwart Chips. The three of us ambled along the coastal walking path in the bright sunshine, discussing my impending finish three days hence.

We stayed the night, the third last of the world run, with Chips and his wife Jenny in Thirroul, just as I had during my Melbourne to Sydney run in 2009. And, on both treks, the nights prior to that had been spent at Barry and Deb's in Kiama. I chose almost identical routes through the region on each occasion, Chips running with me on the same paths both times. No wonder I was feeling a strong sense of déjà vu.

My third last day on the road, 11 September, began with an iconic run. Chips and I headed along the coastal trail north of Thirroul. The highlight was running on the Seacliff Bridge, a recent engineering marvel, suspended over the ocean. This whole section was highly reminiscent of the Big Sur stretch of coastline in California that I had run some eighteen months earlier.

The visits continued unabated, with friends we'd met in 1986 in Rome dropping in at Stanwell Park and staying with us until the end of the day. Running around the world was no longer a lonely affair.

I eventually ascended the climb to Stanwell Tops, where Lawrence Hargraves had conducted so many of his box-kite experiments in the late 1800s. These tests were pivotal in the history of human transport, elucidating the principles of aerodynamics that ultimately led to powered flight. And it was here I entered the Royal National Park, the second oldest national park in the world after Yellowstone.

Running through the Royal National Park is a special experience, with its subtropical rainforest providing a shady canopy throughout. Being a weekday, the traffic was light as Chips and I moved along with a spring in our step. But we weren't to be the only runners for much longer.

Chook, along with his brother Don, as well as their friends Wayne and Rob, had flown over from New Zealand to run with me to the Opera House. Chook had contributed so much to my run already, including his presence on three previous occasions. Now he was back to add even more value. Wayne and Rob had been part of the Hamilton Runners Club contingent that had joined me on the road more than nineteen months earlier and Don had been there as part of the support crew at the end of the North American leg. Now they were all keen to be there for the finish.

The five of us continued along the river valley and climbed up to the suburb of Waterfall for a lunch of fish and chips, having also been joined by Carmel's cousin. Don was driving one car and Carmel another.

The third last day of the world run concluded at McDonald's in Engadine. My five running companions drove back to Chips' place for the night, Carmel and I cruising the short distance to Jo and Dave's for dinner and an evening with their family.

McDonald's in Engadine was a sea of familiar faces when I arrived in the morning. It was my second last day of running around the world, 12 September, and a group of the Tour de Bois who live locally, including Mother, were there to accompany me on their bikes. Add to those the runners—Chook, Wayne and

Rob, as well as Kate—and we had the largest contingent of the whole odyssey. And also in attendance to run was a colleague of Roger Sharp's; a sort of de facto representative of my sponsor, Asia Pacific Digital.

Various people came out to meet us along the road that day. Briefly stopping by to say hello was an old mate from the Tour de Bois, Kit, who'd been my support crew on numerous training weekends in the past, as well as on the Melbourne to Sydney run and the Run to the Sun in Maui.

Those on bikes peeled off after Sutherland, with Kate leaving us halfway through the morning at Sans Souci. The other four ran the whole day with me, covering a relatively short 31 kilometres to Tempe, finishing just after lunch.

These final days were such a 'people experience', it was impossible to be bored. In fact, the days passed so fast, it felt like I was only on the road for 5 or 10 kilometres. And the last day promised to feel even shorter.

I was now a trivial 11 kilometres from the Opera House—and the end of my odyssey.

Being so close, we stayed at home that night—the first night of the actual run I had spent in my bed since the start on New Year's Eve 2011. I had kept myself occupied with several radio interviews that afternoon and a large group of friends met in the evening for dinner at our favourite Vietnamese restaurant, Uyen.

Many of these friends—those from out of Sydney—had started to gather for the finish and the local B&Bs and hotels did a fair bit of extra business that night. Barry and Debbie were in town, as were Annie, Michael, Guen and Jeff from Melbourne. And Bill had also flown in for his third interaction with the run in less than two months, having recently caught me in Streaky Bay and Melbourne. The finish had become a big deal.

The final morning of the world run, 13 September, began with two early national television interviews—*The Today Show* and the *ABC News*. This was followed by breakfast at home with a crew from ESPN, there to film the last leg. And then we were off to the start at Tempe where more television crews had stationed themselves.

Late that morning I commenced my final day of running with Chook, Wayne, Rob, Barry and Jeff—each of them having run with me on multiple days already and with a combined total between them of close to 1000 kilometres.

It didn't take long for a bit of drama to occur. Wayne tripped on the gutter and fell heavily, opening up a nasty gash on his forehead. The claret flowed liberally and we had to duck into a petrol station and ask for help in cleaning him up. And ESPN caught the whole thing on video, much to Wayne's delight. The egg on his forehead was impressive.

Wayne recovered well, though he initially spent some time in the car of Jane and Peter, who had happened by at just the right time (their first appearance since South Australia). As I neared the city we were joined by Grace and four of her friends. At the same time, Roger Sharp's son chimed in. I now had eleven people running with me down George Street, the main thoroughfare of Sydney.

Just 1 kilometre from the finish, I was met by a police escort on bicycles. They were there to clear the traffic and lead me down the street to the Opera House. At the same juncture I was also joined by South Sydney Rabbitohs Club Captain Michael Crocker and some of the club's administrative staff.

There were now fourteen runners accompanying me down Sydney's busiest street during the lunchtime peak hour, led by two police cyclists. The traffic was halted temporarily as we passed, with crowds gathering on the sidewalks to gaze at the strange procession. Some knew what was happening, having heard one of the many interviews during the previous 24 hours. Others were clearly left wondering what it was all about.

We turned into Circular Quay and before I knew it, the Sydney Opera House was in sight. It immediately conjured memories of the last time I had seen this splendid structure, 622 days earlier. I was led by my police escort to the steps, to be joined by the Rabbitohs mascot Reggie Rabbit and then to the official finishing banner, kindly arranged by Oxfam.

Crossing the finish is hard to describe—a feeling of joy, relief and sadness all mixed as one. After beginning at the same place 622 days earlier, it suddenly dawned on me that I'd finally circumnavigated the Earth on foot.

I had run around the world and the adventure was now over.

However, I had little time to savour the emotion. The waiting press scrum was like a scene from a movie. I was surrounded by camera operators and reporters, all scrambling to be the one to ask the next question. Boom microphones were being held aloft from afar as the throng tightened around me. Carmel was there, as were Hannah and Grace, plus the Year 6 class from Carmel's school. The school had raised more than $10,000 for Oxfam during my run.

The questioning went on for about half an hour after which several more impromptu interviews and photo sessions took place. Many friends and relatives turned up as part of a crowd that was perhaps a thousand strong. Apparently a tour group of Japanese were on the Opera House steps at the time; they were bemused as to what was happening but keen to be part of it anyway.

Eventually the crowd began to disperse and I was finally able to head home. Carmel and I hitched a lift with cousin Karen. Home at last, I busily attended to the last round of documentation and daily blog writing of the world run. A quick shower and it was off to the celebrations at the nearby Clovelly Hotel.

What ensued was a worthy finale to any achievement. Hundreds of people turned up to congratulate Carmel and me, and the festivities went on until closing time. I was pretty much 'match fit' from the nightly red wines during the run, though not quite prepared for the excesses of that evening. The next morning I was not at my sharpest.

And then it was over!

I was prepared for the sudden cessation of what had been my life—seven days a week for the best part of two years—but it still felt a little empty. My legs, however, didn't mind.

I had run around the world and it was time to sit back and rest on my laurels for a while. Not for too long, though—just for a little while.

EPILOGUE

A run around the world ends with a bang not a whimper. And like most bangs, this one was very short lived.

The day after the finish I was busily sorting through mail, unpacking bags and attending to the various minutiae inherent in the return of any traveller after an extended trip. The run was over and it was back to real life for me, and for Carmel too. We did have the privilege of attending a special client event held by Asia Pacific Digital in my honour on the Tuesday after I finished. It was a splendid night, continuing through to the early hours of the morning.

But that's where the celebrations ended. I had envisaged a merry-go-round of parties and informal events but the future is often different when its time finally arrives.

From 'go to whoa' it took me 622 days to run the equivalent of 622 marathons. The total distance covered was 26,232 kilometres, amounting to an estimated 40 million steps and entailing a total uphill component that was the equivalent of running from sea level to the top of Mount Everest and back—not just once but a staggering 25 times.

My time of 622 days was the fastest ever circumnavigation of the Earth on foot, eclipsing Jesper Olsen's previous record by 40 days. On the days I ran, I averaged 50 kilometres (the days I ran were defined as those that counted toward the total distance, as there were many days spent flying between continents or spent as planned rest days, when I didn't add to my overall distance).

As per the rules for running around the world, I crossed four continents contiguously from one major ocean to another, passing through antipodal points along the way—in New Zealand and Spain.

I estimate Carmel drove more than 40,000 kilometres in total. Some may say that's no more than they drive in a twenty-month period but virtually every kilometre of Carmel's drive was new terrain to her. That's certainly not something most people do.

And my run helped to facilitate the donation of more than $60,000 to Oxfam which, I have been reliably informed, provided 2400 orphaned and vulnerable children in Africa with meals for a year. This very tangible and worthwhile outcome was one of the most satisfying elements of the entire endeavour.

Imagine you are contemplating a really difficult ultra-marathon. It consists of running three consecutive marathons back to back, culminating in an 1100-metre ascent from the valley floor to the summit of the notorious Alpe d'Huez of Tour de France fame. Okay, so that's 126.6 kilometres of running, ending with a tortuous slog to the top of one of the most feared climbs in the French Alps. Does this sound like a tough challenge?

But hang on. As soon as you've finished this extreme test, imagine you have to do the whole event again. In fact, once you've done it again, do the whole thing another 200 times (yes, that's 200) back to back—sometimes in 60-degree Celsius heat, other times while trudging through the snow in minus 10 degrees Celsius. And when you've finally completed this mountainous 126-kilometre feat a whopping 200 times, you're not finished yet—top it all off with a final 1000-kilometre run to the finish line.

What I've just described—the distance and the climbing—is what my run around the world amounted to. Yet, much of the way I went about the run was unconventional and, perhaps, counterintuitive.

For example, I did not stretch once during the entire twenty months, nor did I do any strength or flexibility exercises. I received just one massage, provided free of charge in San Sebastián. I took no dietary supplements—no gels, protein shakes, performance pills or the like. There were no doctors, dieticians or physiotherapists travelling with me, nor did I consult any throughout the run. I wore nothing special—no 'skins' or other compression clothing. I ran in minimalistic shoes, so light and flimsy it was hardly any different to running in padded socks; I did not have a single blister the whole run. Other than a few occasions when I rolled an ankle or hurt a shoulder in a fall, I took no painkillers or anti-inflammatory drugs. Anti-inflammatories are not a long-term panacea for overuse injuries. And, after running all the way around the world, my knees have never felt better.

I ate nothing special—just whatever was available in the place I was at the time, even when this meant regular meals of oil-soaked burgers (not my preference) or meat pies and Chiko Rolls (occasionally my preference). I drank no coffee (I simply detest the taste) and no tea. However, I did drink red wine every night.

I wore my shoes for a lot longer than is generally recommended, going through just seventeen pairs during the entire run. And some of these had already been 'worn in' during prior training. By the end, my running style had become so efficient and easy-wearing on the shoes that I was able to eke out more than 2500 kilometres per pair and even then I'd generally only change shoes as a precaution. I probably could have managed the entire world run on ten pairs if it had been necessary.

I tried listening to music while running but quickly gave this away, finding I needed my ears to avoid danger. For that reason, I was alone with my thoughts for the majority of the run. This was a lot easier than I had expected. I love company but I guess I'm pretty content with my own company too.

Aficionados of the sport might consider many of these practices eccentric, even naive. It's true that a lot of my habits and routines were not mainstream. And I'm not claiming they were all of benefit to me. Some of my customs were just personal preferences and wouldn't have mattered either way, such as whether I used sports drinks or not. While, on the other hand, certain widely accepted practices that I neglected to employ, such as strength and flexibility exercises, would likely have advanced my cause, perhaps considerably, had they been included in my daily routine (not that I appeared to suffer for their absence).

But some of the avant-garde practices I did adopt were surely beneficial to the run's success, perhaps bordering on critical. The most unconventional of these was arguably my hydration technique.

The litre of milk I consumed before and after each day's run provided my body with a near-perfect electrolyte balance, enabling me to run for eight or more hours each day in temperatures up to 60 degrees Celsius and without any muscle fatigue or the slightest hint of a cramp. And I actually minimised my sodium intake, never once touching a salt shaker. In fact, contrary to the widely accepted old wives' tale, the best strategy for preventing cramps in hot weather is to actually reduce salt consumption, not increase it. This was crucial to my success and a big part of the reason I felt so good throughout. I received all the sodium I required from my diet, including the milk.

During the day I drank plain water and, to a much lesser extent, Coke or Pepsi. Although I consumed some sports drinks in the early days of the run, I found these were unnecessary and expensive. I simply gave them up in favour of water and cola drinks.

The reason was simple. Coke and Pepsi are purchasable at virtually any outlet in the world and they are dirt cheap in most places—sometimes even cheaper than water. And the sugar gave me the junk calories to sustain my effort throughout the day. I rarely drink Coke or Pepsi in normal life but I found them to be quite compatible with running around the Earth.

$$-\text{\textbf{♀}}-$$

A regular question I receive is 'What physiological changes occurred as a result of your run?' On the surface, I can't point to many. Yes, my weight dropped during the run but it didn't take long till I regained my normal pre-run mass.

One persistent change I am aware of, however, is my resting heart rate. When I was young it hovered around 60 beats per minute (bpm). Prior to the world run, and likely in response to the extensive training, it had dropped to about 50 bpm. But since the run my resting heart rate seems to have stabilised at 38 bpm.

And perhaps there are other physiological changes brought on by running around the world that only a sports scientist or doctor can measure. Whether there are or not, I feel no worse for wear as a result.

My sponsor, Asia Pacific Digital, was immensely supportive during the entire escapade. Not only did the company design my website and provide ongoing support, their contribution to costs went a long way toward making the run possible. And it was a pleasure to have my mate and their top dog, Roger Sharp, join up with me in New Zealand and Malaysia.

A goal such as I had can only be attained with the help of others and the Asia Pacific Digital people, along with individuals like Chook and Don, and Jeff and Michael, who gave up considerable time and/or provided their assets, were the ones who made the run possible rather than improbable. There were also the generous people around the world who welcomed us into their homes and provided us with food, shelter and friendship.

And the general support along the way—from the innumerable followers of the blog and Facebook page, to all the friends who joined in the running or as part of the support crew—this was what made it conceivable for me to face each and every new day. Knowing others are interested in what you're doing can be the difference between success and failure at the mental level. All these people played a big part in my victorious circumnavigation of the world on foot.

But obviously the biggest role was performed by Carmel. Not only did she drive the support vehicle, she acted as the official photographer (and what an amazing job she did), arranged accommodation, managed the social and media commitments, attended to a plethora of logistical issues, did the shopping and washing, was there when I needed her with food and drinks and ice towels and all manner of items I desired on the road from time to time, mixed up my chocolate milkshakes in the morning and evening and made my breakfast and often also dinner. And, most of all, she provided the emotional support when I was doing it a bit tough.

Who better than a lovely wife to fulfil this myriad of roles? It was a real team effort.

My state of mind throughout the world run was helped a lot by knowing Carmel was enjoying the adventure as much as I was—perhaps even more. When I finished she asked, 'Why don't you do another lap?'

Maybe one day I will. And, if a second attempt can attract the requisite sponsorship, that day may be closer than I realise.

For the moment, though, I'll leave the world running to the many younger guys who I expect will attempt to break my record in the years to come. If they do, I'd then have a fresh challenge to aim for—reclamation!

In fact, I believe the world record I set is soft and will be broken many times in the decade following my run. With one lap under my belt, I now have the experience to realise that even I could lower it significantly if I gave it another go. But both myself and Jesper Olsen before me treated our runs as adventures, with enjoyment being our highest priority, not the beating of a particular record time. And Tony Mangan, whose four-year run amounts to the most comprehensive circumnavigation of the Earth ever, is no different. Any runner who focuses solely on the world record will not cherish the experience as much as one who does it for the adventure, though I'm sure such an individual would undoubtedly take a sizeable chunk off the record time.

It's clear that the pursuit of encircling the Earth on foot is increasing in interest. Just before I finished my run, a young British guy, Kevin Carr, began his own run around the world with the aim of setting a new world record for the Fastest Circumnavigation of the Earth on Foot. And others have made their intentions known and are planning their attempts too.

As I understand it, however, the attitude of these younger runners is identical to Jesper's, Tony's and mine—the experience comes first, the record is a distant second. Others will follow, no doubt, now that the precedent has been set and running around the world has become an accepted challenge to pursue.

Late in 2013 the World Runners Club was officially established. There were two inaugural members, Jesper Olsen and myself, with Tony Mangan following soon after. The rules for joining the club are relatively simple and essentially the same as the guidelines I followed during my run. And it's expected that each of the subsequent runners who attempt the same feat according to these rules will ultimately become members of this somewhat elite club.

But becoming a member won't be as difficult as many imagine. I'm not a great endurance athlete—I'm a sprinter 'by trade'—and my body shape is definitely not ideally suited to long-distance running. I honestly believe there are countless other people out there who could run around the world just as competently as I did—people who don't even realise they are capable of such a feat.

I'm just a guy who wanted to do it and that's probably the most important quality one needs prior to initiating such a challenge.

Millions are physically capable, but maybe not so many of those millions have the desire and, therefore, the mental willingness to persevere through the tough times. If a task is something you enjoy doing, it's unlikely you'll consider it a struggle. I guess nothing's too hard if you're having fun.

During the planning stage of this run, the enormity of the challenge was at the forefront of my mind on a daily basis. Would I be capable of running around the world? Would I capitulate, either physically and/or mentally? It just seemed like such a big deal and everyone I spoke with at the time was quick to concur.

But I guess human nature dictates that, once a goal has been reached, it doesn't really seem like such an enormous achievement anymore. In the weeks after I finished, people would comment about how impressed they were with what I'd done and I'd offer a flippant reply about it not being a big deal. And I meant it.

One of my main reasons for taking on this challenge was the element of doubt. It was refreshing to be attempting something of which I wasn't sure I was capable. Like the toss of a coin, the uncertainty was destined to collapse into one of two dichotomous states—success or failure. If I'd failed, I guess I would have held the concept of running around the world in even higher esteem. Having attained the goal, however, it now seems far less formidable.

But from time to time I will still latch on to a fleeting memory—a transient recollection of my attitude to the run before I started. On those short-lived evanescent occasions, I'll briefly again be in awe of the achievement. And then the awareness and the sensation will disappear and I'll be left wondering what all the fuss was about.

Throughout the whole event I was often questioned, by the press and public alike, as to my reasons for running around the world. There were several objectives but my principal answer was always the same: 'Because I thought it would be a great way to see the world.' It turned out to be exactly that.

And after having so thoroughly enjoyed the places I ran, the people I met, the experiences I had and the challenges I overcame, it would be easy to fall into a malaise of regret now the odyssey has ended.

Instead, I've adopted a more positive attitude, encapsulated in the words of Dr Seuss: 'Don't cry because it's over; smile because it happened.'

ACKNOWLEDGEMENTS

It goes without saying that an endeavour like running around the world requires the support of many—too many, in fact, to list everyone who contributed to the journey in the main text of this book.

Therefore, I have acknowledged below numerous of these people who made the run around the world easier, more pleasurable or more possible in some way. The list is generally based on the order of appearance in the main text, not upon any perceived order of importance. For the most part, these are people who haven't been mentioned by name in the main text, though there are a few who do get a second mention.

So, thanks go out to the following, many of whom either accompanied me at some point, or provided accommodation along the way:

Tim and Katie Sharp; Heidi and Derek in Dunedin and Will, a friend of Derek's; Cherie and Andrew in Waikouaiti; James and James from Pen-y-Bryn; Ann, Paul and Bridget in Hook; Peter Kalish and Kit Rumsey for support-crew duties in lead-up runs; Kirsty and Scott in Tauranga; Gail and Michael, friends of Chook in Auckland; Zeb from Oxfam; Lyn, another friend of Chook who drove the US support vehicle from Denver to San Francisco to meet us; James, Jacqui, Harry and Buster the dog in Santa Barbara; Valeria and Ronny in Los Angeles; Todor and his colleague Joe in the California desert; Janet and Bob Woods in Cortez; Walter, Nancy, Tania and Neng in Phoenix; Gay and Mike in Santa Fe; Chook's brother Peter and his daughter Vicki in Denver; Walt, Bob and Bob in Boulder; Lisa and Terry in Estes Park; David and Sherla in St Paul; Matt Pruitt in Memphis; Barry from Breakaway Running in Memphis; Craig, Julie and Zoe in Princeton, New Jersey; Tom Haggerty in New Jersey; David, Laura, William and Lindsey in Connecticut; Jason Bennett from ESPN; Charlie Moret in Connecticut; another Charlie, a British expat in Massachusetts; Ana and Frank in Lisbon; Juan Mari in San Sebastián; Felix from the Apalategui Sports Store in San Sebastián; Michele and Patrice in Saint-Élix-le-Château; Stephane and Laurence from Domaine du Vern in Saint-Affrique; Florence and Vincent from Les Coing des Vignes in Mauressargues; and Don Dawson and his daughter Yolanda in Hungary. And a special thankyou to Miles Williams and Ellie Arena from ATECO and Citroën Drive Europe for coordinating the use of the European support vehicle at cost—a lovely brand new Citroën Grand C4 Picasso.

Many thanks also to Robyn for picking us up from Perth Airport; Kim and Brynn Chute's children Keiran and Meg and, later, their younger brother Callum; Julie and Wayne Salter for providing the support vehicle from Perth to Balladonia; Warren and Judy Merritt in the Swan Valley; Kim 'Keith' Robertson in Northam; Rebecca and Toby in Coolgardie; Danielle and Deb the trans-Australian cyclists; Walter the cycling Dutchman; Caroline and Tony Johnson for delivering Carmel's car to us in Port Augusta to use as the support vehicle for the final leg; Clare and her nephew and niece Dougal and Olivia, their mother Georgina and grandparents Bill and Trina; Dave 'Beaver' Drew and his daughter Mel; Brad King and his parents Margaret and Rodger; Darren Lord; Jo Barnes; Maxine Sims, her husband Damian and her kids, as well as her friends Leah, Mick and Heidi; Watson and Marie Curry in Wagga Wagga; Anthony, a farmer from Wagga; Kate Day, Tony and Sue; Ann and Geoff 'Poddy' McMahon; Alan, Nola and Warren Denniss; Kate Day's friend Matt; and Cindy Stevens.

Tuesday 10 September 2013 was a huge day. Thanks for making it so special go out to the following: Principal Tony and Deputy Phil and all the other teachers and students from Lake Illawarra High School who ran with me; my fifth-grade teacher Fay Holbert and Yvonne Carnellor; Hughie Owen, Darren Maquire and Paul Maccabei for accompanying me as I ran alongside Lake Illawarra; Tina, Kerrie, Jackie, Snake and Forbesy for coming along to the school to meet me; Jason Hughes; Linda, Paul, Frank, Mum, Rachel, Mel, Megan, Dratchi, Karen and my mother's lifelong friend Eileen for their cheering, placards and support out the front of Mum's place; Cousin Debbie and her husband Derek, as well as my Aunt Carol and husband Charlie; Matt, a friend of a friend who ran most of that day with me; Jenny and Peter 'Chips' Rafferty; Joanne and Kevin; Carmel's cousin Patrick; Liz and Tony 'Mother' Corben and all the other Tour de Bois who joined me on the second last day of the run; Kit 'Klitty' Rumsey; Kev 'The Moth' Phillips; Graham 'Duane' Brooks; Paul 'Robbo' Robinson; Bill Purkiss; Stuart Turner; Dave Cunningham; and Ken 'The Love God' Challinor.

Thanks also to Peter Hynd, Roger Sharp's colleague from Co-investor for running with me that day; Grace's friends Tessa, Ariane and Emma, as well as Dave and Jo's daughter Meg, all of whom ran the final few kilometres with me; Tim Sharp again; Sarah Brady and others from the South Sydney Rabbitohs; Patrick and Simon from the NSW Police Force; journalist, author, rugby legend and all-round good guy Peter FitzSimons for following my run in his column; St Charles Primary School at Waverley for raising over $10,000 for Oxfam; Libby for her extended support crew contribution in the early months of the run; Michael and Dave for their additional support-crew duties at short notice; Lynell Asher from South Dakota; Fergus Owens from Ireland; and Bob and Janet Woods from Colorado. And everyone else who followed the run so closely throughout; Jimbo from the Tour de Bois for all his help with the maps and data for the web site; and Andrew Sloan for his help with various videos and other technical matters.

Special mention has to be made of the people who ran the greatest distances with me:

• Female aggregate:
Karen (89 kilometres), Kate (87), Sylvia (70) and Grace (46).

• Female 'Most in a day':
Karen (37), Kate (30) and Sylvia (21).

- Male aggregate:

Chook (312), Dave (209), The Hud (195), Barry (150),
Jeff (142) and Eric (106).

- Male 'Most in a day':

The Hud (60), Dave (57), Eric (56) and Chook (55).

- Most countries run in:

Tied for first place with three each—Chook (New Zealand,
United States and Australia) and Barry (Bulgaria, Turkey and
Australia).

- Male 'Most in two days':

The Hud (111), Eric (81) and Dave (79).

- Male 'Most in three days':

The Hud (111—run in just two days), Dave (110) and
Eric (106).

The exact distance run (accurate to the nearest 10 metres) was
26,232.47 kilometres. This is equivalent to 621.7 marathons
and took 621 days, 23 hours and 46 minutes. The latter is, at
the time of writing, the official world record time for the Fastest
Circumnavigation of the Earth on Foot.

ABOUT THE AUTHOR

Tom Denniss is an Australian athlete, scientist and entrepreneur. He has a PhD in Mathematics and Oceanography, has invented a technology to convert the energy in ocean waves into electricity, founded a company to commercialise that technology, played professional rugby league and was a finalist in the 2014 Australian of the Year Award. In 2013 he set a new world record for the Fastest Circumnavigation of the Earth on Foot.

Tom has served on a variety of committees and boards, including as a member of the Global Roundtable on Climate Change, as the Australian Government's representative on the International Energy Association's Ocean Energy Systems Executive Committee and the Australian Government's Advisory Board for the Clean Energy Innovation Centre. He was the first person ever inducted into the Ocean Energy Hall of Fame and in 2005 the technology he invented was named by the International

Academy of Science as one of the Top Ten Technologies in the World.

Tom lives in Sydney, Australia. A former professional musician, he has played to audiences in eight countries. He has written various articles for newspapers, magazines and journals. This is his first book.